The Last Zonian

The Last Zonian
Here's Where the Story Ends
The End of an American Era

Leopold J. Cimino

Oakhurst Publishing, LLC
Altamonte Springs, Florida

The Last Zonian, Here's Where the Story Ends
Copyright © 2024 by Leopold J. Cimino

All rights reserved, including the right to reproduce this book or portions thereof in any form whatsoever without the prior written permission of the author.

Published in Altamonte Springs, Florida, by Oakhurst Publishing LLC
First paperback edition July 2024

This is a work inspired by true events.

Book design and layout: Ryan Cimino, AVANTI Branding
Editor: Lynn Thompson, Living on Purpose Communications
Assistant Editor: Michelle Zeh

All photographs used with the permission and/or copyright transferred to Leopold J. Cimino and family. Photographs of the families are from family members.

Printed in the United States of America

Library of Congress Control Number: 2024913440

ISBN 978-1-7336058-4-7 (pbk)
ISBN 978-1-7336058-5-4 (ebk)

For my parents
Leopold "Leo" and Josephine Cimino,
my family, Rhonda, Ryan, Rachel,
my sister, Liz "Lulu," and brothers
Mike and John

Preface

What is a Zonian? A simplistic definition is "a United States citizen who lived and worked in the Panama Canal Zone." However, there is more to the story of identifying a true Zonian.

A more thorough answer to the question begins with the construction of the Panama Canal, one of the greatest engineering achievements of its time. The Hay-Bunau-Varilla Treaty of 1903 enacted terms between the United States and the Republic of Panama that granted exclusive Canal rights to the US. On May 4, 1904, the Panama Canal Zone became an unincorporated US territory. Hence, the first Zonians came to be.

The Panama Canal Zone was a ten-mile-wide strip of land stretching across the Isthmus of Panama between the Atlantic and Pacific Oceans. On August 15, 1914, the Panama Canal inaugurated its opening to traffic with the transit of the US cargo and passenger ship SS Ancon. The ability for ships to traverse the Isthmus of Panama, connecting two oceans, changed world commerce. During World War II (WWII), the Panama Canal ushered US and Allied ships as a shortcut between the Atlantic and Pacific Oceans.

According to hospital records, the human cost of building the 51-mile-long Canal during the United States construction period was 5,609 deaths. During the French construction period, worker deaths were higher. According to a report by Dr. William C. Gorgas, the US Army Chief Surgeon who implemented mosquito control measures to prevent yellow fever and malaria, estimated deaths were possibly 22,000 workers.

The name of the governing body for the Canal changed a few times, from the Isthmian Canal Commission to The Panama Canal in April 1914. Then, in 1951, the governance was reorganized into two separate operations: the Panama Canal Company (PCC), responsible for Canal operations, and the Canal Zone Government (CZG), which oversaw civil affairs and health bureaus in the Zone. The Zonians performed essential work day and night, seven days a week.

On September 7, 1977, President Jimmy Carter signed two treaties between the United States and the Republic of Panama. First, the Neutrality Treaty ensured the neutrality of the Panama Canal and that the US military could defend the Canal to assure that stance. Second, the Panama Canal Treaty specified that on October 1, 1979, the US unincorporated territory known as the Panama Canal Zone would be abolished and cease to exist. The second treaty additionally stated that on December 31, 1999, complete control of the Canal would pass to the Panamanians.

The execution of the treaty commencing in 1979 is referred to as "The End of an American Era." The US assisted the Panamanians with Canal operations for the next 20 years, between October 1, 1979, and December 31, 1999. However, since the US unincorporated territory ceased to exist, US citizens born in the former Canal Zone or who received employment during that period are not Zonians. Therefore, the commencement of the

The Last Zonian

treaty in 1979 was the end of US persons truly being identified as a Zonian.

Throughout my life, I have encountered innumerable people who have no idea what a Zonian is or have never even heard the term. What is a Zonian? A more detailed definition is a US citizen who lived and worked in the Canal Zone for the Panama Canal Company (PCC) or Canal Zone Government (CZG) or was born in the Canal Zone before its abolishment on October 1, 1979.

While writing this book, the question arose of non-PCC or non-CZG employees and their families who lived and worked in the Canal Zone being Zonians. The fact is that most non-PCC or non-CZG employees, such as military personnel, contractors, and other civilians, rotated in and out of the Canal Zone on a tour of duty, working for other government departments or private agencies. Zonian families remained and raised their children in the Canal Zone, although there are some exceptions with non-PCC or non-CZG employees who stayed and lived there for numerous years. Panamanian locals considered anyone living in the Canal Zone a Zonian, as did some Zonians, who considered military families, and others living there quasi-Zonians, especially the kids who went to the same junior and senior high schools.

A more precise method of identifying a Zonian is through employment. The employee received a pay stub derived from the PCC or CZG. Also, upon leaving or retiring from the Canal Zone, a document with the Seal of the Canal Zone Isthmus of Panama is on a Canal Zone Government and Panama Canal Company certificate of retirement and service.

So, a Zonian is a US citizen who lived in the Canal Zone and worked for the PCC or CZG, including their family members residing there, or was born in the Panama Canal Zone. In other words, any person with a Canal Zone birth certificate is a Zonian. After the Panama Canal Zone ceased to exist, Canal Zone birth certificates were no longer issued. The Department of State issued a Certificate of Birth Abroad in the former Canal Zone (now called a Consular Report of Birth Abroad, CRBA).

Zonians are a diverse group of people from different cultural backgrounds, races, and religions. If you encounter a Zonian, you will likely sense a pleasant and good-natured person.

The Panama Canal workers and their families, known as Zonians, are fading away. Many are no longer with us, and the list of entire Zonian families who are deceased continues to grow yearly. As I researched and gathered information about Zonian families, I realized that, in some instances, I was interviewing the last Zonian for their family.

Writing *The Last Zonian, Here's Where the Story Ends* was more than personal for me. I realized I wanted to write this book after I reached out to friends to assist me in sharing my book *Misty's Tale,* which I had recently published, and then being informed by them of the sad news of Zonians I knew passing away. Hearing about these people I had not seen since I left the Canal Zone, I felt inspired to preserve the stories of a few Zonians who had a role in the day-to-day operations of the Canal and Zone. I gathered the information for this book from various sources, including official documents, the National Archives and Records Administration, news publications, the Internet, and personal accounts. Members of the 20 Zonian families who shared their stories with me are a small representation of a legacy to the tens of thousands of workers who kept the world's shortcut across Panama operational for three-quarters of a century.

Tom Brokaw's book *The Greatest Generation* was also a source of inspiration. In his preface, he writes, "They finished the war determined to have more peaceful and prosperous lives, these children of first a global economic depression and then a war that engulfed the world." Many members of The Greatest

Generation and Korean War veterans pursued life in the Panama Canal Zone, referred to as "a slice of paradise."

Numerous authors have written books about the Panama Canal, Canal Zone, and prominent Zonians. *The Last Zonian, Here's Where the Story Ends* is about ordinary people who had necessary jobs in the Panama Canal Company and Canal Zone Government operations. It is about life in the Canal Zone and the legacy of Zonian families. *The Last Zonian, Here's Where the Story Ends* is about more than an end of an era; it is about honoring the end of a group of people bonded with a unique distinction of being a Zonian.

Acknowledgments

I attended the Panama Canal Society's annual reunion in Orlando, Florida, in July 2019. It was the 40th Anniversary of the Panama Canal Treaty, which took effect on October 1, 1979, officially abolishing the Panama Canal Zone as an unincorporated US territory. I was born in the Canal Zone and have many wonderful memories of my childhood living in the Zone.

Before attending the reunion, I reached out to a childhood friend, Barbara Yerxa Horton, who I had recently discovered lived less than two hours from my home. I met Barbara and her mother, Betty Yerxa, a truly sweet lady, at the reunion for lunch before she re-acquainted me with other friends I had not seen in 47 years.

Old friends quickly remembered me, and some asked if I remembered them. I did, but not as quickly in some instances. Since we were older and did look a bit different than in our youth, I had to gaze more closely at their faces. As we reminisced and shared stories, other friends of friends would come by and talk about the Canal Zone. Barbara and Betty were assisting as volunteers at the reunion, so they left me with some friends conversing and mingling as if we had never left the Canal Zone. Unlike previous reunions, where I briefly connected with a few old friends, we chatted for hours.

Many years earlier, my beautiful wife, Rhonda, and I had attended two reunions, once while we were home in Orlando on military leave and another shortly after retiring from the Army. That day, Rhonda told me to go and enjoy myself and meet more old friends. She was battling cancer and wanted to spend time with her 86-year-old mother (my loving mother-in-law, Lois Watson), our next-door neighbor.

When I got home later that afternoon to help make dinner, Rhonda asked me how it went. During our meal, I shared about who I met and renewed acquaintances. When I told her about being informed of Zonians I had known passing away, Rhonda gave me the push of encouragement that inspired me to write the stories shared by Zonians of our lives in the Canal Zone and our journey after leaving the Zone.

A couple of weeks later, I started putting together a concept and draft outline for the book. I began researching, writing, and gathering information from Zonians on some evenings, but after three months, I stopped writing. Time is so precious, I wanted to spend it all with Rhonda and family. Her health began to decline. The Lord called Rhonda home on December 24, 2019; she was 61.

I began writing the book again 17 months later. I intended to write about 50 families with different occupations from across the Panama Canal Zone, starting on the Atlantic side of the Canal and traversing to the Pacific side. I was doing everything on my own. I was overwhelmed trying to find 50 Zonian families for the book, conducting interviews, gathering information, doing genealogy research, collecting family photos, and traveling to different locations to meet family members. I told my daughter Rachel, "I might have bit off more than I can chew." She gave me the encouragement Rhonda would have given me; try to find someone to ask for help. I ultimately narrowed the book's focus, settling on 20 families primarily living on the Atlantic side. Although there was interest from some families on the Pacific side, it was not sufficient for having jobs across the isthmus, which was the original intent.

After interviewing and gathering information from Maurie Moore about her family, she became my go-to person and information source. I want to thank her and Tom Finneman for assisting in my recollection of living in the Canal Zone.

The depth of my thanks is beyond words for the love of my life, Rhonda Kay (Watson) Cimino, my wife and life partner for 41 years and eight months. Her support and encouragement in my life during and after my Army career helped make me the man I am. I thank the Lord for his union of Rhonda and me and the blessing of having Rhonda at my side, sharing our lives together. To our daughter, Rachel, and son, Ryan, I love you. Thank you for watching over me after the Lord called Mom home.

A special thanks go to friends and beta readers Maurie Moore, Michael Murphy, and Cathy Dewitt. I appreciate your feedback and contribution; it was helpful. And, to my editor Lynn Thompson, thanks for the editorial assistance and insight. Comments from your editorial assistant, Michelle Zeh, during the proofreading stage were invaluable. Your contributions enhanced *The Last Zonian, Here's Where the Story Ends*.

To the Zonians in this book, thank you. I am honored by the privilege of being welcomed into your circle and getting to write a snippet of your family story. And, to all the Zonians who lived, worked, or were born in the Panama Canal Zone, I am grateful to be part of a larger family with different backgrounds and a common identity as a Zonian.

Leopold J. Cimino

Zonian families have the unique distinction of being a part of United States history referred to as "The End of an American Era." Truly, everyone has a unique story to share about themselves as they walk their path in life.

CONTENTS

PREFACE	vii
ACKNOWLEDGMENTS	xiii
MEMORIES	xxi
ZONIAN LIFE	1
A SLICE OF PARADISE	3
OCCUPATIONS AND OPERATIONS	13
THE ZONIANS	15

LELAND DARREL SNIDER   17
Supervisory Admeasurer • Panama Canal Company
US Marine Corps, Korean War Veteran

GERALD OSTER   27
Ship Pilot • Panama Canal Company
US Army, WWII Post Era Veteran

THEODORE LESTER BAILEY   35
Tugboat Captain • Panama Canal Company
US Navy, WWII Veteran

Contents

JOHN THOMAS O'DONNELL JR. — 45
Leader Marine Machinist • Panama Canal Company
US Navy, WWII Veteran

LEIGH CASSIUS "CASH" PAULSON — 53
General Manager Distribution Facilities • Panama Canal Company
US Navy, WWII Veteran

GAYLE GEORGE FORTNER JR. — 63
Police Sergeant • Canal Zone Government
US Navy, WWII Veteran

GEORGE "LANKY" OSCAR FLORES — 69
Fire Chief • Canal Zone Government
US Army, Korean War Era Veteran

DAVID REED JR. — 77
Guard Supervisor Captain • Panama Canal Company
US Army, Korean War Era Veteran

THEODORE MATTHEW & PATRICIA FINNEMAN — 85
Locks Security Lieutenant • Panama Canal Company
US Army, Korean War Era Veteran

JOHN MICHAEL KLASOVSKY — 93
Lead Foreman Control House Operator • Panama Canal Company
WWII Panama Canal Essential Occupation

JACKSON JUDSON BARGER — 101
Locomotive Operator • Panama Canal Company
US Army, WWII Veteran

IRVING IKE SPECTOR — 111
Tugboat Master • Panama Canal Company
US Navy, WWII Veteran

ROBERT GRAHAM & ALICE FORSYTHE — 119
Lead Lock Operator Machinist • Panama Canal Company
US Navy, WWII Post Era Veteran • And The Dressmaker

ROBERT JOHN BLAIR — 127
Lead Foreman Lock Operations • Panama Canal Company
US Navy, WWII Veteran

Contents

CHARLES CUNNINGHAM LOYD Senior Powerhouse Operator – Gatun Dam • Panama Canal Company US Navy, WWII Veteran	137
ROBERT EDWIN MCCULLOUGH High School Teacher • Canal Zone Government US Army, WWII Era Veteran	145
IRIS ESTHER MARY (DEDEAUX) HOGAN Finance Branch Superintendent Postal Operations Canal Zone Government	149
EVELYN (KUINLAM) BARRAZA Otolaryngologist • Canal Zone Government	157
RONALD EDWARD MOORE Obstetrician-Gynecologist • Canal Zone Government US Army, Pre-Vietnam War Era Veteran Civilian Physician, Vietnam War	165
LOIS JEANNE (ARNOLD) NELSON Operating Room Nurse • Canal Zone Government US Navy, Korean War Post Era Veteran	173
THE LOST TOWNS	181
THE ATLANTIC SIDE	183
GATUN: THEN AND NOW	223
COCO SOLO: THEN AND NOW	227
HERE'S WHERE THE STORY ENDS	231
EPILOGUE	233
REFERENCES	235

Memories

In the summer of 1982, ten years after my father, Leopold "Leo" Cimino, retired from the Panama Canal Company, I returned to the former Panama Canal Zone as a soldier assigned to the 193rd Infantry Brigade at Fort Clayton on the Pacific side of the isthmus. There was much elation in my family when I reenlisted and got my area of preference assignment of Panama. Once I arrived, I could hardly wait to show my wife, Rhonda, who joined me after a few months, where I grew up and the places in my childhood stories. My parents were as happy as I was with my assignment to Panama. The choices they made for the family ultimately determined my upbringing. They raised me in a wonderful place like no other: the Canal Zone.

My family story starts with my father, born on March 21, 1910, in Brooklyn, New York. He had seven siblings, three sisters and four brothers. The family moved to New Haven, Connecticut, in 1920. My father's mother, Lucia Scarfata Cimino, died in November 1924 when he was 14 years old. In 1930, at age 20, he worked as an engraver in a print shop. When

Leopold J. Cimino

I was 20 years old and working, he shared with me that living through the Great Depression was a hardship for his family, as it was for hundreds of thousands of families during the 1930s.

My father continued working as a laborer and printer before departing New Haven in 1934 at age 24. He enlisted in the US Army as an infantryman in October 1934 and was stationed in Brooklyn, New York. He reenlisted in September 1937 and was sent to the Panama Canal Zone with a duty station at Fort De Lesseps on the Atlantic side of the isthmus. A year later, in November 1938, he received a promotion to corporal. The following year, his military specialty changed from infantryman to military policeman, and in December 1939, he got another promotion to sergeant. In March 1940, he received an honorable discharge from the Army for government convenience to accept a civil service employment position in the Canal Zone. He remained on the Atlantic side with the Construction Quartermaster at France Field Army Air Station.

Leopold Cimino

The United States, concerned with Nazi Germany's annexations that began in 1938 of Austria, the Sudetenland in Czechoslovakia, and the invasion of Poland on September 1, 1939, that started World War II, took defensive action to protect the Panama Canal. The US Secretary of War recognized that the military forces and equipment were inadequate for defending the Canal. By January 1940, the US had increased troop strength to about 19,500 military personnel, which rose to approximately 21,000 by the end of April.

The surge of troops and equipment required numerous infrastructure construction projects, including new bases, roads, and other facilities. The War Department recruited and employed workers from Panama, Jamaica, Spain, Puerto Rico, Colombia, and El Salvador. While attaining a workforce for the construction projects, the United States entered the war on December 8, 1941, following the attack by Japan at Pearl Harbor, Hawaii.

By the summer of 1942, the recruited workforce of unskilled and semiskilled workers totaled 65,786. Although a small percentage of the total workforce, these workers were essential in the labor needed to complete projects like the trans-isthmus highway. Additionally, there was a need for US civil service workers and contractors.

My father transferred to different civil service positions to better himself. He worked as a truck driver from March 1940 to September 1940 at the France Field Army Air Station. Then, as a truck driver and cable splicer helper from September 1940 to September 1941 with the US Army Signal Corp at Fort Davis. From September 1941 to September 1942, he worked as a wireman for the US Navy at the Coco Solo Submarine Base. There, he got the nickname "Sparky."

I can only speculate that anytime my father had an opportunity to move up, he did. I know he had a strong work ethic that he later instilled in me as a teenager when I began working.

In September 1942, he progressed to an electrician position while working for the US Navy in Coco Solo. He received a Certificate of Recognition of Service in December 1945 from the Department of the Navy for essential wartime work during WWII. He continued working for the Navy until the late 1950s. I often wondered why the Army did not recall him in 1941 since he was an infantryman and military police sergeant. I later discovered that as a civil service employee working in the Canal Zone, he was part of the essential civilian workforce deemed necessary for Canal operations along with military forces needed for its defense.

In July 1954, my father, at age 44, married for the first and only time. The story of his courtship with my mother, Josefina "Josephine" Maria Bequeles Salinas, was clarified to me in February 2020 when I visited family living in Panama. I always thought my parents met at an American-Panamanian-sponsored social function. Well, that was close, but not a sponsored function. During my visit, two of my mother's six sisters, Aunt Deida and Aunt Vilma, told me the story.

Josephine & Leopold Cimino

They met at a party. My father went to the party with a friend, and my mother, who was younger, attended with her boyfriend. Someone introduced my father to her and her boyfriend. I was told there was an instant attraction between Leo and Josefina. A week after the party, he began to pursue her. He showed up at her family's home and introduced himself as a friend. Initially, he visited her at her family's house, and then they went out with one of her six sisters and a friend who acted as chaperones. My mother's previous boyfriend was no longer in the picture; my father had won her over.

They married after a year-long courtship, which I was told may have been longer. My mother, born on April 23, 1935, had recently become 19, a young attractive secretary who fell in love with a man 25 years her senior and a handsome early

The Last Zonian

middle-aged man who fell in love with a teenager. Sounds crazy, but I am glad they did because my sister, two brothers, and I, our children, and our grandchildren would not be a part of my parents' lineage. A year after their marriage, my sister Elizabeth Lucille "Lulu" was born in July 1955, when my parents lived at 77-C Coco Solito in US Navy housing.

In May 1957, due to a Navy reduction in force (RIF) in the Canal Zone, my father attained a job as an electrician and locomotive operator with the Panama Canal Company at the Gatun Locks. I am certain my parents felt blessed to have gotten that job since a month earlier they had a second child, Leopold "Leo" John (me), born in April 1957 at Coco Solo Hospital. My parents were still living in Coco Solito, then moved to Canal Zone Government housing at Coco Solo on Severn Road for a few years before we moved to Gatun, the town adjacent to the Gatun Locks.

My brother, Robert Michael "Mike," entered the world in April 1960. My mother had left her secretarial job years earlier and was a full-time homemaker. In August 1962, we traveled by plane to Miami and then by train through New York City to New Haven, Connecticut, to visit my father's seven siblings. They had not seen him since before WWII, 27 years earlier. The following year, my parents were again full of joy with the birth of my brother, John Joseph, born in June 1963.

Around the time John was born, my father started taking me with him to Sunday morning mass, 6:00 AM, at the Catedral de Inmaculada Concepción, Cathedral of the Immaculate Conception of Mary in the seaport city of Colon, ten miles from Gatun. The church, built in 1934, is within walking distance from Fort De Lesseps, where he was stationed as an Army military policeman at the start of WWII. My father drove to the church in Colon even though there was a small Catholic church in Gatun. He had attended that church since his arrival in Panama, which I am sure reminded him of his early days as a soldier in Panama. He went to that church every Sunday when he was not working at the Gatun Locks.

Sometimes, after mass, our family traveled to Panama City if we had not done so on Saturday. My parents provided us with a better life experience than just the enjoyment we had in the Canal Zone. We appreciated living in two cultures—the Canal Zone and Panama.

My parents were great cooks, so we savored Italian and Panamanian cuisine. They also taught the maids, our help, how to cook. They loved socializing with family and friends. My father regularly took us night fishing at the Gatun Locks bridge crossing and along the northwest shoreline of the entrance of the locks. My mother expressed her joy when we brought home snook that were 28 to 35 pounds. The refrigerator was always stocked with fish.

Growing up in Gatun, we lived in different housing quarters based on family size and seniority: 205 Schoolhouse Road, 243 Sibert Street, and 235 Loma Blanca Place. It did not matter where we lived in the small town; my parents encouraged us to go to the community gym and swimming pool and have fun with our friends. We participated in recreational and competitive sports, from battleball, ping pong, badminton, archery, tennis, basketball, volleyball, swimming, water polo, and sandlot football. My sister, Lulu, was a powerhouse playing sports. Besides organized sports, we each had a group of friends we hung out with. I sometimes hung out with Lulu and her older group of friends. My younger brother, Mike, did the same with me, especially when we went into the jungle exploring and building forts. We spent little time indoors because there was always a new outdoor adventure. John, the youngest of us, sometimes tagged along with Mike and his friends. We all did our share of fishing with the occasional disregard of a no-trespassing sign to get to a good fishing spot. Whatever we did with our friends, we always had fun.

Mike and John, Michael and Richie Murphy, Randy and Eddie Williams, and other friends would drape a dome-shape military parachute, free of its suspension cords, over a small dome-shape monkey bar set, then spread the remaining fabric out in a circular pattern about 15 feet from the playground equipment. They would then bundle and tie some of the material from the round outline to the bottom of the monkey bars, but only on one side. Taking turns, three of the lightweight youngsters would crawl underneath the spread-out loose parachute on the opposite side of the fabric anchored to the monkey bars and find a spot away from each other to maintain the outer circular outline. Each would lie down on the ground and tuck some of the loose material around their body as if to make a sleeping bag. When a wind gust flowed across the ground into the unanchored loose openings, the updraft would fill the canopy and briefly raise the boys two to three feet off the ground, giving them an air-lifting ride.

Mike, Lulu, John, Leo

Visiting my mother's side of the family in Panama City and venturing out of the city was always exciting. Going to El Interior, the interior provinces of Panama, Isla Taboga, Isla Grande, and beaches on the Atlantic and Pacific sides of the isthmus kept us entertained. I also remember having a lot of fun in the city. My relatives always kept a close watch over me since my complexion differed slightly from the rest of the family compared to my sister and brothers, who had a nice tan look as that of my father's Italian and my mother's Greek and Portuguese origins. I stood out as a white kid who sometimes wore glasses. I was considered a "Gringo," a white person from the United States, a foreigner.

We visited our family in Panama City almost every other weekend. My parents purchased groceries and other items in the Canal Zone and brought them to the relatives. My father and mother socialized with my grandmother, aunts, and uncles, chatting and eating for hours. Us kids, we went out to play. My Aunt Nani always told my older cousins Oscar and Miguel, "Cuidan el Gringo," which meant, "Take care of your cousin Leo."

It was fun seeing my cousins and, at times, adventurous. We played "kick the can" in front of the house, along the sidewalk of a busy street, which involved hide-and-seek and freeing teammates. There was no grassy backyard; it was in the city. My cousins watched over me from other Panamanian kids who thought I was a Gringo, but after they learned I was half Panamanian and spoke Spanish, I was good to go. When I was about nine years old, my cousins, along with my sister, would climb over a wall at the back of the house into an alley that led to another busy street to go to a "tienda," a store, to get a Fanta soda and ice cream then we roamed the city streets for a little bit before returning to the house.

Living in the Canal Zone provided Zonians with numerous amenities, a utopia for many Zonians, in stark contrast to life outside the Zone. The Canal Zone was clean, and the buildings, streets, and facilities were well maintained.

In May 1972, my father retired from the Panama Canal Company. He was a leader lock operator and chief electrician with 36 years and two months of government service, of which over 33 years were spent in Panama. He and my mother considered staying close to family in Panama; however, they would no longer have access to the Canal Zone amenities. We moved to Orlando, Florida. My parents chose Central Florida for the warm, sunny weather. They did not want to deal with cold and snowy winters in Connecticut. Orlando was a good halfway location between Connecticut and Panama, and many Zonian families lived in Central Florida and on the coast. Like many retired Zonians, my parents missed life in the Canal Zone and Panama.

When I returned to the former Canal Zone for my tour of duty at Fort Clayton from 1982 to 1985, the decline from its cleanliness and well-groomed former existence was definitely noticeable. Many roads were poorly maintained and lined with trash, overgrown grass, and vegetation, and some buildings and structures needed paint. Passenger coaches from the Panama Railway were dilapidated. It was sad to see the changes and remember how it had been in my childhood.

Rhonda and I celebrated the birth of our first child, Ryan Leo, in January 1984 at Gorgas Army Hospital. Although he was born in the former Canal Zone, Ryan is not a Zonian. When President Jimmy Carter signed the Panama Canal Treaty in September 1977, the Panama Canal Zone was abolished effective October 1, 1979. Meaning, it was the end of any new persons being identified as a Zonian.

The same year Ryan was born, I attended an Army school at Fort Sherman that my buddies and I were keenly aware of when I lived in Gatun in my youth. Whenever we saw paratroopers in the sky beyond the Gatun Locks, we knew soldiers were training at the Army Jungle Operations Training Center (JOTC) at Fort Sherman.

During the Vietnam War era, about every four weeks, we rode our bicycles to the bridge that crossed over the railroad tracks at the Gatun Train Station. We watched soldiers disembark from the train and then load onto military deuce-and-a-half trucks that took them to Fort Sherman for three weeks of jungle warfare training.

As kids, we thought it was neat to see a line of parachutes in the sky. We knew where the drop zone was since we often rode our bikes across the Gatun Locks bridge to find a new adventure in the jungle, including entering the mock Vietnamese village used for training.

My brother Mike also enlisted in the Army. He attended jungle warfare school three years before me in 1981. Mike contacted a childhood friend, Michael Murphy, from our Gatun days, who still lived in the former Canal Zone. Michael told him he saw the paratroopers in the sky as when we were kids. Mike told him he was one of the paratroopers assigned to the 82nd Airborne Division at Fort Bragg, North Carolina. For two days, Michael picked up Mike from Fort Sherman and drove around, showing him the former Canal Zone and Panama, having a good time together. They had a Zonian friendship.

Growing up in Gatun and venturing into the jungle, we learned a lot as kids. During an exercise when I attended jungle warfare training, our platoon came to a sparsely grassy clearing in the jungle. When my boots sunk into the dirt a little, I knew what it was, and I told the platoon sergeant and lieutenant. I informed them that I grew up in Gatun and played in this jungle. They snickered and told the platoon to drop their gear around the edges of the clearing as we prepared to move forward to assault a position. I was a squad leader and told my guys to drop their gear about five feet away from the clearing. When the platoon returned from the exercise and picked up their rucksacks, they discovered that ants had infested them. My squad's gear was ant-free, and we chuckled about the situation. When the lieutenant looked at me, I just smiled, and he acknowledged me with a smile and shook his head.

While living at Fort Clayton, Rhonda met my relatives, and I showed her all the places from my childhood, including visiting the beaches and doing some scuba diving at Isla Grande. We left the former Canal Zone in 1985, a year after I attended JOTC. Our daughter, Rachel Lynn was born six months later, in March 1986, at the US Navy Hospital in Orlando, Florida.

Twelve years after my tour in Panama, I returned with Liz "Lulu," Mike, and John to honor my parents' wishes. My parents were happily married for 43 years. My father, Leopold, passed away on April 7, 1996, in Orlando. He was 86 years old. My mother, Josephine, passed away nine months later, on January 3, 1997, of a broken heart. She was 61 years old. Our family in Panama arranged everything for us during our stay and the celebration of life for my parents. All my mother's family was there—a final tribute to the middle-aged man and the teenager who loved each other to the end. Their ashes were lovingly released in the water, at the north end of Gatun Locks.

Leopold & Josephine Cimino

I am thankful to my parents for my upbringing, instilling in me the moral values and faith I have today. My walk in faith started as a youngster, going to church with my dad, and strengthened as I got older.

There is some humor and more to the story of my father taking me to church with him and the significance of the number

22 in my life. My parents told me that the morning my father decided to take me with him to a 6:00 AM mass, he just wanted some company. My mother watched my siblings and then went to mass when we got home. The mass in Colon was in Spanish. As we got older, my parents sent us to the English-speaking mass at the small Catholic Church in Gatun.

After mass with my father, he took me to a "bodega" (a small store), where he got a cup of coffee, and I got a pastry. When I finished eating, my dad held my hand as he guided us through the streets of Colon. He was very familiar with the streets and some shop owners from his days in the military. As we walked on the sidewalks, he would glance at the "billetes de loteria" (lottery tickets) displayed on vendors' boards outside the various stores and shops lining the streets.

While strolling Avenida Balboa, we stopped at a one-chair barbershop owned by a Jamaican lady, Eunice, near the corner of Calle 11. She had cut my dad's hair since before I was born and mine until we left the Canal Zone in 1972. I visited Eunice once, in 1983, with Rhonda, when I was stationed at Fort Clayton. And again in 1997, when my siblings and I returned to Panama to honor my parents' wishes. Eunice was still cutting hair; she was much older and had the same pleasant demeanor as when I was a child.

The first time I accompanied my father to mass, he asked me to pick some loteria tickets. I picked 2222 and a few other tickets, all having the number 22. Later that afternoon, at 1:00 PM, the selection of the ticket numbers was broadcast over the radio and seen on television. The tickets with the number 22 won. Starting that day, I became a regular, attending early morning mass with my dad, then walking with him as he picked his tickets, and I chose one, always with the number 22.

Throughout my life, I have associated the number 22 with my father. After he passed, I always felt a sense of peace and

The Last Zonian

comfort when I saw the number 22. On occasion, whether driving through a storm or something else, I knew my family and I would be all right when the number 22 appeared in some way.

The most memorable situation occurred after I experienced the worst flight of my life. I flew home to Alexandria, Virginia, from El Paso, Texas, to see Rhonda, Ryan, and Rachel during a four-day weekend holiday while attending the nine-month US Army Sergeants Major Academy.

When I landed at Ronald Reagan Washington National Airport, I told Rhonda that I did not want to fly back. She said, "Honey, you know you have to fly back or catch a bus back now."

I knew she was correct that I had to fly back; it was just the worst flight I had experienced. We enjoyed a wonderful weekend and I was happy to be with my family. I just was not looking forward to the flight back to Dallas and El Paso, Texas.

On the day of my return flight, when Rhonda, the kids, and I got into the van, the temperature gauge displayed 22 Celsius. That was odd because we always had the temperature display set to Fahrenheit degrees. When we arrived at the airport, we parked on level 2 of the garage and when we stopped the music CD, it was on track 2; together, it was 22. When we checked the time of our arrival, it was 1:22 PM. When I checked in with the airline ticket agent, she informed me that my flight would leave from gate 22, and my seat was 22C.

Rhonda knew the significance of the number 22 to me. She said, "Honey, you are going to be fine on this flight." She was correct. I had smooth flights back to my destination. Later that night, when Rhonda and I chatted on the phone, she said she took note of what occurred with the number 22 that day. After she wrote it down on a piece of paper, she noticed the time was 8:22 PM. She also said we had been together for 22 years that year. So, when the number 22 is involved in my life, I know that my dad and now Rhonda are watching over me and the kids.

Leopold J. Cimino

My father and mother were happy Zonians. They said the best times of their lives were living in the Canal Zone, raising us kids there, and being close to visit my mother's family regularly.

What happened to us kids? Elizabeth "Lulu, Liz" worked in insurance for a few years and later sold real estate. Liz married Harold Yeadon. She had four kids: James, Stephen, Jacquelyn, and Kyle. She and Harold later parted ways. In 2009, she suffered a stroke and lives in a medical facility near her former home in Orlando, Florida.

Like my parents, my brother Mike loved life in the Canal Zone, the memories, and being a Zonian. His upbringing, being an altar boy at Catholic mass, and his friends all helped in shaping his life. After leaving the Army, he worked in home construction for many years before becoming a subcontractor with two of his own crews. Having a kind heart, he was extremely generous to strangers. He married Pamela Girouard, adopted three children: Matthew, Rodney, and Nicole, and had one together, Robert. Sadly, Mike passed away in June 2006 at age 46 in Orlando, Florida.

John, the youngest, reminisces about the fun times of his childhood living in Gatun. He is an easy-going, great guy. I know it is from our upbringing and he, too, was an altar boy. John married Sheila Perrine and had three children; twins, John Jr. and Kelly, and Alicia. He worked in county government for 35 years and owns an irrigation business. After retiring, the county asked him to return and he did. John and Sheila live on two acres, where they have had large vegetable gardens, chickens, a heifer, and bloodhound dogs over the years. They are active, always doing something or going somewhere. They live in Orlando, Florida.

After living throughout the US and abroad, I retired from the Army as a sergeant major. Rhonda, the kids, and I moved to Altamonte Springs, Florida, and built a home next door to her

The Last Zonian

mother, the last of our parents. Having loving parents and being raised in families with modest means, Rhonda and I were the first in our families to attain college degrees. Rhonda received a bachelor's at Hawaii Pacific University, and I attained a bachelor's from the University of Maryland University College and a master's at the University of Central Florida. Our kids, Rachel and Ryan, went on to get their master's degrees. Rhonda and I enjoyed hosting family reunions, getting together with friends, traveling, and Bible study.

ZONIAN LIFE

A Slice of Paradise

The Canal Zone was home to thousands of US citizens who lived in towns and military installations, along with non-US citizen workers and their families who lived in designated towns on the Atlantic and Pacific sides of the Isthmus. The residents of the towns, like most people anywhere, wanted to live in communities that were safe with basic public services and amenities.

Many Zonians thought living in the Canal Zone was a slice of paradise. What made it so special? The tropical ambiance, a sense of community, a great place to raise a family, and the many amenities. To begin with, the Panama Canal Company maintained the Canal Zone territorial area, infrastructure, and its communities. The Zone was clean and orderly, free of loose trash and graffiti, and no billboards or commercial advertisements visible anywhere. Residents worried not about home repairs or cutting their grass since that, too, was done by a maintenance department. There was law and order in the Canal Zone with a low crime rate. And, there was no unemployment or homelessness because in order to live in the Canal Zone, the head of the household had to have employment in the Zone. Therefore, when a person retired or left their employment, they had to leave the Canal Zone. Lastly, there was always something to do or attend year-round, be it enjoying the beaches and other water recreational activities, sporting competitions, community gatherings, church-sponsored events, social occasions, and holiday functions. The activities and camaraderie in communities developed lifelong bonds between residents.

Most of the towns bordered the jungle, a playground for many of us. The tropical vegetation was home to numerous animals and bird species. It was common to see and hear flocks of the green Panama yellow-head amazon parakeet chatting loudly. Or, see a band of 20 coatimundis, members of the raccoon family, exit the thick tropical brush, frolicking in a clearing as they traveled across the opening, and then disappear back into the jungle. And, seeing an iguana speedily race across a yard, then rapidly scamper up a tree. There was a calmness in living next to the jungle. The local news never reported an alligator in a yard, a black bear going through a trash container, or a mountain lion strolling through a residential area as seen in stateside news stories nowadays. It was pleasing to see a royal blue butterfly fluttering after a rain shower. Plus, many Zonians had fruit trees in their backyard to readily pick avocados, papayas, guavas, and bananas.

A town's basic services and amenities differed based on the number of residential dwellings and the proximity to other larger communities. Besides housing quarters, other services and facilities might include a police and fire department, healthcare clinic and dental care, gas station, post office, a church, recreational facilities (gymnasium, swimming pool, tennis courts, other sports playing fields, bowling alley, picnic areas, and boat launching ramps), schools, commissary, company retail stores, cafeteria, snack bar, movie theater, restaurants, yacht club, and a golf course and country club. There were two hospitals in the Canal Zone, one on each side of the isthmus.

The Atlantic side of the isthmus was home to the Gatun Locks, the biggest of the three locks with three pairs of chambers, Gatun Lake, which is 180 square miles and a major part of the Panama Canal, Gatun Dam known as "the spillway," and Coco Solo Hospital. The primary towns, in September 1979 for US citizens, included Gatun, Margarita, and Coco Solo, with smaller residential areas of France Field and New Cristobal. The military bases with residential areas were Fort Gulick, Fort Davis, and Fort Sherman that was home to the Jungle Operations Training Center (JOTC) for jungle warfare training. There were other smaller military facilities with barracks and housing, some already deactivated, such as Fort Randolph, Fort De Lesseps, Army France Field, and Coco Solo Navy Annex. The one non-US citizen town was Rainbow City. Brazos Heights was another small residential area for persons employed by shipping agencies and other nongovernmental employers.

The following maps identify the Panama Canal Zone territorial boundary area, along with most of the towns and military installations, and the route ships traverse to cross the Isthmus of Panama. A ship entering the Panama Canal from the Atlantic side and the Caribbean Sea passed through the breakwater into Limon Bay near the seaport city of Colon. Then it made its way to the Gatun Locks to enter Gatun Lake, cross the isthmus to pass through the Pedro Miguel and Miraflores Locks, and then proceed to pass the Bridge of the Americas (originally named the Thatcher Ferry Bridge), and exit on the Pacific side.

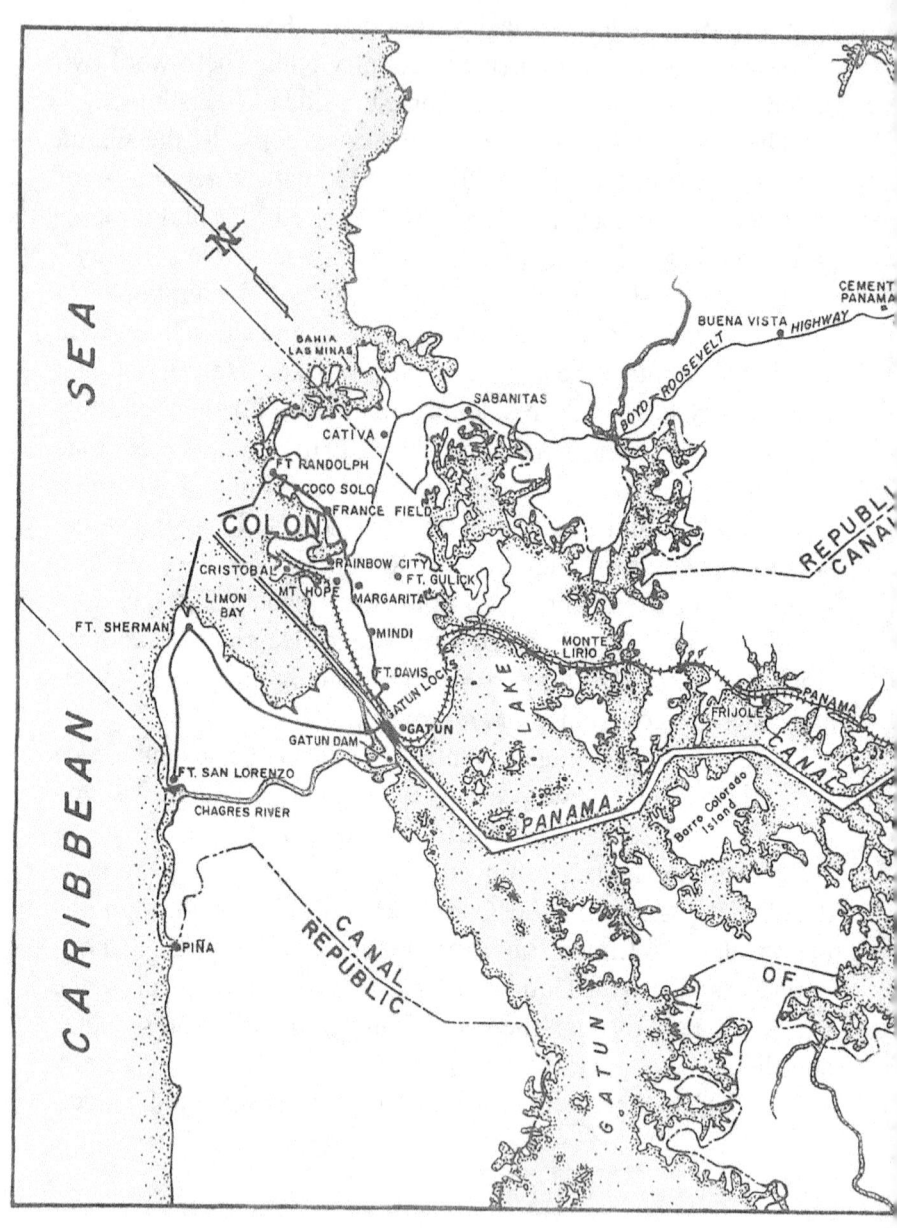

Panama Canal Zone: Atlantic side north

The Last Zonian

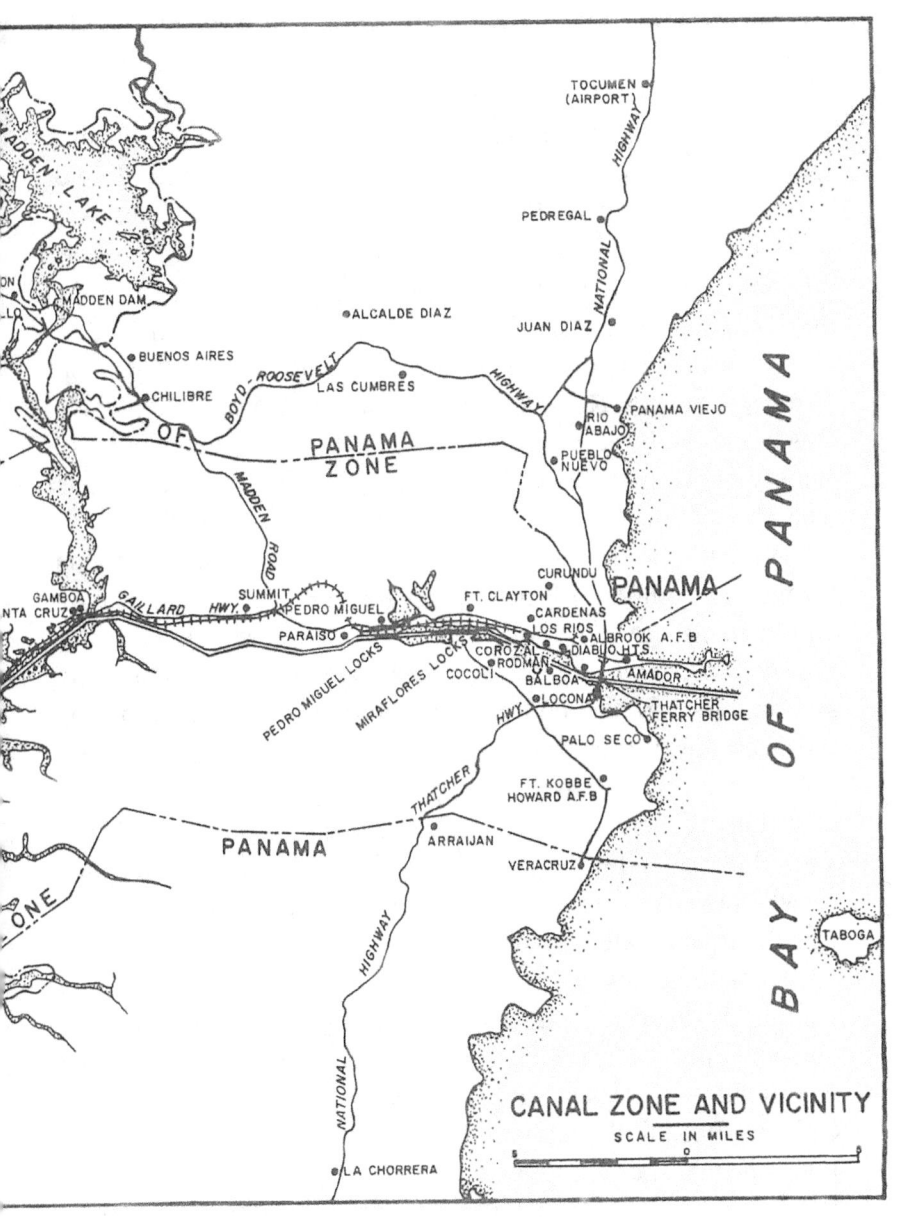

Panama Canal Zone: Pacific side south

The Pacific side of the isthmus had Pedro Miguel Locks with one pair of chambers and Miraflores Locks with two pairs of chambers. The Panama Canal Company and Canal Zone Government administration building was located in Balboa, the US military headquarters was at Quarry Heights, and Gorgas Hospital, the main healthcare facility in the Canal Zone, was located at Ancon. The towns for US citizens included Balboa, Ancon, La Boca, Cocoli, Los Rios, Diablo, Cardenas, Curundu, and Gamboa. The military installations with residential areas consisted of Quarry Heights, Fort Amador, Fort Clayton, Fort Kobbe, Corozal, Rodman Naval Station, Howard Air Force Base, and Albrook Air Force Base. The other smaller military facility, previously deactivated with no housing, was Fort Grant. The non-US citizen towns were Paraiso and Pedro Miguel.

A visitor to the Canal Zone riding in a vehicle passing through a neighborhood during a non-school day or after school would likely see kids riding their bicycles or skating, playing hopscotch, sandlot football, or having fun at a community swimming pool. The pool was normally open one night during the week. It was a hangout for many kids to play water tag, water polo, jump off a diving board, play foursquare, or just sit and chat. On weekend nights, kids teamed up to play Ringalevio. They hid under hibiscus bushes, evaded the other team, and slowly moved stealthily to get closer to home base to rescue and free their teammates captured by the opposing team.

Weekends saw a heap of additional activities, including visiting the beaches in the Canal Zone and the numerous sandy getaways outside the Canal Zone in Panama. Some favorites were Shimmy Beach, Devil's Beach, Pina Beach, Maria Chiquita Beach, Playa Langosta, Playa Blanca, and Isla Grande for its beach, snorkeling, and scuba diving on the Atlantic side. Popular beaches on the Pacific side were Amador Beach, Playa Coronado, Playa Gorgona, Playa Rio Mar, Playa Santa Clara, and Isla Taboga. Families traveled to the opposite sides of the isthmus to enjoy a day of fun in the sun, depending on how far they wanted to drive.

Many Zonians reveled in water activities, including sailing, water skiing, canoeing, swimming, and hanging out at one of the various yacht clubs. At the Gatun Yacht Club, kids would swim out to buoy "A," a marker for ships traversing Gatun Lake, and then climb to the top of the buoy to attempt rocking it from side to side.

Fishing enthusiasts relished having some of the best fishing in the world, including deep-sea fishing, spear fishing, and angling for peacock bass at Gatun Lake. Fishing was a part of life for many of us, although using fishing tackle or having a fishing line wrapped around a stick were not the only ways to fish for snook. The Barger boys, with friends at times, did some rock fishing. The Finneman boys, with the same friends, had another method: stick fishing. And, a Klasovsky kid once used a golf club. Their unusual and comedic methods of fishing without a rod and reel were fairly effective, some more than others.

Besides the abundance of water activities, folks spent time at the golf courses, tennis courts, horse riding stables, motocross dirt trails, and the gun and skeet club ranges. There was something for most everyone to do and enjoy, including a square-dancing club, bridge card playing, bowling, visiting the roller skating rink, and then going to the cafeteria. Hot French fries served in a small brown bag were an appetizing snack for kids. They would add ketchup, close the bag, and shake it all together to enjoy eating.

During the summer months, for families not on "home leave" vacation stateside, the community swimming pool, recreational fields, and gymnasium became hot spots for many kids, partaking in archery, baseball, volleyball, basketball, battleball, kickball, badminton, and ping pong (table tennis). A non-organized sporting activity for kids in neighborhoods with hills was sliding down them on their bottom. Another preferred method was using a torn cardboard box as a sled, which was a faster ride and cleaner, so kids didn't have to explain to their mother (or the family help) how they got the grass stains or ripped the bottom of their pants.

The towns across the Canal Zone were unique in their own way, based on location and amenities. There was a sense of pride about where residents lived and a competitive spirit. Many towns had sports teams that competed against each other at the gymnasium, recreational sports fields, and swimming pool. The Atlantic side swim teams included the Coco Solo Sharks, Margarita Marlins, and Gatun Gators. My participation on the Gatun Gators swim team prepared me for later being on the Gatun Boy Scout Troop 12, the 200-meter relay team, that won a gold medal in a Canal Zone Boy Scout Olympics. The Pacific side teams included the Balboa Barracudas, Curundu Crocodiles, Gamboa Dolphins, and Los Rios Sting Rays. The experiences gained in these sports activities built confidence and teamwork.

Besides the usual sporting events, there was one competition that was a highly esteemed achievement: the annual Ocean-to-Ocean Cayuco Race that started on the Atlantic side of the isthmus and ended on the Pacific side. What began in 1954 as a Boy Scout Explorers event of an approximately 50-mile grueling Cayuco Race expanded in 2000 after the US turned the Canal over to Panama. Cayucos are boats similar to canoes. They were originally made from dugout large tree trunks and used as a form of transportation. The Panamanians continued the annual tradition with minor changes and different categories, including a juvenile and an open group. This unique race is the only one of its kind in the world to have international teams enter the competition. The Boy Scout Explorer crews and others who competed in the race possess a life-long memory that not many others have had the opportunity to experience.

Once the summer months ended and the school year began, kids from the various elementary schools joined adolescents and teens at Cristobal Jr. Sr. High School in Coco Solo on the Atlantic side, or Curundu Junior High School on the Pacific side, before moving on to Balboa High School in Balboa. Local non-US citizen towns attended their own schools, although some non-US citizen families living in and out of the Canal Zone paid tuition to send their kids to US schools in the Zone.

The start of the school year was the continuation of competitive sports activities. Instead of town teams competing against each other, school teams competed, representing the opposite sides of the isthmus.

Attending a football game between Cristobal Jr. Sr. High School from the Atlantic side and Balboa High School or Canal Zone Junior College on the Pacific side was different than just driving across town. Students either traveled with their family by car 50 miles across the Roosevelt Transisthmian Highway or rode on the Panama Railway Student Association Train, chartered specifically for those events.

Prior to the event, students bought their train tickets in their homeroom class. The tickets were color-coded for a designated train coach. However, students swapped their tickets with other students to be in the same coach as their friends.

Students were explicitly informed and forbidden from leaving the Canal Zone to enter Panama City. But of course, some ignored it. I recall a time a group of us skipped a football game and ventured off walking down a street through Ancon to get to Gorgas Hospital, then strolling down a hill and crossing the street into Panama City to eat at a little place called Napoli's Pizzeria on Calle 1. If anyone had caught us, we would have been in big trouble with school officials, who would likely have given us a three or four-hour detention on a Saturday, and our parents, with grounding at home.

The end of the calendar year, starting with Halloween, transitioning into the holiday season was as fun and festive in the Canal Zone as it was stateside. Following Thanksgiving, families adorned their residences with colored bulbs and decorated real Christmas trees. December brought out the evening gowns and formal attire for Zonians attending a gala and ball event.

At the start of the new year, community residents gathered for their annual after-Christmas tree bonfire with games, music, and more competitiveness. Teams from the town would collect the discarded Christmas trees throughout their neighborhoods and sometimes from other towns. Some crews would attempt to locate other teams' hidden trees by following the decorative tinsel into the jungle. The January event culminated with teams hauling their stockpile of trees to a designated location, supervised by the fire department, to make a huge mass for the bonfire. The winning group with the most trees received movie tickets with free popcorn. It was never about getting the tickets; it was about the challenge and having fun.

Living in the Canal Zone within the Republic of Panama was special and wondrous. I will venture to say that most Zonians remember the Canal Zone as a marvelous place to raise their children. Families enjoyed the splendor of life and amenities in the Canal Zone and the wonders of beautiful Panama, from its beaches to the picturesque highlands of El Valle and mountainous areas in Volcan and Boquette. Although, as with everything in life, nothing lasts forever. The unincorporated US territory known as the Panama Canal Zone ceased to exist on October 1, 1979. What endures are the lifelong bonds forged, the memories, and being a part of a legacy derived from our parents, grandparents, or great-grandparents.

Occupations and Operations

The Panama Canal Company (PCC) and Canal Zone Government (CZG) required myriad occupations to maintain the Panama Canal Zone. The PCC and CZG were a composite of different bureaus and divisions.

The PCC consisted of bureaus, including the Office of the Comptroller, Personnel, Community Services, Supply and Service, Industrial, Railroad and Terminals, Engineering and Construction, and Marine. Visitors to the Canal Zone or transiting by ship across the isthmus saw the most visible and publicly photographed divisions from the Marine Bureau at work, consisting of Navigations, Locks, and Dredging.

The CZG had the Civil Affairs and Health Bureaus. The divisions within the two bureaus included the Division of Schools, Postal, Customs and Immigrations Division, Police, Fire, Hospitalization and Clinics, and Dental Clinics. Some of these divisions and others from the PCC provided the services that made the Canal Zone a great place to raise a family.

Additionally, the PCC and CZG non-US labor workforce was essential to operations throughout the Canal Zone. They held numerous positions that assisted with daily operations. Also, many Zonian families cherished the local ladies they employed as their help. These ladies did household chores, including cleaning, dusting, laundry, ironing, cooking, and some assisted in raising the children. I credit Elida, our live-in help during my childhood, for never smoking. When I was nine, I asked her for a cigarette. She responded with "No" and that I could not and should not smoke. After annoying her to let me try a cigarette, she did. I got a vile reaction. Looking at me sternly with a slight smile, she said, "I told you so, no smoking."

The following stories are snippets of the lives of PCC and CZG employees and their families who lived in the Canal Zone. The overwhelming majority of these Zonians called it home. Some of the family stories include their home address, house number, and street name, which you can locate by navigating the town maps in "The Lost Towns" chapter.

THE ZONIANS

Leland Darrel Snider
Supervisory Admeasurer • Panama Canal Company
US Marine Corps, Korean War Veteran

Leland "Lee" Darrel Snider was born on October 9, 1931, in the small agricultural community of Logan, Kansas. He added to the population of fewer than 900 people, where, in high school, he played football, basketball, and baseball. In 1949, less than a year after graduating, Lee left the small rural town and, in 1950, enlisted in the United States Marine Corps (USMC). After completing his Marine Corps boot camp, he shipped out to the Korean War. In September of that year, Lee was a part of the USMC amphibious landing force at the port of Inchon. He received the Purple Heart for wounds he sustained during the battle.

Returning to the United States marked a significant turning point for Lee while stationed in Bremerton, Washington, where he met his future wife, Kathleen "Kathy" Ann Wenzl. Her friend, John Triggs, introduced them at a church social. Kathy was born in Clovis, New Mexico, on December 6, 1931. Her family moved to Bremerton during World War II, where her father worked as a welder in the shipyard.

Leopold J. Cimino

Following a four-month courtship, Lee and Kathy married in September 1952. Lee left the Marine Corps in 1954, at the end of his enlistment. They had their first child, Michael "Mike" Lee, born in March 1954. The following year, the family grew with the birth of Patricia "Patty" Marie in June 1955. Then, in October 1956, Elizabeth "Beth" Ann joined the family. The family had more additions in January 1958 with the birth of twins, James "Jim" Edward and Thomas 'Tom" Edwin. Two years later, in April 1960, the family added Theresa Lynn to the roll call.

Following his discharge from the Marine Corps, Lee worked as a machinist apprentice at the Puget Sound Naval Shipyard. He remained active in sports, playing softball and basketball. Lee also coached youth league basketball and football at his church parish school.

In early 1963, Lee was offered a job in the Panama Canal Zone. He and Kathy jumped at the chance for several reasons: they had friends there, Panama offered excellent fishing, cheap housing, maid service, a 25 percent increase in salary, free shipping of their household goods and vehicle, travel expenses, warm weather, and adventure.

Accepting the job in the Canal Zone required a two-year commitment with an all-expenses paid return trip to the United States after the completion of the obligation. Or, the family could pledge to an additional two years and get a paid vacation to travel back to Bremerton. Lee and Kathy felt it was worth the gamble. They knew they could handle two years.

So, in March 1963, Lee and Kathy, with their six children, set off on a road trip in their nine-passenger Ford station wagon with their luggage and Lee's machinist toolbox on top of the vehicle. They visited family in Logan, Kansas, en route to the seaport of embarkation. After arriving in New Orleans, Louisiana, they boarded and loaded their car on the SS Cristobal for their voyage to the Canal Zone.

Upon arriving at the Port of Cristobal, a friend, Cecil Caudill, waited for passengers to disembark. He asked the purser, "Are there any Sniders aboard?"

"Yes, a whole boatload," the purser responded with a smile.

Initially, Lee worked as a marine machinist, repairing, adjusting, and installing equipment. Two years later, he took a position as an admeasurer assistant, a boarding officer, the first point of contact for vessels awaiting in the harbor. In this position, he facilitated the smooth entry and departure of ships, ensuring they fulfilled statutory formalities and the required declarations. In early 1968, he advanced to an admeasurer position. The job entailed examining blueprints and taking physical measurements of a ship, figuring out the tonnage of a vessel, and then calculating the rate a vessel is charged to transit through the Panama Canal.

Kathy stayed busy raising the kids and later worked in several government positions with the Canal Zone Government, Panama Canal Company, and the Department of the Army. She started in inventory at Coco Solo Hospital, then as a secretary at the US Army School of Americas, and in the telephone office at Fort Davis. The furthest distance she drove was approximately ten miles when she took a position as a secretary at the Gatun Locks. She jumped at the opportunity to work in the library at Cristobal Jr. Sr. High School, which was less than a mile from home. A year later, she got another pay increase when she took a job as the secretary for the Army Alcohol and Drug Abuse Office at Fort Davis.

Kathy and Lee welcomed their seventh child, William "Bill" Carl, born at Coco Solo Hospital in May 1967. Maintaining a household with seven children did not slow them down from enjoying life with their kids.

Having help from a locally employed maid, Una Samuels Smith, greatly assisted the family. Una rode a colorfully painted "chiva" bus approximately four miles from the seaport city of Colon to Coco Solo. Employed in 1965, Una worked Monday through Friday doing household tasks, including laundry, sweeping and mopping floors, cleaning windows and bathrooms, polishing door knobs, washing dishes, ironing clothes, and nursing the kids when they were sick. She did everything but cook. She loved the kids, and they adored her.

The family loved playing cards and board games together. Lee and Kathy also enjoyed playing bridge, taking family outings, and attending the kids' sporting events as they grew older. The kids participated in almost all sports, including volleyball, swimming, diving, football, tennis, baseball, track, soccer, and rugby. The girls also took ballet, tap, and jazz lessons for years from Ann Downing School of Dance. Patty, Beth, and Theresa were also cheerleaders.

The Snider family: (top left) Bill, Lee, Kathy, Patty, Mike, Beth, Jim, Theresa, Tom

Living in the Canal Zone was a wonderland for water activities. The family took water safety seriously, and in time, most of the kids became lifeguards. Family members water-skied almost every weekend. Pina Beach was a hangout for them with friends, and they visited various other beaches to go snorkeling and skin and scuba diving. They regularly fished for peacock bass at Gatun Lake and enjoyed going deep sea fishing. Fishing at night for tarpon on the Chagres River was a thrill.

The Last Zonian

On one occasion, before the kids were teens, the family was fishing for tarpon on the river in their boat, El Barco Borracho, "The Drunk Boat," when the excitement of trolling changed abruptly. Standing at the stern, nine-year-old Jim stumbled on a piece of equipment and fell overboard with four lines rigged with large triple hook lures trailing the boat. Lee instantly dove into the water to get Jim. No one else on board knew how to drive the boat. Luckily, the boat began moving in a circular pattern around Lee and Jim, although this caused the four trolling lines with the lures to slowly tangle and get closer around them. Fortunately, the eldest son, Mike, found the switch to turn the boat engine off. All turned out well, and family members learned how to drive the boat.

At age sixteen, Mike won the annual Tarpon Club fishing tournament in two categories: the biggest fish caught by a student and the biggest fish caught during the tournament. The silver tarpon weighed 87 pounds.

Lee and Kathy provided their children with a home filled with love and faith. The family was actively involved with Holy Family Church, the Catholic Church in Margarita. They exemplified a famous quote by Catholic Priest Patrick Peyton, "The family that prays together stays together." Family dinners were also important, so it was best not to be late.

In 1981, Lee retired after 30 years of government service, four in the USMC, eight at Puget Sound Naval Shipyard, and 18 years with the Panama Canal Company. Lee and Kathy returned to Washington State with their son, Bill, who was a freshman in high school. The other kids had already left the household, living their own lives.

After retiring from the Panama Canal Company, Lee worked in quality control and admeasurement. As an admeasurer and surveyor, he traveled extensively throughout the Northwest, Alaska, Australia, the Pacific Islands, and England. Kathy joined him on the long hauls, enjoying their time together on the adventurous trips. Sadly, after 56 years of marriage, Lee passed away on December 19, 2008, at age 77.

The Sniders: (top) Lee, Patty, Kathy
(front) Jim, Beth, Theresa, Mike, Tom, Bill

Kathy lives in Bremerton, Washington. She and Lee, blessed with seven children, have 25 grandchildren and 50 great grandchildren. Three of the seven children live fairly close to her.

After graduating from Cristobal High School (CHS) in 1972, Mike earned a bachelor's degree from Washburn University in Topeka, Kansas. He went on to attain a Juris Doctor degree. He is an attorney at his law firm, Snider & Seiwert LLC. Mike married Joan Kirkpatrick and had two sons, Carl and Nicholas. They live in Wichita, Kansas.

Patty graduated from CHS in 1973 and attended Washburn University in Topeka, Kansas. She and her husband, Kenneth Morgan, met on a blind date. They married and had three daughters: Bridgette, Leslie, and Katie. Patty worked in healthcare as a certified nursing assistant, electrocardiogram (EKG) technician, echocardiogram (ECHO) technician and cardiology technician supervisor. She attained a bachelor's and master's degree in social work. She works as a social worker in a hospital. Ken retired after a career with the State of Kansas. Patty and Ken live in Topeka, along with their three daughters and their families.

Beth graduated from CHS in 1975 and married Stephen Earnest, a Canal Zone College student. Steve enlisted in the Army, and they got stationed at Fort Hood, Texas. They had two kids, Michele and Stephen Jr. Upon completing his military enlistment, they moved to Houston, where he received a civil engineering degree at the University of Houston. He opened his own construction company, MRE Builders, Ltd., and named it after their daughter, Michele Ranae Earnest. Steve Jr. later became a construction supervisor at MRE Builders. Beth and Steve's union dissolved, and she took a job in Colorado. After years of experience in inventory control and as a production manager, she made a career change to the dental field as an office manager. Beth married Shayne Hutchinson, and after sixteen years, they split. In 2008, she relocated to be near her daughter and grandchildren in Newport, Oregon. She worked for the State of Oregon as a business service representative until her retirement. Beth lives in Topeka, Kansas.

Jim, a CHS graduate of 1976, attended Canal Zone College. A competitive athlete, he twice paddled in the grueling annual Ocean-to-Ocean Cayuco Race, once in high school and again in college. Jim completed a production machinery mechanic apprenticeship in Houston, Texas. In 1985, he took a job at the Puget Sound Naval Shipyard (PSNS) in Bremerton, Washington, to be closer to his parents and assist with his younger brother, Bill. Jim is a third-generation worker at the shipyard. He had a successful career as a mechanic and manager. He married Mary McGregor, and they had two daughters, Kerry and Shannon. Years later, Jim and Mary parted ways. They co-parented the girls and are immersed in their kids' lives. Jim, now retired, enjoys playing cards, watching and attending sporting events, and doing some traveling.

Tom graduated from CHS in 1976 and attended Canal Zone College. He married Evelyn Barraza, a Zonian from France Field. He resided in and traveled to different locations, with Evelyn being a physician in the US Army. They had three children: Kristin, Kyle, and Ryan. They live in Fox Island, Washington.

Following Theresa's CHS graduation in 1978, she attended Canal Zone College for a year, then took a secretarial position in the Panama Canal Company Construction Division. She started dating Timothy "Tim" Herring, a Zonian and 1967 graduate from CHS. There were a few raised eyebrows when she, a 19-year-old, and Tim, a 30-year-old, started dating. They married a few months later. He had previously served in the Army with a tour in Vietnam before returning to the Canal Zone in 1971. Theresa was also a preschool teacher for a few years, although, in time, she became a full-time homemaker and mother. Tim retired as a Panama Canal Company ship pilot in 1999, and the family moved stateside. They had thirteen kids: Tom, Christopher, Mary, Joe, Monique, James, Bernadette, Madeline, Angelica, Rebecca, Anna, Stephanie, and Cecilia, a baker's dozen. They live in Silverdale, Washington.

Bill was in a serious car accident in his senior year of high school in October 1984 before his graduation in 1985. An active young man, after sustaining a traumatic head injury, he had to wait until he recovered enough to attend his graduation in 1986. A sports enthusiast, he attended numerous sporting events with his brother, Jim. After Bill moved to Gilroy, California, Jim enjoyed celebrating Bill's birthday by taking him to Reno,

Nevada. In 2021, Bill relocated to be closer to family. He lives in an adult care group home in Bothell, Washington.

Una, the help, remained with the Snider family until 1981, when Lee and Kathy retired and left the former Canal Zone. Una then went to work for Theresa, who was five years old when her family initially employed Una in 1965. She stayed with Theresa and Tim until their departure in 2000. She was with members of the family for 35 years. The Snider kids took turns sending Una money monthly until her death.

In December 2016, Kathy wrote a Christmas letter to her family: "Our family went on to live eighteen wonderful years in 'Paradise.' We thank God for the adventure and the opportunity. It truly was a remarkable place to raise our growing family as we added Bill in 1967. Living there helped make us who we are today through the unusual living circumstances, closeness of friends, and wonderful faith community."

Gerald Oster
Ship Pilot • Panama Canal Company
US Army, WWII Post Era Veteran

The year 1929, when Gerald "Jerry" Oster was born on April 29, ended a thriving period for his birthplace in the Bronx Borough of New York City. What followed was The Great Depression, which commenced in August 1929 and lasted until March 1933. The borough slowly declined and would not see a resurgence for half a century. Fortunately, his father, Arthur Oster, had employment as a taxi driver.

Jerry worked odd jobs as a teenager. At age 18, he dropped out of school and enlisted in the US Army in September 1946. After his military training, he was sent to Japan following its surrender a year earlier on September 2, 1945. He served as part of the Allied occupation of Japan, which lasted from 1945 to 1952.

After completing his enlistment in September 1948, Jerry remained in Japan, taking a job with the Military Sea Transportation Service (MSTS) at the Yokohama Port. Shortly after that, the outbreak of the Korean War began in 1950. The port and MSTS where Jerry worked played a vital role as a transport terminal for United Nations forces.

In 1952, in Fukuoka, Japan, Jerry met Toshiko Takiuchi through a friend, and they started dating. Toshiko, born in Fukuoka on April 21, 1931, was a young teen when she witnessed the Allied strategic bombing that began in 1944. Following the turmoil of the war, meeting Jerry was a great joy for Toshiko.

The Korean War ended in 1953. Jerry and Toshiko married in April of that year. Their son, Stanley Arthur, was born in August 1954 in Yokohama, Japan. Three years later, Toshiko gave birth to a second son, Robert "Bob" Leonard, * in July 1957, also in Yokohama.

Jerry worked for MSTS in various positions, progressing in rank from an able seaman (AB) to becoming a fourth officer aboard the cargo ship USNS Private Leonard C. Brostrom. He made numerous seafaring round trips from Japan to the United States during that time.

In June 1965, he moved his family to the Panama Canal Zone after accepting the Panama Canal Company's offer to receive Canal ship pilot training. The family initially moved to the town of Coco Solo on the Atlantic side of the isthmus for a few months before moving to France Field, about two miles away. The neighborhood, although small, had its charm.

When Jerry completed his intense training and received his unlimited Panama Canal pilot's license in January 1967, the family had settled into living in the Canal Zone. Being a Panama Canal pilot came with enormous responsibility. Jerry would be ferried to a ship awaiting transit through the Panama Canal. Then, he took responsibility for its navigation in Canal waters, which usually took about ten hours to cross from one side of the isthmus to the other.

Although he worked long hours, Jerry and Toshiko did their share of socializing and barbecuing with friends and other pilots, many of whom they knew while living in Japan, including the Sandrock, Robertson, McDonald, Katsumoto, Pritchard,

Uyeshiro, Keller, and Tyler families. They, too, received recruitment offers for positions with the Panama Canal Company.

Jerry was always doing something for entertainment. He frequented the Cristobal Gun Club and range. The Brazos Brook Golf and Country Club was a good place to relax with family. He and Toshiko spent time chatting with friends, plus it was a decent place for family dinners. A favorite activity was getting out to eat and enjoying different cuisines at restaurants in and out of the Canal Zone. The Breakers Club in Coco Solo provided a great view of the bay and the city of Colon. The Gatun Yacht Club at Gatun Lake was another hangout; the boys could also go swimming. There was no slowing Jerry down. Being mechanically inclined, he stayed busy fixing cars.

Toshiko, on the other hand, was more mellow. She enjoyed gardening, reading, cooking, and spending time with her friends. However, on one occasion, she jumped into action when called upon to assist as an interpreter for a Japanese seaman who was rushed to the hospital following an accident aboard a vessel that severed one of his legs.

The family stayed occupied on weekends when Jerry was off work and during summer breaks. Visiting the numerous beaches on both sides of the isthmus provided tranquility for Jerry and Toshiko, especially when the boys were younger. Shimmy Beach at Fort Sherman on the Atlantic side was a relaxing recreational site for many families since it had a snack bar, changing facility with showers, and lifeguards. Pina and Maria Chiquita beaches were other short-day excursions. Beach getaways to the Pacific side to Rio Mar and Santa Clara were day trips or overnight stays. The family's fun beach days lessened as Stanley and Bob got older and were doing their own thing with friends.

Periodic travel stateside, brought excitement and a change of scene. When Jerry enlisted in the US Army and left the Bronx in September 1946, he had no idea where his journey would take him. Later, he and the family occasionally visited his relatives up north. He knew he would never return to live in the Bronx, though, with weather being one factor. They vacationed more in the south with its warmer climate. Miami, Florida, became a desired locale with its tropical vibe. Additionally, while visiting the city, coincidentally or not, Jerry almost always attended a coin collection show since his hobby was coin collecting after his son, Bob, introduced it to him.

While family outings and life changed somewhat when the boys entered high school and became more independent, the family's close bond was evident. When able, Jerry joined Toshiko at the boys' sports events. They both played football and ran track in high school, and Bob was also on the baseball team. Hanging out with friends, going to the beach, and the Gatun Yacht Club occupied much of their time.

Stanley initially got around riding his Yamaha 175cc motorcycle. Musically talented, he played the drums, bass guitar, and an organ. He played bass in a band with Jaime Barraza, Gaspar Sayoc, and Julio "Papo" Aponte. The band was featured on the Southern Command Network television in the Canal Zone.

Bob also relished riding his Yamaha 360cc motorcycle and going dirt biking. The nearby France Field airstrip was a perfect place to ride minibikes until being spotted and chased by military police (MP) in the no-trespassing area. Eluding the MPs was exciting, especially when they disappeared into tall sawgrass, where the police vehicle had to stop its chase, allowing Bob and his friends to flee back to the neighborhood.

Living in the France Field housing area was mainly quiet and peaceful. However, during crab mating season, it was a nuisance for many residents having to deal with the numerous crustaceans roaming the neighborhood. The Oster family help, maids Ida and Maria, did not mind the crabs, which they happily plucked, boiled in a large pot, and enjoyed eating.

After Jerry became the President of the Panama Canal Pilots Association in 1973, the family moved to Los Rios on the Pacific side. Jerry had an active role during negotiations for Panama Canal pilots, including trips to Washington, DC, to meet with federal government officials to discuss ship pilot safety and seek better equipment to transit ships through the Canal.

Moving to the opposite side of the isthmus meant acquainting themselves with new places. Jerry was always up for going out to eat at different restaurants in Panama City and the Tivoli Hotel in the Canal Zone. He enjoyed getting together with fellow pilots for dinner and drinks. Toshiko liked shopping with her friends and occasionally trying her luck on the slot machines. At home, she found tranquility in her gardening and stayed occupied taking care of Terry, the family dog, and astutely watching over her son Bob to make sure he was being safe. Bob was getting around in a high-performance Z28 Camaro, partying with friends at the Balboa Yacht Club, the Fort Amador causeway, and discotheques in Panama City.

Stanley & Bob Oster

In 1976, as President of the Panama Canal Pilots Association, Jerry played a key role in the effectiveness of an employee "sick-out." The pilots' union responded to a possible employee wage base freeze with support for the "sick-out," which prevented ships from transiting the Canal. It was the first shutdown of the

Panama Canal since 1915, when a massive rock slide closed the passage for nearly seven months.

Jerry retired in December 1979 after 29 years of government service. He and Toshiko moved to Thousand Oaks, California. He worked for Chevron Shipping Company for several years in California before transferring to Honolulu, Hawaii, to become the port captain. Life was grand for them. They enjoyed island life, treasured visits from family and friends, and getting out to restaurants. Jerry spent time at the gun range, remodeling their home, and working on cars. As always, Toshiko enjoyed shopping with friends and gardening.

Jerry & Toshiko Oster

Jerry passed away on February 2, 1998, in Honolulu at age 68. Toshiko remained in Honolulu for many years. In 2020, her son Bob insisted she move closer to him in California. Toshiko completed her life at 90 in Torrance, California, on May 22, 2021.

Stanley graduated from Cristobal High School in 1972. He attended college in Salinas, California, for a year and later enlisted in the US Navy and served from May 7, 1975, to January 10, 1978. When he returned to the Canal Zone, Stanley worked in Gamboa for a while and then married Marissa. They had three daughters: Sandra, Sarah, and Abigail. He moved to Los Angeles, California, and worked for the US Postal Service. Stanley and Marissa parted ways, and he relocated to Honolulu. He enjoyed working on and fixing up cars. After his mother passed away, he moved to be closer to his daughter Sandra in

The Last Zonian

Goose Creek, near Charleston, South Carolina. Stanley passed away on November 13, 2021, at age 67.

In 1976, after graduating from Balboa High School (BHS), Bob moved stateside to attend San Antonio College in Texas with other Zonian friends. He transferred a year later to the University of Tampa in Florida. Attaining an associate degree, he transferred to Florida State University earning a bachelor's in criminology in 1980. He married Christine Harrington in May 1982. She had also attended BHS. They moved to Los Angeles for job opportunities and to be somewhat closer to his parents, who lived in Hawaii. They had two kids, Brandon and Ryan. Bob retired as an insurance investigator. Chris works as an operating room surgical tech. Bob and Chris live in Torrance, California. They enjoy traveling to Hawaii, visiting family on the East Coast, and attending the annual Panama Canal Society Reunions.

Bob, when asked what he thought about the Canal Zone, replied, "Living in the Canal Zone was paradise. There was wildlife and vegetation people will never experience unless they grew up in a tropical place. Surrounded by water, we enjoyed the beaches, swimming, and fishing. There was hardly any crime. As kids, we could stay out all day and not have to worry about anything. We made friendships with people from all over the States, especially with military dependents who lived there for three or four years and then moved back to the States. We also got to taste a variety of foods from different nationalities. I miss the place, the beauty, and all the people there as I was growing up."

* Bob is the last Zonian in the Oster family.

Theodore Lester Bailey
Tugboat Captain • Panama Canal Company
US Navy, WWII Veteran

April 21, 1923, was a pleasant sunny day, not muggy at all, when Melville Maximilian Goldstine Jr. was born in New Orleans, Louisiana. His mother later changed his name to Theodore Lester Bailey. A few twists to this story involve a young Lester Floyd Bailey, who fell in love and assisted an older co-worker, Edith Florence Silvera Goldstine.

Years earlier, at seventeen, Edith married Arthur J. Stewart in August 1908, and they had one child, Earl Stewart. By January 1920, she and her son were already living with her parents when she became a widow.

Melville Maximilian Goldstine, a soldier from Chicago, Illinois, returned home in July 1919 after serving a year in France during WWI and attaining the rank of first sergeant. Five months later, he reenlisted at the rank of private, and was stationed in New Orleans. While in the city at Jackson Barracks, he met Edith. They married on March 9, 1920, before he shipped out in April to the Panama Canal Zone. Edith followed him shortly thereafter.

Lester Bailey, a soldier from Kittery, Maine, arrived in the Canal Zone in November 1920. In May 1922, upon completing his tour of duty, he returned stateside. At the time, he had yet to meet Edith.

Edith left the Canal Zone in October 1922 to live with her parents in New Orleans, where she gave birth to her second son, Melville Jr., in April 1923. Melville Sr., by then a sergeant, completed his Army enlistment in December 1922 and started working as a civilian government employee that same month. Unable to get family government quarters in the Canal Zone, he traveled to New Orleans in November 1922 and on August 16, 1923, to see Edith before she returned to the Canal Zone.

Lester completed his Army enlistment in September 1923 and returned to the Canal Zone, where he initially worked as a clerk. After Edith returned to Panama, she gave birth to her daughter, Marjorie Edith Goldstine, on June 10, 1924, at Gorgas Hospital, Ancon, Canal Zone. Less than a year later, while Edith was raising her young children during Melville Sr.'s time in jail for fraud, she got a job at the same location as Lester. He fell in love with Edith and assisted her while Melville was in jail.

Melville, after being incarcerated for a year, from January 1925 to January 1926, immediately departed the Canal Zone upon his release. Edith and Melville legally parted ways in August 1926. Edith and Lester married in Panama City on December 8, 1926.

Edith changed her son's name from Melville Maximilian Goldstine Jr. to Theodore Lester Bailey in honor of her brother, Captain Theodore Alexis Silvera, a WWI veteran who passed away in August 1926, and Lester Bailey, her new husband, who helped her during a turbulent time. She changed Marjorie Edith's last name from Goldstine to Bailey.

Melville never remarried. He later moved to Texas and reenlisted in the Army, serving from 1927 to 1930. He passed away on January 31, 1932, in San Antonio, Texas. Lester became an accountant in the Panama Canal Industrial Division, and Edith worked as an operator in an accounting department. Lester officially adopted Marjorie when she was 18 years old. He and Edith were happily married for 43 years.

In 1941, at eighteen (and no longer known as Melville Maximilian Goldstine Jr.), Theodore "Ted" graduated from Balboa High School and went stateside in September to attend college at the United States Merchant Marine Academy in Kings Point, New York. Ted received a commission as an ensign in the US Navy in January 1944. He served in the North Atlantic during WWII.

After the war, he worked for Standard Oil (Esso) aboard ships. While living in New York City, he met Patricia "Pat" Regina Sinclair. Pat was born on July 11, 1930, in New York. She lived in the Bronx with her parents, Edward and Mary Sinclair.

Ted later moved to Fort Lauderdale, Florida, while working out of Port Everglades. He and Pat married in July 1949 in Broward County, Florida. Due to Ted's extensive absences aboard ships in the Caribbean, Pat temporarily moved back to the Bronx to stay with her parents. Pat and Ted celebrated the birth of their son, Ted Edward, in August 1950 while living in Hollywood, Florida.

Bailey family: Ted, baby Ted E., Pat

Ted visited his parents, Lester and Edith, in the Canal Zone a few times between 1948 and March 1952 when he and Pat went together. Ted was taking a job with the Panama Canal Company that would allow him to be home with his family rather than being away for extended absences. In February 1953, Pat and their two-year-old son, Ted E., joined Ted in the Canal Zone.

Ted took a position with the Navigation Division as a tugboat captain and then as a Canal ship pilot for a short time. The family lived on the Atlantic side of the isthmus, initially in New Cristobal for a year before moving to Margarita on the same street with Lester and Edith for a year and then to Gatun. There, Pat worked for the Physical Education and Recreation Branch as a manager at the Gatun swimming pool.

In 1956, Ted returned to be a tugboat captain. It was truly what he wanted to do since he was six years old, after seeing the ceremonial launching of three new tugboats on the Pacific side in the Canal Zone. When he was in the first grade, during the holiday season, as other children made cards with everything Christmas, Ted drew tugboats on his Christmas card. His childhood fascination led him to become a tugboat training officer, highly respected, especially by his apprentices, who spent time with him in training and at his home.

In 1957, Pat and Ted parted ways. She and Ted E. moved to Balboa where she worked as a manager at the swimming pool. A year and a half later, in 1959, she and Ted E. moved to Coco Solo upon her transfer to be a manager at that swimming pool. In early 1960, Pat and Ted remarried and lived in Coco Solo for a year before moving to Gatun.

Pat and Ted celebrated the birth of their second son, Bill Lester, born in July 1962 at Coco Solo Hospital. Hortense, a Jamaican gal, was the hired help and greatly assisted the family. She helped with chores and the boys. She watched Ted E. grow up from the sixth grade through high school graduation to his move stateside. And she watched Bill from a newborn to his teenage years.

The Last Zonian

Ted and Pat were known in Gatun since they previously lived in the community. He also served a stint on the Gatun Civic Council and she was known from her prior employment at the swimming pool. They spent time with their close friends, the Spilling and Paulson families, playing cards, having cookouts, and attending social events.

Although Ted lived adjacent to Gatun Lake, a world-class fishing location, he preferred saltwater fishing. While living in Coco Solo and Gatun, he and his buddies would go on fishing trips to the Pacific side and return home with coolers full of red snapper. He gave most of his share away to the neighbors since he preferred eating corbina. He did quite a bit of lobstering, using his boat to get close to the Atlantic breakwater and reefs, a short distance from the shoreline, near Fort Randolph on the Caribbean coast.

Catching small freshwater fish was another fun quest. The family had several fish aquariums in their home. So, whenever Ted went on escapades into the Interior of Panama, he often brought home small fish that he netted from a mountainous stream.

Traveling stateside on vacations was always an adventure, although, at times, the boys were impatient to get to their destination. This stemmed from Ted's curiosity while driving from New Orleans to Ft. Lauderdale. He tended to stop numerous times along the way at locations of interest, which extended the duration to get to their ultimate destination.

Ted E., when knowing the family would travel stateside by sea on the SS Cristobal, would prep empty bottles with a note in each, then seal the caps with wax. On one occasion, traveling to New Orleans, he dropped four bottles overboard, one each day. An indigenous man from Nicaragua found a bottle, could not read the note, and walked three days to see someone who translated it. Three months later, the Bailey family received notice that someone found a bottle. Ted, being a seafarer, sent the man $50.00 for his concern initiated by the actions of his son, Ted E.

Ted, Pat, and the boys did "stay vacations" with friends in the Interior of Panama as well, renting lodging at Santa Clara beach to enjoy fishing, horseback riding along the shore, and evening cookouts. Life was grand.

At home, Ted had a passion for astronomy. He had a nice telescope to view the night sky with the boys. Viewing the stars is something he did during his many years traveling aboard ships. The sea is what Ted had known most of his life. Keeping to his liking of the sea, he taught the boys boating and bottom fishing. They became avid fishermen and skin divers, learning the best fishing spots.

Bill & Ted Bailey

Most Atlantic siders had several favorite fishing locations. When not in a boat, Ted E. would go fishing at the Gatun Locks's north end in a building with an inner boat dock. The building had a no-trespassing sign, but he ignored it like other Gatun kids and found a way to sneak into the fishing spot. Once, while fishing, he heard a car on the gravel road pulling up to the building. Peeping out a window, he saw a police car and hid. What he heard next was, "I know you're in there, Teddy." It was Policeman Gayle Fortner. To Ted E.'s surprise, the policeman gave him a duplicate key to the building. Policeman Fortner was also a fisherman, and he, too, often fished there with his family.

Bill also spent a lot of time near or in the water. He liked fishing for tarpon. He and his buddies fished at the lake and the Chagres River. They would haul in silver king tarpon 5 or 6 feet long. He also participated in the grueling Ocean-to-Ocean Cayuco Race.

Pat devoted more time to her artistic talent of painting. In July 1970, one of her paintings and two others from her friends and painters, Sonia Schack and Evelyn Miesse, were placed in a museum in the city of Colon. Having a religious upbringing, Pat volunteered with the Catholic Church's Society of St. Vincent de Paul organization assisting in a low-income community. She also frequently visited the Palo Seco Hospital, once a leprosy colony, which was later converted and used for the palliative care of elders and children with disabilities.

Ted retired in April 1985 after 33 years of federal government service. He and Pat moved to Florida, settling in Dunnellon, a location of interest that he stopped at during a stateside vacation. They were happy relaxing at home, reading, attending church, and taking occasional trips to see their Zonian friends, the Spillings in New Orleans, and the Paulsons in Tallahassee.

Pat and Ted parted ways for the second time in early 1992. Two years later, Ted passed away on May 7, 1994, at age 71, in Dunnellon. The ashes of the tugboat captain, respectfully considered by many as "The Old Man of the Sea," were returned to the former Canal Zone. In a ceremony with family and friends held aboard a tugboat at Gamboa, where the Chagres River flows into the Panama Canal, his ashes joined the water gently drifting in both directions of the Canal, leading to the Pacific and Atlantic oceans. Two years later, Pat passed away on February 3, 1996, in Dunnellon, at age 65.

Ted Edward graduated from Cristobal High School (CHS) in 1968, then moved stateside. Having an adventurous disposition, he traveled extensively for a couple of years, working various jobs. While working as a seaman aboard a ship crossing the Pacific, Ted E. dropped 100 empty bottles with notes in them overboard. However, after waiting for years, he never received one response. He attended Humboldt State College in California, majoring in oceanography. While there, he met another student, Pamela Gay Wilcox. They married in October 1971. They had two children, Matthew and Samuel. After switching his major, Ted E. earned a bachelor's in civil engineering and a master's in mechanical engineering at California State University in Sacramento. He worked in engineering for over 30 years with a few companies, ending with NTN Technical Center, Inc., in Ann Arbor, Michigan. He and Pam enjoyed spending time together, going out to dinner, the movies, visiting a museum, and sightseeing. Sadly, after 50 years of marriage, Pam passed away on June 17, 2021. Ted is semi-retired and works as an engineering consultant, teaches flight science seminars, substitutes as a science and math teacher in local schools, and manages an online webpage specializing in boomerangs and flight devices. A NASA spin-off publication recognized his technical expertise in 1992. Ted E. lives in Ann Arbor, Michigan.

Bill graduated from CHS, class of 1980. He attended Purdue University in Indiana for a short time before earning a bachelor's in electrical engineering from Florida Atlantic University in Boca Raton. He worked for General Dynamics Electric Boat in Connecticut and, later, Schlumberger Oil Company. He lived and traveled extensively abroad, including Trinidad and Tobago, Patagonia in Argentina and Chile, Brazil, and the Amazon River. After leaving Schlumberger, his exploratory spirit led him to travel and live in New Zealand, Australia, and the South Pacific Islands. He later moved and settled in the northwest. While Bill never married, he has a longtime girlfriend. Bill lives in Bellevue, Washington, and enjoys kayaking.

The Last Zonian

Ted E. conveyed that he thought Gatun was like living in a magical place with a real sense of community. His family had wonderful memories and stories, and they could tell many more about life in the Canal Zone.

John Thomas O'Donnell Jr.
Leader Marine Machinist • Panama Canal Company
US Navy, WWII Veteran

When John Thomas O'Donnell Jr. was born on June 29, 1920, in Philadelphia, Pennsylvania, the city was overcrowded. A large populace worked in textile factories filled with child labor, and the ratification of the 18th Amendment (Prohibition) to the United States Constitution of 1919, banning the manufacturing, transport, and sale of alcohol, was in effect. By 1925, the city was dealing with political and economic issues. Four years later, Philadelphia felt the severity of the economic downturn with The Great Depression.

Fortunately, John Jr.'s father, John T. O'Donnell Sr., had left Philadelphia and arrived in the Panama Canal Zone in the early 1920s. He worked as an accountant. Shortly after, his wife, Agnes Callahand O'Donnell, and their four children, Maria, John Jr., Daniel, and Robert joined him. While living in the Canal Zone, John and Agnes added three more children, James, Paul, and Thomas, to their large Catholic family.

When John Jr. graduated from Balboa High School in 1938, he secured an apprenticeship with the Panama Canal to train as a machinist. Upon completing his apprenticeship, he became a certified machinist working with Mr. George King in the Mechanical Division in Balboa on the Pacific side of the isthmus. George, 20 years older and with years of experience as a machinist, became a mentor to John. Off work in his early twenties, John got around riding a motorcycle, his prized possession.

After the United States entered World War II, John attempted to enlist in the US Navy several times but was denied. His employment with the Panama Canal made him part of the vital workforce needed for Canal operations to ensure US and Allied ships could transit between the Atlantic and Pacific oceans. Finally, on January 3, 1945, he got his enlistment in the Navy and was assigned to the 15th Naval District, Balboa, Canal Zone. He served aboard the USS PC 1221, a patrol craft and submarine chaser, in the Caribbean. Four months later, Germany surrendered on May 7, 1945, followed by Japan on September 2, 1945, ending WWII.

While stationed at US Naval Station Balboa, John was able to leave the base when off duty to see family and friends. The Canal Zone was home for him. One evening, in the spring of 1946, the red-haired, freckled young man knocked on the door to the residence of his mentor, George King, to see if he wanted to get something to eat and drink. As the story goes, a hot 20-year-old babe opened the door. She was George's daughter, Edna Mae King, born on August 29, 1925, in Easton, Pennsylvania. She arrived in the Canal Zone

Edna & John O'Donnell

with her mother after graduating from Easton High School to join her father in January 1944 and worked as a clerk. Edna had briefly returned to Pennsylvania in early May 1946 before coming to live in the Canal Zone. John was unaware that his mentor had a daughter. The rest is history. Shortly thereafter, John and Edna married in Easton, Pennsylvania. When John was discharged from the Navy on June 5, 1946, he returned to his machinist position.

After becoming a family man, he sold his Indian motorcycle and settled for an automobile. He and Edna added to their family with the birth of their daughter, Mary Frances, in February 1947 while living on the Pacific side of the isthmus.

They moved to Margarita on the Atlantic side when he took a machinist position at Mt. Hope in the Industrial Division. He later attained additional skills as a hard hat diver marine machinist. There, he worked on ship overhauls and engines, constructing new parts with a lathe machine, resolving emergency ship situations, and making prop repairs above and below the water to ensure a ship could safely transit through the Panama Canal and continue on its voyage. He received accolades for his expertise and knowledge with a decompression chamber that saved a man's life.

Mt. Hope was less than a mile and a half from their living quarters, 8514 Campana Place in Margarita, so John could quickly get home to take Edna to the hospital for the birth of their daughter, Kathleen "Kathy" Margaret, in May 1948. When Mary was born, Edna had ceased working as a clerk and became a homemaker. With the birth of Kathy, she had a full-time occupation caring for her infants.

As the girls got a little older, John and Edna enjoyed taking them to events hosted by the Elks Club, their church, and other town activities, including fish fries, spaghetti dinners, holiday celebrations, and the after-Christmas annual tree gathering bonfire. By the time Ann Marie was born in May 1957 at Coco Solo Hospital, Mary and Kathy were already riding bicycles, playing outdoors, swimming at the community pool, and attending little league baseball games with friends. Additionally, when Mary and Kathy became young teenagers, John took them to the gun range and taught them gun safety and how to shoot a rifle.

The occasional travel stateside to visit family was a joyous time, especially for the girls to see and experience something different from the Canal Zone. Sadly, one of the trips to Pennsylvania was to attend the funeral for Edna's father and John's mentor, George King, who passed away in October 1960. Because of knowing George, John met Edna and was enjoying life together with her and their family in the Canal Zone.

O'Donnell family: John, Kathy, Ann, Mary, Edna

Although John was a workaholic, they still managed to have some fun times. With her adventurous and athletic disposition, Edna expanded the family outings with her three daughters. Because of work, John missed out on exciting trips that were more than just going to the Gatun Yacht Club at Gatun Lake and Shimmy Beach at Fort Sherman near the breakwater at the Atlantic entrance of the Canal. Edna took the girls on escapades to various tourist sites on the Pacific side, visiting Summit Gardens with its small zoo, Isla Taboga, Isla Contadora, and beaches along the Pacific coastline, an hour from Panama City.

She did the same with the girls on the Atlantic side, going to Caribbean beaches outside the Canal Zone, visiting remnants of an old Spanish fortress at Portobelo, and traveling to the San Blas Islands, which is home to Kuna indigenous people known for their colorful handmade fabric molas used as pieces of clothing. As an athlete, Edna also got the girls involved in sports activities.

Mary and Kathy, known for being good, proper girls, dabbled in a little mischievousness, having more independence in their teen years. For example, partaking on a team during the after-Christmas annual tree gathering free-for-all, the girls collected and, at times, swiped trees from other teams' stashes to increase their team's total at the town's bonfire event. Having one car to share with the family meant that Mary and Kathy did not get many chances to drive, so they caught rides to the beach with friends. And, occasionally, they had a Panama Cerveza beer while hanging out.

The family cohesion began to change after Mary left the nest and moved stateside, followed by Kathy the following year. When Ann saw her older sisters moving on with their lives, she knew that she would leave the nest someday, too.

As time passed, Ann went from zipping around on skates and riding her bicycle in the neighborhood to venturing into the jungle with friends. Although a novice jungle explorer initially, she learned a hard lesson like others before her. She stood in a small sparsely grassy clearing in the tropical foliage where her shoes sank a little into the dirt. Within minutes, she felt the bites of red ants crawling up her legs in her pants and she immediately fled the clearing.

Edna served as a Girl Scout leader when Mary and Kathy were Girl Scouts. She later had Ann join the Girl Scouts to learn new skills and experience some camping. During one of these camping trips, Ann got the unwanted title of having the most mosquito bites: sixty. Ann preferred playing sports like volleyball, basketball, softball, bowling, and golfing. Edna, an avid golfer, taught Ann how to play, leading Ann to compete in golf tournaments.

John and Edna were happy living in Panama. However, all good things come to an end. And that was certainly a fact of living in the Canal Zone.

All Zonian employees knew that upon their retirement, they had to leave the Canal Zone. This fact was also known by companies, banks, and municipalities seeking to recruit and promote their interest to retirees returning stateside. That was the case with the seminar and pitch from a bank to approximately 180 Zonian families, touting how Dothan, Alabama, was a great place to live with good weather. Many Zonians did retire to the Dothan area.

John and Edna were one of those families. Following John's retirement as a leader marine machinist in July 1977, after 37 years of government service, they left the Canal Zone and moved to the Dothan area to settle with other Zonians. They enjoyed socializing with Zonian families, meeting for coffee, gathering for monthly dinners, holiday social events, annual Zonian reunions, and golfing, which Edna thoroughly liked. John was an avid reader and took up the hobby of woodworking. He spent many hours making small items that he gave to his friends who visited.

John passed away on May 23, 1987, at age 66, a month after he and Edna celebrated 41 years of marriage and 10 years of retirement from the Panama Canal Company. The once red-haired, freckled young man who got wide-eyed upon first seeing Edna open the door at her parents' house lived 52 years of his life in the Canal Zone.

Edna remained in Dothan, staying busy with church and spending time with friends, bowling, playing bridge, and traveling. She relocated in 2007 to live with her daughter, Ann, and son-in-law in Wyoming for 13 years. She then moved back to her place of birth in Easton, Pennsylvania, to be near her daughters, Mary and Kathy, and her other grandchildren. Edna passed away in Easton on August 9, 2023, at age 97.

After Mary graduated from Cristobal High School (CHS) in 1965, she attended Canal Zone College for a year and then moved to Mount Bethel, Pennsylvania, to reside with her grandmother. She became a cosmetologist and later taught at a cosmetology school. She married James A. Ceraul and they had three children: Janice, Toni, and Peter. She and James live in the small town of Pen Argyl, Pennsylvania. In their earlier years, they enjoyed the outdoors and camping.

Kathy graduated from CHS in 1966, and she, too, moved to Mount Bethel, Pennsylvania, to stay with family. She attended East Stroudsburg State College for a bit, then worked for a printing company. She married Larry Helman and had two kids, William and Leann. Their family enjoyed visiting her parents in Dothan, Alabama, and became Alabama Crimson Tide fans. Kathy and Larry live in Easton, Pennsylvania, which is fairly close to her sister, Mary. Retired, they spend more time at home with their black Labrador Retriever "Bear."

In 1975, Ann graduated from CHS. She moved to Pennsylvania in June 1976, a year before her parents departed from the Canal Zone. She then moved to Mississippi and married Steve Barger, a Zonian from Gatun she had known since the fifth grade. They had two children, Samantha and Kyle. Ann retired from the US Postal Service. She and Steve live in Casper, Wyoming, although they spend the winters with their dogs in Arizona and haul their motorcycle to enjoy riding there.

Reflecting on life in Panama, Ann stated that if her father could have stayed in the Canal Zone, he would have. It was all he knew. It was his paradise.

Leigh Cassius "Cash" Paulson
General Manager Distribution Facilities
Panama Canal Company
US Navy, WWII Veteran

Born in the small town of Corry, Pennsylvania, on August 17, 1918, Leigh Cassius "Cash" Paulson enjoyed sports. He and his three brothers grew up swimming and playing football in the summer, with ice skating and ice fishing in the winter. President of the Boys Student Council, Cash played football and was a member of Pep Club Cheerleaders in high school. After graduating, he worked for a few years at the Aero Supply Manufacturing Company, a local iron metal mill.

Cash entered the US Navy on September 9, 1942, and then shipped out to the Pacific Theater during World War II. There, he served with Navy Squadron VP-72 as an aircrewman on a Catalina PBY flying boat manufactured by the Consolidated Aircraft Corporation. The Navy acronym PBY means "PB" patrol bomber, and the "Y" was the manufacturer code. The amphibious aircraft was primarily utilized for anti-submarine warfare, search and rescue missions, and other missions, such as cargo and personnel transport. On June 29, 1944, Aviation Machinist Mate Leigh Paulson received a citation as an aircrewman on a PBY and for rendering aid to a rescued fighter pilot shot down in action off Pagan Island. The PBY was within range of the enemy-held island.

At age 26, while home on military leave in 1944, Cash met a young lady visiting the town of Corry. That encounter would change where and with whom he would live the rest of his life. Mary Jane White, visiting from the Canal Zone, was staying with her Aunt Mayme Baker in Corry. Smitten with each other, they went out on a couple of dates. Mary Jane, who was already engaged to another fellow, broke it off, knowing that she and Cash had more of a connection and deep enamored feelings for one another. After Cash's military leave ended and he returned to his Navy duties, they wrote letters to each other.

Born in Ancon, Panama Canal Zone, on April 24, 1923, Mary Jane graduated from Balboa High School in 1941. After graduation, she worked several temporary positions in the Canal Zone Administration Division. In the fall of 1941, she attended Mildred Elley Business School in Albany, New York. In early spring 1942, she took a clerical position at the Aero Supply Manufacturing Company in Corry, Pennsylvania, where her aunt lived, and pondered about her future. It was a couple of years later when she met Cash. When he returned to his Navy duty assignment, Mary Jane applied to the Panama Railroad Company, and they hired her in September 1944. She traveled to Brownsville, Texas, departing by ship back to the Canal Zone. She worked as an operations stenographer in a war service temporary position until the end of WWII. Mary Jane returned to Pennsylvania in March 1946. The exchange of letters that she and Cash wrote to each other and the long separation from one another fortified their feelings and desire to be together.

Cash returned to his hometown of Corry after being discharged from the Navy as a petty officer first class in January 1946. The following month, in February, his mother, Flossie, passed away after a lengthy illness. Cash then took a job with the Aero Supply Manufacturing Company. Shortly thereafter, Mary Jane joined him, and he asked for her hand in marriage. They married on May 15, 1946. They honeymooned in Paradise, Upper Peninsula of Michigan, a long drive from Corry. Cash's brother, Harry Jr., and his wife, Thelma, accompanied them on the journey, which was a regular occurrence in those days. No more than ten months later, the newlyweds' first child, Judith Ann, was born in March 1947. Mary Jane then became a homemaker. Two years later, following Judy's birth, their son, Leo Walter, was born in January 1949.

Mary Jane endured the cold weather and snowy winters in Corry, approximately 30 miles from the shores of Lake Erie in northwestern Pennsylvania. After several years, she was ready for a warmer climate and wanted to return to the Canal Zone. Cash, too, was looking for a change and a better prospect for his family. He saw his future in the thriving state of California. He wanted to start a sheet metal business. So, in June 1949, Mary Jane persuaded Cash to first visit her family and take a vacation in the Canal Zone, rather than setting off traveling overland. That visit lasted 30 years.

Cash took a storeroom position with the Panama Canal, Supply and Service Bureau, Commissary Division, in Balboa on the Pacific side of the isthmus and got housing on Williamson Place. Mary Jane was happy to be home. Cash held several positions, from commissary supervisor to assistant supply officer, to supervisory supply officer.

Shortly after getting settled into life in the Canal Zone, the family grew with the addition of Mark Andrew, born in June 1950. A couple of years later, a fourth child, Jane Mary, was born in April 1953. Mary Jane gave birth to both children at Ancon Hospital. Cash and Mary Jane spent much of their time with her family, who enjoyed living in the Canal Zone.

In 1956, Cash became the assistant manager for the Commissary Division at Mt. Hope on the Atlantic side of the isthmus. Upon taking the position, he and Mary Jane relocated to the town of Gatun, at 255-B Limon Place. The following year, they added their fifth child, Jill Elizabeth, born at Coco Solo Hospital in March 1957. They later moved to 114 Lake View Place on a hilltop with a great view of Gatun Lake.

Cash Paulson

At Mt. Hope, Cash set up a civil defense station in a secure location within the warehouse complex, part of the Canal Zone Civil Defense Program equipped with ham radios. Participants received civil defense classes, including ham radio operations and Morse code. Licensed radio operators stayed vigilant to the airways during global tensions.

Cash later became the general manager for Distribution Facilities at Mt. Hope. The warehouse facilities operations included receiving incoming goods from stateside, inventory control, and distribution of goods to all the Panama Canal Company commissaries across the isthmus. Additionally, a bakery for the Atlantic side at the warehouse complex produced bread, pastries, pies, cookies, and other baked goods.

With their brood of five children, Cash and Mary Jane were enjoying life in Gatun, making friends and becoming part of the Gatun community, where practically everyone knew each other. In 1960, Cash was the manager for the Atlantic Little League, American Legion Team; Caleb Clement was the assistant coach.

That same year, the family of five grew to six with the birth of Larry Michael "Mike" in November 1960.

Living in Gatun, the family spent time at the Gatun Yacht Club, swimming, barbecues, holiday parties, and much more. As the kids grew older, all became excellent swimmers and spent a lot of time around the water. The boys received two cayucos for Christmas one year. Fishing was another favorite activity, angling for tarpon down the Chagres River and peacock bass at Gatun Lake. A Sunday afternoon family picnic at Devil's Beach provided some relaxation while basking in the sun, enjoying the scenery, and walking in the swallows at the north end of the beach in search of sea urchins. On occasion, the family enjoyed a weekend at Pina Beach at the Jorstad and Corrigan families' house overlooking a small private beach.

Visiting the beaches on the Pacific side was normally more than a day trip. Cash and Mary Jane, with close friends Hod and Janet Jenner, would rent a duplex at San Carlos Beach for their families. They would purchase fresh fish and lobsters from local fishermen and then pick up delicious micha bread, baked daily, from a local bakery to feast on during their stay. Hod, an early riser, was up every morning whipping up and cooking a batch of perfectly golden beer pancakes for the families. They referred to their stay at the beach as "Paradise vacation!"

Cash and friends also took weeklong fishing trips to Isla de las Perlas, "Pearl Islands," Archipelago on the Pacific side. They reveled in catching loads of fish, having some drinks, and lots of laughs. Upon their return home, a fish fry always followed with family and friends.

Other get-togethers with friends included playing the card game Canasta and preparing great meals. Mary Jane, with friends Mary Connard and Rose Deaton, enjoyed baking and cooking.

The fun and adventures were not limited to life in Panama and the Canal Zone. The family occasionally traveled back to the US to visit relatives. Stateside, there were long road trips, typically starting with a visit to Mary Jane's parents, Walter and Helen White. They had moved to DeLand, Florida, after retiring from the Canal Zone in 1959. Following a short stay, it was on to visit Cash's family in Pennsylvania. Along the way, Cash would pull into a hotel with a swimming pool and restaurant. It was necessary after driving a long distance and hearing six kids chatting all day, Cash just wanted to rest. He would get rooms near the swimming pool and let the kids go play.

On one occasion, the hotel manager informed Cash and Mary Jane that the kids could not be at the pool alone. So, Cash informed the kids and told them to go swim some laps. The kids were excellent swimmers. The manager, seeing their swimming abilities, said, "Okay," and walked away.

The pool was a means to release the kids' energy after a long day of being cooped up in the car and the nearby restaurant was perfect for just walking a short distance. After visits in Pennsylvania and DeLand, they headed to New Orleans, Louisiana, to embark on the SS Cristobal for their return journey to the Canal Zone.

Over the years, the enjoyment of ham radio operations continued, with Cash and Mary Jane installing equipment in their housing quarters. Mary Jane received her amateur radio license in 1969, with the call letters KZ5MP. She helped numerous families with calls to the US. Long-distance phone calls to the States were expensive, so ham radio communication was a workaround. She would make contact with a specific location where a ham radio operator on the other end would then patch in the family with local call rates. Additionally, she connected families with loved ones who were away for prolonged periods recovering from an injury or surgery at Walter Reed Army Medical Center. In 1976, Mary Jane received an Honorary Public Service Award for her humanitarian efforts connecting families with their loved ones.

In 1978, after 30 years with the Panama Canal Company, Cash retired. He and Mary Jane and their son, Mike, left the Canal Zone. They moved to Tallahassee, Florida, to be close to family. Their daughter, Jane, and her husband, Milton Martin, lived in the area. Their daughter, Jill, attended Florida State University (FSU) in Tallahassee.

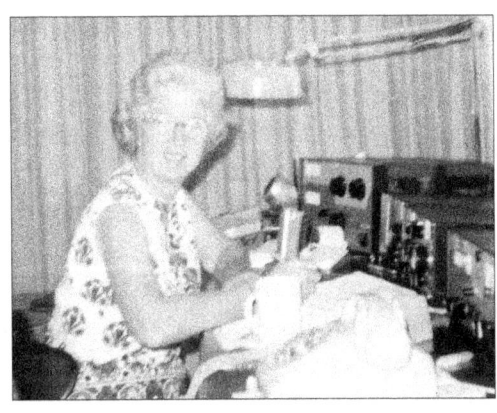

Mary Jane Paulson

With their large swimming pool, Cash and Mary Jane's home became known as "The Grand Central Station," an open house for family and friends. Cash and Mary Jane were elated to have some of their children and grandchildren always around them. Mary Jane and Cash also enjoyed operating their ham radio in Florida. After 26 years of happiness with family and friends in Tallahassee, Cash passed away in his home on February 6, 2004, at age 86.

Although the Paulson kids were grown and living their own lives, some remained in or relocated to Tallahassee to be closer to the family. Mary Jane was the core of the family.

After Judy graduated from Cristobal High School (CHS) in 1965, she attended Saint Leo College in Florida and later received a master's degree at Western State College of Colorado in Gunnison. Judy married Marty Weaver after they met at grad school. In the fall of 1974, she returned to the Canal Zone as Mrs. Weaver and taught English at CHS. Judy and Marty had a son, Brian, in 1979. A year later, the family returned to the US, working in Oregon and Idaho, then moved to Tallahassee, where Judy taught English at a local high school. Marty passed away in 1988. The following year, Judy and her son, Brian, moved to Beaufort, North Carolina, where she built her dream home. While in Beaufort, she taught English at the local community college and worked at a realtor's office. In 1999, an opportunity to fulfill another dream arose, so she and her partner, Wilson McCray, moved to Costa Rica. There, she taught English at a private European K-12 school. She and Wilson married in July 2014 and returned to Florida to be close to her son, Brian, settling in Fort Myers. After a long illness, Judy passed away on August 14, 2019. She was 72.

Leo was an all-star football player at CHS. He graduated in 1967. While attending college, he returned to the Canal Zone in 1968 and '69, working summer jobs. He received his degree from Saint Leo College in Florida in 1970. In 1971, he married his college sweetheart, Barbara Nelson, and then moved to Garden City, New York. They had two children, Lisa and Naren. They relocated to New Mexico, Arizona, Alabama, and Florida, finally settling in Tallahassee in 1978. Leo and Barbara's union eventually dissolved, and he later married Cynthia Varner. He and Cynthia had one son, Dustin. They later parted ways. Leo and his three children have a close relationship. He lives in Crawfordville, Florida.

Mark graduated from CHS in 1968. He enlisted in the US Navy and served aboard the USS Haleakala (AE-25) from February 1969 to October 1970 during the Vietnam War. After completing his military service, he stayed in San Francisco, California. Mark and Maria Gonsalves were in the Canal Zone on vacation, and once Mary Jane met Maria, she offered an heirloom engagement ring to Mark. He proposed to Maria, and they decided to get married right away. There is something special about a paradise wedding. Mary Jane and Cash had a wedding and reception planned in a week. Mark and Maria married in August 1977 in the Canal Zone. They have four children: Corey, Casey, Kristin, and Cody. Mark and his family live in San Francisco. He has a career in restoring San Francisco historic homes and businesses.

After Jane graduated from CHS in 1971, she attended Canal Zone College for a year before relocating to Tallahassee, Florida, in 1973, where she moved in with a Zonian friend, Toni Klasovsky. She later met Milton Martin. Jane and Milton married in May 1974. Jane worked for the State of Florida Department of Revenue for five years, then took a hiatus to raise her children, Alan and Jessi. She returned to the workforce in 1987, working at Florida State University, providing administrative support in several departments. Jane retired from FSU in 2019 from the Information Technology Services Department. She lives in Crawfordville near Tallahassee.

Jill graduated in 1975 from CHS. She received her bachelor's from FSU in 1979. After completing her degree, she moved to Miami and worked for Burdines as an assistant buyer for three years. In 1983, she returned to Tallahassee and worked with the State of Florida for several years. On December 31, 1987, Jill and Skip Berger, a Zonian and CHS graduate of 1966, married. Following their union, within 24 days, they returned to Panama, making their home in Margarita. Between October 1, 1979, and December 31, 1999, the US and the Panamanian government transitioned the Canal Zone operations to Panama. Jill worked in a US military civilian position from 1988 to 1999. In 2000, she and Skip started a tourism business, Gold Coast Travel, and they remained in Panama, where they still live. They had one child, Joseph, who is also in the travel and tourism business.

Mike, the youngest of the children, completed his high school senior year and graduated stateside in 1979 after moving to Tallahassee with Cash and Mary Jane in 1978. He remained in Tallahassee and worked several jobs. In December 1986, he married Cindy Barber. They raised three daughters: Sarah, Deanna, and Mary. Mike became the family genealogist, researching and sharing his findings with the family. Sadly, Mike passed away in March 2018, at age 57, and Cindy passed away in June 2022, both from cancer.

On January 18, 2020, Mary Jane White Paulson passed away at age 96 in Tallahassee. Her family has a long Zonian legacy with Panama Canal service and has Roosevelt Medal recipients on both sides of her lineage. Frank J. Shay, her maternal grandfather, medal holder #3252, was employed with the Panama Canal from 1907 to 1930 in the Division of Terminal Construction and Panama Railroad Company. Her father, Walter W. White, worked in the Canal Zone from 1919 to 1950. Her paternal aunt, Harriet White Trout, and her husband, Earl, worked for the Commissary Division from 1927 to 1954. Charles P. Shay, her maternal uncle, also worked with the Commissary Division from 1930 to 1953. Mary Jane's paternal uncle, George B. White, medal holder #6767, worked as a firefighter from July 1910 to February 1914; he later retired from the Panama Canal.

Cash and Mary Jane started a beautiful legacy with their brood. The Paulson children are the 4th generation of Zonians.

Gayle George Fortner Jr.
Police Sergeant • Canal Zone Government
US Navy, WWII Era Veteran

The Panama Canal was operational for a little over a decade when Gayle George Fortner Jr. was born on June 23, 1927, at Gorgas Hospital in Ancon, Canal Zone. His father, Gayle June Fortner, from Owenton, Kentucky, arrived in the Canal Zone as a US Army soldier. He was a private first class in 1920, stationed at Camp Gatun on the Atlantic side of the isthmus. His mother, Daisy Dill Fortner, was from Galesville, Wisconsin. She arrived later and worked as an elementary school teacher. By 1930, Gayle Sr. was working as a policeman, and the family lived in the town of Pedro Miguel.

In August 1944, Gayle Jr. was sent stateside to attend Galesville High School in Wisconsin. He returned to the Canal Zone after completing the 11th grade. In May 1945, at age 17, he completed an application for enlistment in the US Navy. On June 25, 1945, two days after his 18th birthday, he was inducted into the US Naval Reserves. The following week, on July 4, 1945, Independence Day, he entered active service at US Naval Station Balboa, Canal Zone. Two months later, World War II ended on

September 2, 1945. Subsequently, Gayle received his honorable discharge as a seaman first S1 on July 23, 1946. Ironically, the following day on July 24, 1946, Gayle completed a military draft registration card DSS Form 1.

After leaving the Navy, he attended Balboa High School in the Canal Zone. His yearbook identifies him as "Our tall, easy going Navy man ..." Gayle was an all-star in football and baseball, as well as athletic in basketball, water polo, and swimming. He began dating a classmate, Mavis "Bunny" June Beall. She, too, was athletic, playing volleyball, softball, and basketball. They both graduated in 1947.

Mavis was born in Bournemouth, England, on April 27, 1929. Her father, Cyril Beall, worked for British Petroleum (BP). Shortly after her birth, he was transferred to Panama. He, his wife, Willy Mary Broers Beall, and their daughter moved to Panama City. Growing up in the city, Mavis had many Panamanian friends, one of whom was a young Roberto "Tito" Arias from a prominent political family, who later became a well-known Panamanian lawyer and diplomat.

Following their high school graduation, Gayle and Mavis married in Pedro Miguel on September 2, 1947. They initially lived in the town of Cocoli. Gayle got a job as a policeman with the Canal Zone Police Division.

Being an exceptional athlete, Gayle played in the Panamanian Baseball League for a brief time. He received an invitation from the St. Louis Cardinals to spring training, but he passed on the offer. He and Mavis opted to stay in the Canal Zone, although he later played a lot of softball.

As a young couple, they enjoyed socializing with friends, sitting around the table, and chatting for hours on Saturday nights. Getaways to the Pacific Coast beaches and fishing trips twice a year provided an escape from the daily routine of life at home.

The Last Zonian

They later moved to the town of Gatun on the Atlantic side adjacent to the Gatun Locks. Initially, they got living quarters at 39 Lighthouse Road, then moved a few more times to 119-B Lighthouse Road, 144-A Bolivar Highway, and 400-A Laurel Street. Gayle and Mavis were outgoing and friendly, and with Gayle being one of the town's policemen and Mavis attending local events, they easily met new friends. Their active social lives slowed down a bit with the birth of their son, Kenneth "Ken" Gayle, in April 1954 at Colon Hospital in the seaport city of Colon. Having friends over to play cards and chatting was just a bit quieter with an infant. Mavis enjoyed the peacefulness at home to work on her crafts of sewing, knitting, crocheting, and painting.

As Ken got older, Gayle taught him how to ride a bike, catch a baseball, bowl, and fish. Being an avid fisherman, he and the family spent many hours fishing in a good spot at the north end of the Gatun Locks. It was at a boat dock inside a locked building, restricted to the public, to which Gayle had a key, being a policeman. He shared a spare building key with other passionate fishermen. Although he was aware of Gatun kids sneaking into the building in ways other than the front entrance, he never chased them out of that prime fishing spot since he knew who they were and where they lived.

Police Officer Gayle Fortner

Gayle and Mavis, athletes since their high school days, continued an active lifestyle. He was a powerful bowler and played for many years in the Margarita bowling league. Mavis loved going to the swimming pool. And, Ken participated in various activities and sports.

Gayle was great with the neighborhood kids. During the school year, he parked his patrol car at the corner of Jadwin Road and Laurel Street to ensure kids could safely cross the road on their way to the Gatun Elementary School. He played a game with the kids waiting at the crosswalk. If they could guess how much loose change he had in his hand or pocket, he gave it to them. Of course, the kids liked the game, but they also liked Policeman Fortner.

Although the family enjoyed a happy life, there were those times when it was not all hunky-dory. On one occasion, Ken's misbehavior led to Mavis chasing him down the street with a belt. The next day, his friends who saw it chuckled and told him, "You must have done something wrong."

During the January 1964 Panamanian anti-American demonstrations and riots, an elusive shooter shot at Gayle while he was performing his police duties. Luckily, he found cover. That same year, in May, he was elected president of the Canal Zone Police Lodge No. 1798, American Federation of Government Employees (AFGE) Union.

In June 1968, the family moved to the town of Gamboa. Gayle, a senior police sergeant, transferred to the Canal Zone Gamboa Penitentiary, closer to the Pacific side of the isthmus. Two years after his arrival, he was engaged with the security of Panamanian military officers brought to the facility. They were seeking political asylum for their involvement in an attempt to overthrow Panamanian leader Omar Torrijos, who was successful in a coup of Panamanian President Arnulfo Arias after his election in 1968. It is thought that the Panamanian military officers were later transferred to a ship passing through the Canal near the Gaillard Cut adjacent to the penitentiary.

The Last Zonian

Away from work, Gayle and Mavis were huge fans of Leroy Lewis, a master organist, at the Hotel El Panama Hilton, where they occasionally went to dinner and enjoyed the music. Gayle liked playing cards at the Elks Club in Balboa and sometimes visited the hotel-casinos, with the Hilton as a favorite. Mavis spent much of her time with the ladies from church and visiting with neighbors. They also kept in touch with and visited good friends living in Panama City.

Gayle was a big fan of Ken playing football in his junior and senior years at Balboa High School, which selected Ken as an all-star. Gayle attended the games, sitting in the bleachers and observing the field action where he had once been an all-star football player at the same high school. Although Mavis was an athlete, too, she was terrified Ken would get hurt.

Gayle worked and lived in Gamboa until his retirement in July 1977, after 31 years and 6 months of government service and living in the Canal Zone for 50 years. He and Mavis moved to Orange City, Florida, adjacent to their good friends, Dick and Louise Soyster. They were looking forward to enjoying life after retirement, with plans to do some traveling. Sadly, the following year, Gayle passed away on July 18, 1978, at 51 years old.

(L-R) Dick & Louise Soyster, Mavis & Gayle Fortner

Mavis remained in Orange City, staying busy with her Canal Zone friends, being actively involved with the Orange City United Methodist Church, and attending the Panama Canal

Society annual reunions. She later moved about six miles to DeLand, Florida. Mavis passed away at home on March 24, 2009, at age 79.

Ken graduated from Balboa High School (BHS) in 1971. Athletic like his parents, he was a Canal Zone All-Stars football player. He attended Auburn University, earning a bachelor's in civil engineering. He entered the US Navy as an ensign and married DeLight Nelson, a Zonian born in Ancon and a BHS '75 graduate. They had two children, Charisse and David. While in the Navy, he served in various leadership positions and attained a master's in civil engineering from Georgia Tech. As a civilian, Ken worked for CH2M Hill, Inc., an engineering company that had a major role in the Panama Canal expansion of the third locks. Ken was a project manager for the Pacific side third locks expansion, Cocoli Locks. While working in Panama, he resided in the town of Diablo. Ken retired from the Navy and his professional engineering position. After parting ways with DeLight, he later married Renee Floretta Potloff. They stay busy traveling. Ken and Renee live in Keizer, Oregon.

George "Lanky" Oscar Flores
Fire Chief • Canal Zone Government
US Army, Korean War Era Veteran

George "Lanky" Oscar Flores was born on September 28, 1928, in San Carlos, Costa Rica, a municipality in the Alajuela Province, a major supplier of produce and dairy products for the country. The agricultural and dairy lands surrounded the Arenal Volcano, one of the world's most active volcanoes. In contrast to his birthplace, he would forge a life living adjacent to the world's shipping gateway between two oceans.

His father, Juan Angel Flores, was born in Puerto Rico and migrated to Costa Rica sometime before his son's birth. The Flores family left Costa Rica with two-month-old George and moved to Panama. At age four, George's sister Melva joined the family while they lived in Cristobal on the Atlantic side of the isthmus.

George received a nickname as a young teenager while in the Boy Scouts. He was standing at the end of the line in a squad when his scoutmaster called out to him, "Hey there, you lanky on the end." From then on, the nickname, "Lanky," stuck.

Leopold J. Cimino

Although World War II ended on September 2, 1945, George, an 18-year-old senior in high school, completed his military selective service registration card on September 30, 1946. The following year, he graduated from Cristobal High School (CHS), where he played softball, baseball, basketball, football, and track. He held the records for the 50-yard and 100-yard dash for several years.

After graduating, he was a civilian employee for the US Navy, working as a radio mechanic. While no longer in high school, he met Patricia "Pat" May Geddes, a CHS sophomore.

Pat was born on May 1, 1933, in the Borough of Queens, New York. At age seven, she traveled with her mother, Florence, and one-year-old sister, Dianne, aboard the SS Cristobal to join her father, Robert Geddes, who met them at the Port of Cristobal as they disembarked on September 25, 1940. Robert was a bulldozer operator working for the Panama Canal. He arrived from New York earlier that year with his father, Thomas, and brothers, Al, Bill, and Frank. Thomas (Pat's grandfather) worked in the construction of the Panama Canal in the early 1900s before the official opening of the Canal on August 15, 1914.

Pat graduated from CHS in 1951. Like Lanky, she was athletic, playing volleyball, basketball, and softball. She was an all-star in all three sports and was the Football Queen in her senior year.

Lanky and Pat dated for quite a while and wanted to get married, but he did not have a job. His father, Juan, worked as a barber at the Hotel Washington, a swanky place for its time. The hotel was less than a mile from the Port of Cristobal, at the end of Front Street, with a great view of Limon Bay, and various dignitaries frequented it. Wanting to assist his son in attaining a job, Juan got the opportunity with a visiting one-time customer.

A chance arose during a US congressional visit to the Canal Zone. A congressman, wanting a haircut and shave, sat down in Juan's barber chair. Juan, who enjoyed chatting with his customers, conveyed that his son was engaged and now looking for employment. When the grooming was done, the congressman left the barber shop and made a telephone call. Later that afternoon, Lanky was offered a job and informed to report to the personnel administration office in the morning.

Lanky initially worked as a locks guard, then transferred to the Fire Division and became a firefighter. Shortly thereafter, he and Pat married in June 1951. They lived in New Cristobal until 1952 when he got drafted into the US Army.

The Korean War, which the United States entered on June 27, 1950, was ongoing. Lanky was sent to basic combat training (BCT) at Camp Polk in Leesville, Louisiana, referred to as "The pipeline to Korea." After completing BCT, he stayed at Camp Polk, and Pat joined him. The Korean War ended on July 27, 1953. In November 1953, their daughter, Wendy Marie, was born. Nearing the end of his enlistment, Lanky wrote a letter to the post commanding general (CG) requesting a reassignment to work at the fire department on post to utilize his firefighter skills. The CG granted his request. In 1955, Lanky, Pat, and Wendy returned to the Canal Zone.

Lanky returned to his firefighter position in the Fire Division, and the family moved to Gatun, initially to their house at 201 Schoolhouse Road behind the Gatun Elementary School. They moved a few more times while living in Gatun to 261-B Sibert Street in the New Town neighborhood, 196 Pamarosa Street next to the elementary school, and Laurel Street. All the houses were close to the fire station. As a firefighter, Lanky responded to fires, controlled burns, and other emergencies. In November 1956, he was promoted to fire sergeant. A few months later, he and Pat had another child, Lori Ann, born in February 1957.

Pat joined the Panama Canal Company workforce in 1962, when Lori started kindergarten, working in an administrative position. In February 1965, she received a superior service award as a clerk-stenographer in the Industrial Division.

The hired help, Carmen, a Jamaican gal, took care of the girls when Pat began working. Ironically, Carmen only spoke English, no Spanish, even though she had been living in Panama.

Due to a reduction in force (RIF), Lanky took a job with US Customs at the Port of Cristobal. By February 1965, he had gone from being a customs enforcement officer to a contraband control inspector. Working at the port, he often received invitations to have dinner aboard cruise ships with his family. They thoroughly enjoyed visiting the ships and getting treated like royalty.

Pat with Wendy & Lori

Simultaneously, Pat's career continued to flourish. By March 1967, she received a promotion to a staffing specialist and then to a supervisory administrative services assistant.

The girls were blossoming, as well, with the occasional mischievousness. On more than one occasion, the school bus driver, who transported the Gatun fifth and sixth graders to and from Margarita Elementary School in the adjacent town, returned to the school, prompting the principal to board the bus and scold the rowdy students. Those few kids, including Lori, received assigned bus seats in the front rows under the watchful eye of the driver. As a result, Lori and her friend, Bill Kern, decided to carry out a spiteful deed on the last day of the sixth grade.

The Last Zonian

They got off the bus at one of the first stops in Gatun and climbed the hill to get to Lori's house at 406 Laurel Street. They immediately went into the kitchen and took four raw eggs from the refrigerator. When Carmen learned why they needed the eggs, she told them, "No" and threatened to call Lori's parents at work. Nevertheless, Lori and Bill took the eggs and waited at the top of the hill for the bus to finish dropping off all the kids and head back out of town. As the bus passed below them, Bill threw an egg at it. The egg cleared the bus and splattered across the windshield of a gold Cadillac traveling in the other lane. As the bus continued on unscathed, the Cadillac driver slammed on her brakes and looked up the hill, seeing the culprits as they took off running. Within minutes, Mrs. Danielsen, a neighbor from further down the street, was in Lori's driveway. Bill had run home. Carmen sent Lori, who attempted to hide in her room, out to the driveway to face a very angry Mrs. Danielsen. Their punishment was to wash her car, which they did.

When not working, Lanky and Pat enjoyed spending time with the girls, going to the Gatun Yacht Club, beaches, motocross races, and, later, to high school football games and seeing Wendy perform on the Girls' Drill Team.

The family spent a lot of time at the Gatun Saddle Club, horseback riding, showing horses, and attending horse shows. The girls had several horses over time. Wendy had Beauty and Noel. Lori had Marie, Paint, and Dancer. Lanky also had his horse, Duke, then Fury. He liked going to the stables to ride with the girls. Pat loved helping with the horse shows. She spent numerous hours typing up programs, serving as an evaluating judge keeping score, and as the club designee presenting top competitors with ribbons and prizes.

Lanky and Pat also hung out with friends Jerry and Shirley Boswell, Jack and Shirley Alexaitis, and Carol Coe who attended high school with Pat. Dressing up to attend the Policemen and

Firefighters Balls was always fun. And, they often socialized with Lanky's sister and her family, who lived in Colon.

Lanky's hobby as a licensed ham radio operator allowed him to communicate with operators in other countries as well as in the United States. It was beneficial when he would do phone patches with operators stateside to speak with relatives in the US for free.

Pat enjoyed playing tennis and swimming. At home, she liked working on her hobby as a seamstress, sewing clothes for the girls and their dolls.

By 1969, Pat was already an administrative officer in the Industrial Division at Mt. Hope. She and Lanky worked hard and played hard, as the saying goes, and the family also attended Catholic mass every Sunday.

In 1971, Lanky accepted a position and promotion as a fire lieutenant and returned to the Fire Division. The family moved to La Boca on the Pacific side of the isthmus. He worked shifts, 24 hours on and 48 hours off. One of his crews' primary responsibilities was to fight ship fires on vessels in Canal Zone waters at the Pacific isthmus port or transiting through the Canal. After controlled brush fires, Lanky collected grasshoppers for his pet squirrel monkey, Paco.

Living on the Pacific side, Lanky and Pat bought a beach house in Las Guias, about one hour and a half from Panama City. They spent many exhilarating weekends at the beach house with Lori and her teenage friends, relaxing in the sun, playing volleyball, swimming in the surf, and eating lobster for breakfast, lunch, and dinner.

Lanky and Pat parted ways after several years on the Pacific side. They remained there as their careers continued to excel. In 1977, Lanky became the Fire Commander of the Balboa District and then was promoted to the Panama Canal Commission Fire Chief. Pat culminated her career as the administrative officer with the Engineering and Construction Bureau. She married Robert "Bud" J. Risberg, a civil engineer.

When President Carter signed the Neutrality Treaty and Panama Canal Treaty in 1977, directing the abolishment of the Panama Canal Zone by October 1, 1979, and the turnover of the Canal to the people of Panama by the year 2000, Zonians knew what their future held. A record number of retirements ensued.

Chief Lanky Flores

Lanky, at age 52, with 31 years of government service, retired in December 1980. He remained in Panama for a couple of years, then moved to Sarasota, Florida. He enjoyed traveling, playing golf and tennis, and visiting with his daughter Lori and his grandchildren. He married Judith Morgan in June 1992 and later moved to Virginia. Lanky passed away in Moon, Virginia, on January 12, 2014, at age 86. His daughter Lori stated she had a loving father. He loved animals and always had a dog or two.

Pat retired after 20 years of service in May 1981. Her husband, Bud, also retired in 1981. They moved to Titusville, Florida, to a home they purchased in 1978 in preparation for their retirement. They enjoyed traveling, seeing each other's families, attending the Panama Canal Society reunions, going to the Royal Oak Golf and Country Club, spending time babysitting Lori's two children, and, for Pat, playing bridge with her lady friends. On March 28, 2011, Bud passed away at age 89 in Titusville. Pat lives in Orlando, Florida, near her daughter Lori and her family.

Leopold J. Cimino

Before graduating from Cristobal High School in 1971, Wendy was the 1970 Football Jamboree Queen, like her mother, Pat, who was the Football Queen in high school. Wendy moved into the dormitory with other Atlantic side girls while attending Canal Zone College. Tragically, Wendy was killed in a car accident on July 28, 1972, at only 18 years of age.

Lori graduated from Balboa High School in 1975 and attended Canal Zone College. She moved stateside to complete her schooling at Florida State University, receiving a bachelor's degree in Dietetics. She met Zonian William "Scott" Roche when she returned to Panama to visit her parents during a two-week Christmas break from college. They hit it off, and, after dating for a while, Scott moved in to live with her in Tallahassee. What she did not know when she picked him up at the airport was that he also brought his black Labrador Retriever. The rest is history. Lori and Scott married in November 1982 and they had two children, Daron and Lauren. Lori worked as a chief dietitian in hospitals before retiring. She and Scott live on five acres in Orlando, Florida, with their three horses and four dogs. They enjoy being with family and traveling from time to time.

Pat expressed how fortunate and blessed she feels to have lived in the Canal Zone and raised her children there. As for many Zonians, it's a place of nostalgia for her.

David Reed Jr.
Guard Supervisor Captain • Panama Canal Company
US Army, Korean War Era Veteran

Born on February 19, 1930, during the Great Depression, David Reed Jr. grew up in the small agricultural town of Brinkley, Arkansas. The town was less than 75 miles in each direction between the cities of Little Rock and Memphis.

In his youth, David worked at the local movie theater. In June 1948, he left his hometown of around three thousand and enlisted in the US Army. After completing basic combat training, he was sent to the Panama Canal Zone. Initially, he got stationed on the Atlantic side of the isthmus at Fort Sherman, assigned to a harbor defense battery. The following year, the Korean War commenced. The United States sent military forces to aid the South Koreans from invading North Korean forces and stop the expansion of communism. David remained in the Canal Zone with a reassignment to Fort Kobbe on the Pacific side of the isthmus across the Bridge of the Americas from Panama City.

On weekends, when not on duty, he did something different than other military personnel. He found a part-time job on one of his days off and began working for a Panamanian businessman,

Mr. Julio Garcia, delivering produce to the local market. David was in the vicinity when he overheard a gentleman ask Mr. Garcia if he could take his daughter, who graduated from college in the US, out on a date. Mr. Garcia told him, "No." David then realized that his part-time boss had a daughter.

Early one morning, while David and Mr. Garcia prepared to go to the market, the businessman's daughter was chatting with him from an open window on the second floor about picking up some items for her. That was the first time David saw the attractive 22-year-old daughter. Beatriz "Betty" Garcia, born on March 25, 1927.

On the way to the market, David asked Mr. Garcia if he could take his daughter out on a date. Mr. Garcia said, "Yes, under one condition." So, when David arrived to pick up Betty, he opened the door for her to sit in the front passenger seat, then opened the rear passenger door for Mrs. Garcia, who sat in the back seat and accompanied them on their date. David and Betty dated for a short time and then got engaged. They married on December 23, 1951.

At first, David and Betty lived in Panama City. When he got out of the Army in June 1952, they moved to West Memphis, Arkansas. David got a job with the US Army Corps of Engineers making mechanical repairs to tugboats and other water vessels. Unfortunately, while living there, they encountered some racism. The following year,

Betty & David Reed

they celebrated the birth of their first child, Carmen Mary, in February 1953.

Three months later, in May 1953, the family relocated and returned to Panama. David's father-in-law, Mr. Garcia, had friends working in the Canal Zone who helped David get a job with the Panama Canal Company. As an Army veteran who previously served in Panama, David welcomed being a security guard with the Protection Division at the Gatun Locks on the Atlantic side of the isthmus.

Upon their return, the family lived in various locations, initially residing in New Cristobal. Within a year, their daughter Helena was born in June 1954. They moved to Coco Solo, then to Cristobal next to the seaport. In January 1956, Danny David was born at Coco Solo Hospital.

In 1957, they built a concrete and block house in the Panamanian town of Sabanitas, close to checkpoint Charlie, a Guardia Nacional Panamanian police station located on the Roosevelt Transisthmian Highway approximately five miles outside the Canal Zone territorial boundaries. David and Betty were happy to be back in Panama and able to see her parents, who had moved and relocated their business from Panama City to the city of Colon on the Atlantic side.

Having three toddlers did not slow them down from exploring and finding things to do on the Atlantic side. Plus, they liked visiting Betty's parents' farm in Buena Vista, about ten miles farther on the Roosevelt Transisthmian Highway. And, they got to know their Panamanian neighbors, store owners, and the local police. David and Betty were well-liked in the community. The family grew again with the birth of Ronny in June 1959. Living a happy and quiet life in Sabanitas ended after seven years.

On January 9, 1964, a confrontation between Panamanian and American students and the Canal Zone police escalated in the media. The issue of flying the Panamanian flag next to the

American flag at Balboa High School, located in the Canal Zone, led to violent riots along the Canal Zone territorial boundaries, primarily in Panama City on the Pacific side of the isthmus and Colon on the Atlantic side.

The rioting mobs, some armed, burned, looted, and destroyed property. The US Army 193rd Infantry Brigade stationed in the Panama Canal Zone deployed troops to protect lives and property. Americans living in Panamanian neighborhoods fled back into the Canal Zone, others sequestered and hunkered down with Panamanian friends. Local Panamanian policemen, friends of David and Betty, came to their home and notified them that rioters were looking for Americans. They escorted David back to the Canal Zone lines while the family awaited his return. David and a friend arranged an exit plan for his family from Sabanitas by boat via Gatun Lake at the back of the neighborhood. While implementing the plan, Betty and the kids evacuated to the Canal Zone with the assistance of her mother, who drove through crowded streets to get her daughter and grandchildren to safety. After three days, the rioting ended on January 12, resulting in the death of four American soldiers and twenty-two Panamanians.

Shortly thereafter, David and Betty sold their house and moved back into the Canal Zone, first to the town of Margarita and then to Gatun, at 245 Sibert Street, on the corner with Limon Place, where they remained. Living in Gatun adjacent to the Gatun Locks, David was just minutes from home. Several years later, David and Betty added two more children to their team of youngsters: David Lenard, born in October 1966, and Jimmy Lin, born in November 1969.

David progressed to the position of guard supervisor captain. The job entailed ensuring the security of the Canal premises and Cristobal shipyard.

Their house was a hangout for many Gatun kids, with the family having a billiard table on the ground floor in a breezeway patio next to the garage. Additionally, being a motorcycle enthusiast and mechanic, Danny often rode his 50cc minibike through a trail cut by a bush hog mower in a field of tall sawgrass. He let his friends ride it as well. It was fun, but riders who wiped out on the trail got their share of cuts from the sawgrass.

Captain David Reed

When David and Betty took their kids to the beaches, especially those on the Atlantic side, Maria Chiquita, Pina, and Shimmy Beach at Fort Sherman with a shark protection barrier, they always took neighborhood kids with them piled into the back of a red utility truck. David and Betty enjoyed spending time with close friends Ken and Acis Hill, Don and Amy Sperling, Richard Kresgie, and Ted Finneman. They were all security personnel.

David spent time at a hobby shop tinkering with anything mechanical and teaching others. He repaired cars, motorcycles, and fixed bicycles for neighborhood kids. Betty enjoyed cooking and, at times, fed the kids who hung out at the house. Betty worked at the Gatun Theater as a ticket taker, so she knew the town's kids, and they knew her. The Reed kids engaged in all types of activities with friends, mostly innocent, although, at times, not so much, like at the military drop zone when Danny drove an Army bulldozer with a friend while others watched, and they didn't get caught.

Leopold J. Cimino

David retired after 29-and-a-half years of government service. With their two youngest kids, he and Betty left the Canal Zone in August 1979. They initially relocated to Pangburn, Arkansas, then moved in and out of state before settling in Searcy, Arkansas. David continued with his enjoyment of tinkering as a mechanic, attending family reunions, and visiting Zonian friends in Jonesboro, Arkansas. Betty loved spending her time together with David and cooking. She did work for a bit as a nurse's aide in a nursing home. After 57 years of marriage, David died on July 6, 2009, at age 79. Betty passed away on September 5, 2019, at age 92.

After graduating from Cristobal High School (CHS) in 1972, Carmen married Ken Suttle, a soldier stationed at Fort Davis, and moved to California, then Florida. They had a son, Kristopher. The marriage dissolved years later. In 1985, she relocated to be closer to her family in Arkansas. In 1992, she married Lanis Parish. She worked in medical services handling insurance claims for most of her career. Carmen and Lanis live in Rose Bud, Arkansas, and are actively involved in their church.

Helena graduated from CHS in 1974. Two years later, she moved to West Memphis, Arkansas, to live with family. She worked as a beautician for 39 years. She lives in Heber Springs, Arkansas. Semi-retired, Helena enjoys doing crafts, drawing portraits, and painting. She volunteers and works part-time at a hospital.

Danny graduated from CHS in 1975. After leaving the Canal Zone, he lived in Arkansas and California and enlisted in the US Navy for three years. He is now doing what he enjoys the most, fixing and building mechanical machines. He married Deborah Yarbrough and has three stepchildren: Craig, Mandy, and Jeff. Danny and Debbie live in Searcy, Arkansas.

The Last Zonian

Ronny, a 1977 CHS class graduate, left the Canal Zone shortly thereafter. He became a semi-truck driver. He married, though the marriage dissolved. He lives in Little Rock, Arkansas.

After leaving the Canal Zone with his parents in August 1979, David graduated from high school in Pangburn, Arkansas. He married Allison Bonner Null. They have no children. David and Allison live in Memphis, Tennessee.

Jimmy, the youngest, also left the Canal Zone in August 1979. After graduating high school in Pangburn, Arkansas, he served three years in the US Navy. He attended college at Arkansas State University. He married Misty Parks, and they had three daughters: Samantha, Tiernan, and Alexandra. He later married Johanna Mathis. They had no children and lived in Hot Springs, Arkansas. Sadly, Jimmy passed away on June 11, 2016. He was 46.

Carmen shared that her parents thought living in the Canal Zone and Panama was like living in a slice of paradise.

Theodore Matthew & Patricia Finneman
Locks Security Lieutenant • Panama Canal Company
US Army, Korean War Era Veteran

In the winter that Theodore "Ted" Matthew Finneman was born on December 26, 1929, in St. Cloud, Minnesota, the small city had below-freezing temperatures, as in previous years. After graduating high school, Ted worked as an auto mechanic and truck driver and took up boxing. At age 18, he enlisted in the US Army on January 3, 1947 at Fort Snelling, Minnesota. After his basic military and specialty training, he was stationed in the Panama Canal Zone, arriving in May 1947 at Fort Clayton. He was assigned to Battery A 903d AAA (Antiaircraft Artillery) AW (Automatic Weapons) Battalion on the Pacific side of the isthmus.

Shortly after arriving, he met a young lady, Patricia Ann Cicero, a high school student, at a dance. Patricia "Pat" was born on June 27, 1932, in Atlantic City, New Jersey. She came to Panama with her parents in 1945.

Her father, Joseph "Joe" John Cicero, was a professional baseball player who played with the Boston Red Sox, Philadelphia Athletics, and Cincinnati Reds. In 1945, during the off-season, Joe went to Panama to play in the Panama Baseball League. Joe liked the vibe in Panama and stayed. He got a job as a security officer at the Miraflores Locks. He thought living in the Canal Zone was a wonderful place for his family and raising his two kids.

Ted and Pat dated briefly and began discussing marriage. After completing his tour of duty at Fort Clayton, where he was a Golden Gloves Boxer for the US Army in Panama, he returned stateside. He received his honorable discharge on January 6, 1950.

At age 17, Pat graduated early from Balboa High School then left the Canal Zone in February 1950 to join Ted in Minneapolis, Minnesota. He was living with relatives, and Pat lived as a lodger with another family and worked as a clerk stenographer for an insurance company. Ted worked as an auto mechanic. She and Ted officially took residence together after her 18th birthday and married 18 days later, on July 15, 1950. In February 1951, their first son, Jerome "Jerry," was born, and Pat became a homemaker. While in Minnesota, their second son, Michael "Mike," was born in July 1952.

PFC Ted Finneman

The family returned to the Canal Zone in March 1953 and initially lived on the Pacific side. Ted took a position as a security guard at the Miraflores Locks, conducting identification checks of all personnel entering the premises. Pat, having an infant and a toddler, was glad to be closer to her family. She and Ted later moved to the Atlantic side and made their home in Gatun, settling into family quarters at 223 Bolivar Street.

Living adjacent to Gatun Lake and near the Gatun Dam allowed Ted to do a lot of fishing. In October 1955, he and Billy Poindexter, a fellow locks guard, were spearfishing near the apron of the Gatun Dam's spillway. It was a great place to catch snook. Seeing the movement of a fin behind a rock, Billy fired his spear and hit his target. Unfortunately, what he thought was a fish was one of Ted's diving fins. The spear penetrated Ted's foot. He was taken to the hospital, treated, and released the same day.

Two months following the accident, Pat gave birth to a third son, Thomas "Tom," born in December 1955. The family grew with the addition of two more boys, Joseph "Joe," in April 1959, and David in December 1960. By then, the two oldest boys began participating in Little League baseball.

In September 1961, Ted became a guard supervisor lieutenant in charge of security for the Gatun Locks, its bridge traffic entries, along with the Gatun Dam and spillway. In 1964, Pat began working with the Postal Division at Gorgas Hospital on the Pacific side, commuting 50 miles in each direction across the isthmus. Shortly after that, she transferred to the Cristobal Post Office as a window clerk on the Atlantic side.

As busy as Ted and Pat were working in their careers and raising their children, they were both baseball enthusiasts. Ted coached the Veterans of Foreign Wars (VFW) Little League team, and in 1966, his team, with his son, Tom, on the roster, won the Atlantic side VFW Championship. Pat served as the secretary and treasurer for the Atlantic Little League.

Later that year, Pat gave birth to another son, Lawrence "Larry," in November 1966. Ted and Pat had their hands full raising six boys, half a dozen, enough to field an ice hockey team in Minnesota. Although, they were in no hurry to get back to the cold winters. The family liked the warm tropical weather in

Panama. Plus, Ted, Pat, and their "mischievous boys," a title they attained in Gatun, were having fun with baseball and living life in the Canal Zone.

In 1968, Ted again took his Little League team, with sons Tom, Joe, and David on the roster, to the Atlantic side VFW Championship game. They placed second.

Ted with sons (L-R) Joe, David, Mike, Tom

There was more than just baseball for this happy couple. Ted and Pat liked getting together with friends and going to Maria Chiquita Beach, outside the Canal Zone on the Caribbean coast. Together with the Reed family, they would load the back of two pickup trucks with kids from the neighborhood and go to the beach. Ted liked the Maria Chiquita Beach area, so he later purchased property near the old historic town of Portobelo that had remnants of a Spanish fortress. Plus, they invited neighbors' kids when the family went to Shimmy Beach at Fort Sherman Army base, approximately 11 miles from Gatun.

In 1969, an incident occurred when Tom, who was a 13, ran an errand. His father sent him to buy ice at the American Legion Post. Having a bar and restaurant, military personnel frequented the Legion, which was also a hangout for locals and kids to eat and play the pinball machine. While Tom was buying ice at the bar, a soldier told him to leave and pushed him. When Tom returned home, he told his dad. Having been a soldier, Ted had a lot of respect for military personnel. However, he would not tolerate an adult pushing any kid. So, Ted returned to the establishment with Tom. Needless to say, when the soldier bucked up against Ted, the former Golden Gloves boxer disciplined the soldier's misconduct and knocked him out.

Enjoying life with family and having others partake in their fun was visually evident, whether taking kids to the beach or a little league picnic. Ted and Pat always included others. Ted won the Panama loteria a few times. His winnings afforded him and Nick Olsen, a fellow locks security officer, to co-own land and build a house close to the cold rushing waters of a river in the picturesque mountainous region of Volcan, near the Panama and Costa Rica border. Here, too, the family invited friends and got permission from other families to take neighborhood kids on mini vacations to the mountains.

The boys were also adventurous, getting out and exploring the terrain surrounding the town of Gatun. Along with other kids, they knew when military exercises were complete, so they would hike into the jungle and procure as much equipment as they could carry out. This included military clothing, new jungle boots, foot powder, mosquito repellent, camo sticks, cases of C-rations, parachutes, and flash-bang and smoke grenades.

Even though the family had a house in the mountains, water activities were a regular part of their lives, and they spent a lot of time around the water—going to the community swimming pool, the numerous beaches, snorkeling, and spearfishing. The Gatun Yacht Club, less than a mile from their house, was a great hangout for all of them. However, the older boys having their driver's licenses had their own hangouts with friends.

Fishing for peacock bass at Gatun Lake, tarpon in the Chagres River, and snook along the Canal's banks at the north end of the Gatun Locks was common. However, fishing for snook with friends in unauthorized and no-trespassing locations was exciting and bountiful for the boys.

Leopold J. Cimino

One of these unauthorized locations was the Gatun Dam spillway, where they used an unorthodox method of stick fishing and hand-catching snook. In addition to being illegal and involving trespassing, it could be dangerous, especially if the boys did not vacate the area upon hearing the warning horn when a gate opened to release water. When all the dam gates were closed and the water level was shallow, Joe and his friends would walk onto the spillway (the concrete deck where water flows) to catch fish. The snook that remained in the shallow water on the spillway after the gates closed floundered, trying to skim along the deck to reach the deeper waters of the Chagres River at the end of the spillway apron. The boys took advantage of this opportunity to hit the fish with a stick, knocking them out or catching them by hand. They would stuff as many fish as possible in knotted T-shirts and ride their bikes home.

Similarly, Tom and his friends would do the same thing. However, they packed the fish into the trunk of a car and then sold them to the American Legion Post. On one occasion, Gatun Policeman Al Goguen caught them trespassing with fish. He was a US Marine Corps WWII veteran and Silver Star recipient. He gave them a stern warning and then let them go with their catch.

Ted and Pat also had their share of (legal) fun. They frequented the Margarita bowling alley and enjoyed going out with friends. Pat, being a swimmer, conveniently lived across the street from the Gatun Swimming Pool. Plus, she liked playing volleyball and was an enthusiastic bingo player.

In August 1976, Pat became the finance branch superintendent in charge of postal operations at the Gatun Post Office. She progressed through various postal positions and worked at different postal locations, including Gorgas Hospital, Gatun, Fort Gulick, and Cristobal.

Ted retired in May 1984 and stayed in the former Canal Zone until Pat retired from the Panama Canal Commission in

1985. They moved to Dothan, Alabama, where they had Zonian friends. Sadly, two years later, Ted passed away on September 20, 1987, at age 57. His ashes were returned to the former Canal Zone and released from the bridge that crossed over the Gatun Dam spillway. The waters at the end of the spillway that poured into the Chagres River was one of Ted's favorite fishing spots—where his boys caught floundering snook on the spillway deck. Pat stayed busy and remained involved with the St. Columba Catholic Church. She died from an automobile accident at the age of 63 on July 1, 1995.

Jerry graduated from Cristobal High School (CHS) in 1969. He moved to California. After his high school sweetheart, Ann Cirulli, a Zonian from Coco Solo, sustained serious injuries in a car accident, he enlisted in the US Army and married Ann to cover her medical treatment. They had two children, Nathan and Ian. After being stationed stateside, the family received reassignment orders to Fort Gulick, in the former Canal Zone, close to where Jerry and Ann grew up. They were able to spend time with Ted and Pat, who were still working in the Zone. Sadly, Jerry died in a motorcycle accident near Fort Davis on November 15, 1981. He was 30 years old.

Mike graduated from CHS in 1970. He moved stateside and never married. He lives in St. Augustine, Florida.

Tom is a CHS class of '74 graduate. After completing an enlistment in the US Navy, he went on to receive a bachelor's from Eastern Kentucky University, which led to him being a commissioned officer in the US Army. Following his military retirement, he worked for the Transportation Security Agency for 20 years until his retirement. He and his wife, Rochelle Blount, a Zonian from Gatun, live in Florida. Retired, they play golf, do some fishing, enjoy getting out to entertainment venues, and visit family and friends.

Leopold J. Cimino

Joe graduated from CHS in 1977. He became a physical therapist. He married Patricia "Trish" Hardy and had one child, Sidney. Joe is a songwriter in his spare time, writing "Back To Panama," "Rose Apple Tree," and "The Atlantic Side," to name a few. He enjoys playing in a band. He and Trish live in Covington, Louisiana.

David, CHS class of '79, became a police officer in New Orleans before becoming a deputy sheriff. He and his wife Marsha Boker had two sons, Matthew and Patrick. After 25 years in law enforcement, he retired. Living a more relaxed lifestyle, he enjoys reading, cooking with Marsha, the tranquility around the house with their dog Sadie, and playing racquetball and golf. David and Marsha live in Jefferson Parish, Louisiana.

Larry graduated from CHS in 1985, when his parents, Ted and Pat, relocated to Dothan, Alabama. He never married and works in maintenance at the University of South Alabama in Mobile, Alabama. Larry is fishing, golfing, or playing at a pool table when off work. Being the youngest of the boys and a competitor, Larry tries to beat his brothers in any activity every chance he gets.

The boys stay in contact and occasionally visit each other. Sometimes, they attend the Panama Canal Society reunions with Zonian friends, a fun gathering to share wonderful memories.

John Michael Klasovsky
Lead Foreman Control House Operator
Panama Canal Company
WWII Panama Canal Essential Occupation

John Michael Klasovsky was born on June 10, 1915, in Aliquippa, Pennsylvania, between the once-industrial steel mill hub city of Youngstown, Ohio, and the large steel production mills in Pittsburgh, Pennsylvania. After graduating high school in Youngstown, he worked for the Civil Conservation Corps planting trees, then attended Bliss Electrical School in Takoma Park, Washington DC, to become an electrician.

In October 1940, he completed his military draft registration card. Eight months later, he moved to work at the Norfolk Navy Shipyard in Virginia. While there, he was recruited to work for the Panama Canal. John arrived in the Canal Zone in October 1941. He worked as an electrician at the Gatun Locks and lived in bachelor quarters in the town of Gatun. After the United States entered World War II, he was never called for military service, being part of the Panama Canal essential workforce needed for the war effort.

One evening, during a stateside visit to see family in Youngstown, John and some of his buddies went to a local bar, the

Hollywood Tavern. There, he met Margaret Dorothy Maruskin, the daughter of the establishment's owner. She was assisting her father at the bar. Margaret was born on December 30, 1921, in Youngstown and attended Kent State University. John and Margaret began dating and soon married on August 28, 1944.

Returning to the Canal Zone, they got family quarters in Gatun, initially at 76 High Street, where they lived for years, with other moves to 107-B San Lorenzo Place, 126-A Santa Rita Court (both in the Old Town neighborhood), and 249-B Limon Place in the New Town neighborhood.

They celebrated the birth of their son, Michael "Mike" Edward, in June 1945 at Colon Hospital in the seaport city of Colon. The following year, Ivan John was born in October 1946. In August 1950, their son, Nicholas "Nick" Alexander, was born in Colon. And daughter, Antonia "Toni" Marie, joined the family in March 1953.

The summer of 1953 brought more good news. John received a promotion from lock operator leader wireman to control house operator at the Gatun Locks. His duties included operating the valves that regulated water flow in the three pairs of chambers, which raised and lowered ships passing through the locks.

In 1959, Margaret began working as a substitute teacher at Cristobal Jr. Sr. High School in Coco Solo. Having Ida, the help, made life more manageable by assisting with household chores and the kids. When Ida passed away, her sister, Chichi, became the help. Her husband was a line handler at the Gatun Locks. She sometimes brought her children to the house to play with the Klasovsky kids.

In the warm, humid climate, housekeeping in Gatun was not easy without air conditioning. Doing laundry and hanging clothes out to dry had to be done in the morning, especially during the rainy season from mid-April to mid-December, to avoid afternoon showers. The later use of dryers was a tremendous improvement. Additionally, the kitchen always had to be clean to prevent ants, with the floors swept and mopped, countertops wiped down, and food properly stored.

John actively participated in the Panama Canal Employee Suggestion and Incentive Awards Program. He received cash awards several times. In 1964, he got $700 for his suggestion of installing a safety device on the locks control house operating board to avoid the early opening of valves that regulated water flow into the chambers. Also, as the union president of the local International Brotherhood of Electrical Workers (IBEW), he devoted many hours writing to government officials regarding improvements he felt were needed for the locks and workers. When not at work or thinking of more job improvement suggestions, he spent time reading and listening to short-wave radio broadcasts from around the world.

Margaret stayed busy gardening, sewing, playing bridge with friends, and assisting at the Gatun Catholic Church, where the family attended on Sundays. She helped the kids care for the family pets, including cats, "Turvy" being one, parakeets, tropical fish, and a baby caiman that later escaped from the boys' enclosure. She and the kids enjoyed feeding birds pieces of bananas, oranges, and stale bread from the second-floor back porch entrance of the house. They were amazed to see the different varieties of birds swoop in to feed.

Klasovsky family: (L-R) Nick, Ivan, John, Toni, Margaret, Mike

A flock of 30 to 40 Panama green Amazon parakeets would fly in and eat everything within minutes, and then quickly fly away. In the backyard, they fed packs of coatimundi that would emerge from the jungle. They could hear parakeets chatting in the trees, and occasionally, they saw a sloth on a tree branch, slowly moving along.

Family outings included trips to both sides of the isthmus. On the Atlantic side, they liked going to Devil's Beach and having picnics at Fort San Lorenzo, an old Spanish fortress on a promontory overlooking an inlet and the entrance to the Chagres River. Both places are on the Fort Sherman Army base. Picnicking at the old fortress provided the opportunity to explore the ruins, and John enjoyed hunting for relics and old bottles at the base of the fort. A favorite trip to the Pacific side was renting a cottage at Santa Clara, where they rode horses on the beach.

Summer fun for the kids included participating in the community gym recreational program and competing in sports activities, including ping pong, volleyball, basketball, and archery. And, becoming advanced swimmers at the Gatun Swimming Pool.

As the kids became teenagers, they were doing outings on their own. Mike and Ivan got into hunting. Mike, the eldest, was the first to get around driving one of the two family vehicles, a Chevy and a van. Nick was known for riding his Vespa motor scooter everywhere, including traveling ten miles to the Coco Solo Teen Center. Toni's enjoyment of sewing clothing in high school became a hobby. She always had an interest in the arts. They all liked going to the Gatun Yacht Club and Gatun Pool where Ivan became a lifeguard, and hanging out at the various beaches with friends. Pina Beach on the Atlantic side was a favorite for bodysurfing and partying.

Besides the beaches, the boys did their share of snorkeling and skin diving with spearguns to catch lobster at reefs along the Fort Sherman coast and the road leading to the old historic port town of Portobello with ruins of another Spanish fortress. Also, fishing in both fresh and saltwater was world-class. A favorite location was at the Gatun Dam on the sides of the spillway apron, joining the Chagres River. Fishing on the concrete spillway deck was prohibited and could be dangerous, but kids ignored it. In addition to using a rod and reel, some kids had unique methods of fishing on the spillway deck when the water was shallow, including using sticks and rocks to hit the fish. On one occasion, Policeman Weiselogel caught Nick and his friend, Brian Plaisance, hitting snook on the spillway with a golf club. Whether they used a 3-iron golf club to strike the fish is unknown. Nick had many fishing adventures with friends Flip Whitney, Brian Plaisance, Billy Geddes, Steve Radel, Steve Jackson, and the Finneman boys. The Klasovsky boys kept the freezer stocked with fish and, at times, sold their catch to buyers in the seaport city of Colon.

While an encounter with wildlife was not uncommon living in Gatun, whether exploring in the jungle or seeing critters in the backyard, having a close encounter was a different story. One night, Nick took a garbage bag downstairs to the carport. He turned on the light switch when he reached the bottom of the steps. With the carport lit up, he looked across it to see a large, startled jaguar looking back at him. Both spooked, they quickly ran away in opposite directions.

In June 1971, John retired from the Panama Canal Company after 30 years of government service. He and Margaret initially moved to St. Augustine, Florida, while house hunting, then moved to Ocala. Liking the warmer weather in Florida, they did not want to live in Youngstown, Ohio. John worked for the City of Ocala as an electrical inspector for several years. They relocated and settled in Merritt Island, Florida. There, they had

Leopold J. Cimino

Zonian friends and a friend from Youngstown, Ohio, who lived in Cocoa Beach, approximately ten miles away.

Fully retired, John enjoyed relaxing, reading, and doing some fishing. He spent time on ecological issues to stop the development of some areas on the island and stayed involved with political issues of the county. Margaret continued with her gardening, sewing, and embroidery. They traveled some around the country, and Margaret went abroad twice to visit relatives on her side of the family. They attended Zonian picnics and socials with friends from the Canal Zone living in the vicinity. Sadly, John passed away on May 5, 1992, at age 76, in Merritt Island. Margaret stayed in Merritt Island until she joined John 15 years later, on July 30, 2007. She was 85.

Margaret & John Klasovsky

Mike graduated from Cristobal High School (CHS) in 1963. He attended Canal Zone College for a year and then left the Canal Zone in 1965 and moved to Youngstown, Ohio. He became a carpenter. In 1967, he married Marsha Foundoulis, and they had a son, Ian. While living in West Middlesex, Pennsylvania, they purchased a 78-acre farm and grew hydroponic plants and vegetables in greenhouses. They enjoyed traveling abroad, riding their dirt bikes, and spending time with their dogs. Mike passed away at age 57 in October 2002.

Ivan graduated from CHS in 1964. He received his bachelor's from Nova University in the Canal Zone. He then completed an apprenticeship in facilities engineering in July 1970. He met a tourist, Barbara "Chrisse" Harwanko, who was visiting

Panama, and they later married. The couple bought property on Isla Grande on the Atlantic side and at El Palmar on the Pacific side. They had two sons, Adrian and Oliver. He and Chrisse later parted ways. Ivan became the Chief of Plans and Property Branch, Directorate of Engineering and Housing for the US Army in Panama. After the US handed over full control of the Panama Canal on January 1, 2000, to Panama, he relocated to Miami, Florida. He married Lizabeth "Liza" Murillo. They lived in Germany for a few years due to her government position and traveled extensively in Europe before returning to Miami. Sadly, Ivan passed away at age 63, on April 18, 2010, in Miami.

A CHS graduate in 1968, Nick worked a summer at the Mt. Hope shipyard as an outside machinist helper before leaving in September to attend Kent State College in Ohio. The following summer, he worked at the shipyard again, returning stateside in September 1969. He traveled around the US and then, in December 1970, returned to the Canal Zone and worked on the Gatun Locks overhaul until June 1971. He assisted his parents with their move to St Augustine, Florida, before returning to Ohio to work and attend welding school. In 1973, he married Nancy Ebel. They had two kids, Daniel and Jean. Along the way, he completed his bachelor's from Kent State. He became the head technical writer for Nordson Corporation. He and Nancy later parted ways, remaining friends until her death in 2010. He married Kathleen Schue, and since their marriage dissolved, they are still friends and go out from time to time. He was an avid kayaker, but nowadays, he enjoys attending local festivals and doing some traveling. Nick lives in the town of Amherst, Ohio, a few miles from Lake Erie.

After graduating from CHS in 1971, Toni attained a bachelor's in art from the University of Florida. She married and had a daughter, Sonya, in 1983. Toni became a well-known artist for her portrait paintings. She later married again and had a daughter, Julia, in 1988. Toni enjoys the outdoors and traveling and is an avid kayaker. She still paints from time to time. She lives in Pine Mountain, Georgia.

John and Margaret had mixed feelings about living in the Canal Zone. They liked raising their kids in the small town of Gatun, and there were things they enjoyed about living in the Canal Zone, including outings to Panama. However, they did not like the climate, and they missed the convenience of being closer to family stateside.

Jackson Judson Barger
Locomotive Operator • Panama Canal Company
US Army, WWII Veteran

Jackson "Jack" Judson Barger was born June 6, 1922, in Harrisburg, Illinois, where coal mining was the primary industry and largest employer for the small city. His father, Joseph Barger, worked as a laborer, unlike many of the neighbors who were coal miners. At age 18, Jack realized if he stayed in Harrisburg, he would likely be working in the coal mines or as a farm laborer, which he had already been doing since after his junior year in high school. He worked in farming for a couple of years until shortly after 1940, and then moved to Detroit, Michigan, to live with his older brother, Frank. There, he worked for Ajax Steel & Forge Company.

Jack signed his World War II draft registration card in June 1942 following the Japanese attack at Pearl Harbor, Hawaii, on December 7, 1941, and the United States' declaration of war the next day. He enlisted in the US Army on February 16, 1943. He served in the European Theatre of Operations during the Rhineland Campaign and was subsequently sent to the Asiatic

Pacific Theatre of Operations. After WWII ended, Jack, a Tec 5, received his military discharge on March 14, 1946.

After returning home from the war, Jack went to Algonac, northeast of Detroit, Michigan. A friend set him up on a double date with an attractive young lady. After only two dates with Ina, Jack told her he was going to marry her.

Williamina "Ina" Forsth Reid Proctor was born in Broxburn, Scotland, in February 1924. She immigrated to the United States in February 1936, at age 12, with her mother, Grace Proctor, two sisters, Grace and Amy, and brother, Johnny, by ship to Halifax, Canada, before moving on to Detroit, Michigan. There, they reunited with her father, John Proctor, whom they had not seen in six-and-a-half years, and an older sister, Jeanne, who joined her father years earlier. John Proctor immigrated to the US through Ellis Island in June 1929.

Jack and Ina married in October 1947 in Highland Park, Michigan. They remained in the Wayne County area, where Jack worked primarily in tool and die manufacturing for a steel and forging company.

The family grew while living in the Detroit area with the birth of their first child, Jack Jay, in August 1948 and then with Gary Neil in January 1950. They added identical twin girls in June 1952; the first was Donna Lou, followed by Daryn Lyn. The family's "every two years" addition continued with the birth of Michael "Mike" Dennis in March 1954. Two years later, Steven was born in February 1956. With her Scottish roots and Steven having the same birth month as Ina, she lovingly gave him the nickname "Wee Stevie," as he was the last child of the clan. It was a family nickname that his friends never knew. Shortly thereafter, the family moved to Algonac.

One summer afternoon, while Jack Sr. was in the yard, an automobile pulled into the driveway. The Hill family was asking for directions to an annual pickerel fish tournament and festival.

The Last Zonian

As the conversation carried on, Mr. Hill revealed they were visiting family while on vacation from the Panama Canal Zone. From that friendly encounter, it is believed the Barger family went to Panama.

After submitting an employment application several times, Jack arrived in the Canal Zone in June 1965. He initially worked as a machinist for six months and then as a lock operator machinist. He later worked as a locomotive operator at the Gatun Locks, Locks Division. The locomotives, known as "mules," ensured ships moving through the three lock chambers maintained the proper cable tension on a vessel in assisting Panama Canal ship pilots with traversing through the locks.

Ina and the kids followed a year later, arriving in the summer of 1966 aboard the Panama Canal Company ship SS Cristobal. They received living quarters in Gatun, at 263-A Barro Colorado Place. Ironically, they had previously met one of their neighbors who lived one house away, at 261 Barro Colorado Place, on the corner with Sibert Street, the Hill family, whom they conversed with years earlier in their driveway in Michigan.

Jack and Ina looked forward to their new lives in the Canal Zone, although they knew that their eldest son, Jack Jay, would be returning stateside within three months. For the other kids, arriving in the summer gave them the opportunity to meet new friends and participate in recreational programs within the town, which included swimming, basketball, volleyball, battleball, badminton, ping-pong, tennis, and archery. The friendships they made that summer and at school became lifelong bonds.

Quickly getting accustomed to the weather, they were enjoying living in the Canal Zone. Ina was known for her pleasant demeanor and riding her bicycle everywhere in town. Kids liked it when she joined them riding in the neighborhood. When Jack was at work, she would make him lunch and ride her bike to the Gatun Locks adjacent to the town to see him and drop off his meal. That act of love was known by many in town. It could be a scene in a romantic movie, the pretty Scottish lady with a basket on the bicycle handlebar riding to see her husband to light up his day. At times, the twins accompanied her on bikes to see their father.

The boys hung out with friends, exploring and venturing into the surrounding jungle and playing baseball and sandlot football at a field behind the Finneman family house. Exploring their artistic talent for drawing, at 15, the twins were more mellow and enjoyed reading and going with friends to the roller skating rink in the nearby town of Margarita. In addition to participating in town activities, Donna and Daryn spent a summer volunteering as nurse aides (the Pink Girls) at Coco Solo Hospital.

Having adventurous spirits, Jack and Ina kept the family engaged during the summer by taking the kids in their customized van on weeklong vacations to explore El Interior of Panama, the mountainous regions of the country. Other Zonian families did the same, renting lodges or camping in the picturesque highlands, and "stay vacations" at the Pacific side beaches.

It was a given that many families spent time around the water, going to the swimming pool, the numerous beaches, Gatun Lake, yacht clubs, and fishing. The Barger boys and their friends fished with traditional tackle of a rod and reel. They also went rock fishing. It was similar to another group of their friends who did stick fishing. So, what was rock fishing?

Rock fishing was a fun way to try to catch fish, but being in that location was illegal. From the bridge that crossed over the spillway at the Gatun Dam or from down within the spillway while walking along on a ledge on each side of the concrete structure, Steve and his friends would drop big rocks to hit fish swimming in the shallow water of the spillway deck. When a fish was hit and stunned, it floated to the end of the spillway, where another lad would snatch it up. Being there was trespassing and

The Last Zonian

hazardous. If they were not caught for trespassing by the police, they were good to go. But, if the police snagged them, they were in deep trouble.

Another way they caught fish was with a speargun. They would sell their catch to the American Legion Post, a hangout for many Zonians and military personnel since it had a bar, a small restaurant, and a pinball machine. In addition, the boys and their friends spent time roaming through the jungle. They would gather avocados, guineps, banana stocks, and other fruit and haul them on their bicycles about a mile to sell them to the Chinese fruit and vegetable market near Fort Davis. Then, in a comical twist, the Chinese market would sell it back to the boys' parents and other Zonians.

In time, the boys went from riding a bicycle to get around to riding minibikes on trails and then to driving a car for outings, dates, and school events. The twins also took turns driving the green van or white Chevy, sharing with their brothers.

Jack and Ina were very supportive of their teenagers' endeavors. They enjoyed attending Mike's high school sports events, seeing the twins perform on the majorette squad

Ina, Mike, Jack, Donna

with Daryn being a squad leader, and applauding the girls' participation in an annual talent show competition amongst the two Canal Zone high schools and a junior college. Donna tied for first place with her performance as a wind-up doll, similar to that in the movie *Chitty Chitty Bang Bang,* and Daryn took third place with her dancing skills routine.

When not at work or with Ina, Jack spent time at a hobby shop tinkering with a vehicle and shooting the breeze with his close friend, Gerald Hamm, a soldier stationed at Fort Davis. At times, it was more chatting than repairing.

In the summer of 1973, Jack and Ina embarked on a big adventure with Donna, Daryn, and Steve. In their vehicle, they traveled over 6,000 miles from Gatun through Central America to Lemoore, California. There, they visited Mike and dropped off the twins, who moved in with him to assist in watching over the place while he was away in the military. Jack, Ina, and Steve continued traveling to visit family in Michigan before ending their vacation. They drove approximately 10,000 miles in total, finishing in New Orleans, Louisiana, where they boarded and loaded their vehicle on a Panama Canal Company ship for their trip home to Gatun.

Several years later, Jack got more involved with the town as an elected member of the Gatun Civic Council. Ina stayed busy enjoying everyday life and riding her bicycle. She and Jack continued their vacations to the El Interior of Panama as empty nesters.

In June 1982, Jack retired after nearly two decades of living in the Canal Zone. He and Ina moved to Louisville, Alabama, an hour north of Dothan. They purchased the property next to their close friends, the Hamm family.

Ina & Jack Barger

The Last Zonian

The property became a home base for the two. Jack and Ina spent most of the time traveling with their camper across the country, visiting and staying with family for weeks and months at a time. It was during one of these trips, while visiting family in Harrisburg, Illinois, that Jack unexpectedly passed away on March 11, 1985, less than three years after retiring. He was 62.

Ina initially moved to Casper, Wyoming, to live with her son, Steve, and daughter-in-law, Ann, for a while. She then relocated to Seattle, Washington, to live with her daughter, Donna, and be near Daryn, who also lived in the area. Ina relocated a couple of times to be with family, living the majority of it with Donna. She and Donna traveled to Scotland to sightsee and visit Ina's birthplace. Returning to Seattle with Donna, Ina remained and lived alone for several years after her girls moved away from the area. She then moved back to Casper, to live with Steve and Ann for a couple of years. Then, Donna helped Ina relocate near Bowie, Maryland, to have her mother closer to her family. Ina passed away in her birth month, on February 6, 2016, at age 92.

Jack Jay left the Canal Zone shortly after the family arrived. He had already graduated from Algonac High School in Michigan and enlisted in the US Army. He did a tour in Germany as a military policeman and then returned to Algonac and took a job working in a factory. His engagement to marry sadly ended after he was diagnosed with a rare medical condition. He succumbed to the illness on December 5, 1970. He was 22 years old. Unbeknownst to the family, in the three months Jack spent in the Canal Zone in the summer of 1966, he met and befriended a young lady. Fifty-three years later, she found Jack's brother, Steve, and sister-in-law, Ann, on Facebook. Hearing about Jack's passing, she wanted to inquire about his life. The brief interlude she and Jack spent together that summer left such a lasting impression that she visited Jack's grave in Algonac, Michigan.

After Gary completed his junior and senior years at Cristobal High School (CHS) graduating in 1968, he left the Canal Zone and moved back to Algonac. He married and had three children: Jay, Krystal, and Ezekiel. He and his wife parted ways and he raised his children on his own until they became adults, and then he relocated to Houston, Texas. Gary passed away on April 16, 1991, at age 41, in Houston.

Donna graduated from CHS in 1970. She moved to Lemoore, California, in 1973 with her sister Daryn to live with their brother Mike. She relocated to Tulsa, Oklahoma, working in a factory for a while. She later moved to Seattle, Washington, to be near her twin sister. In the late 80s, Ina joined Donna, who assisted her mother for many years. Donna later moved to Alexandria, Virginia. A church friend set her up on a blind date. Two months later, in April 1998, Donna married her blind date, retired US Air Force officer Thomas "Tom" Fontana. They adopted a child, Joe. In 2005, Donna went to culinary school and became a pastry chef after graduating in 2006. She and Tom live in Bowie, Maryland. They enjoy traveling and exploring the US, although their favorite place is Cape May, New Jersey.

After graduating from CHS in 1970, Daryn remained in the Canal Zone until 1973, when she moved to Lemoore, California, along with Donna. She then relocated to the Seattle, Washington, area and married Daniel Richardson, a soldier from the Canal Zone. They had four children: Samuel, Jack, William, and Alexander. After parting ways with Daniel, Daryn later married Timothy "Tim" Haslett. They had a daughter, Tralayna. Daryn is a freelance storyboard and animation artist with over 20 years of experience in the industry. She and Tim live in Seattle, Washington.

After graduating from CHS in 1972, Mike enlisted in the US Navy. He was stationed in Lemoore, California, and served in Vietnam. While in Lemoore, his sisters, Donna and Daryn, moved in for a time. After completing his military service, Mike relocated and settled in Tulsa, Oklahoma, and became a helicopter mechanic. Donna joined him there. She introduced him to a friend and co-worker who became his wife. He married Cindy Simmons, and their son, Nicholas, was a year old when Mike passed away on November 14, 1987, at age 33.

After Steve, the youngest, graduated from CHS in 1975, he attended welding school in Cleveland, Ohio. After completion, he returned to the Canal Zone for almost a year, working part-time before returning stateside and disembarking with his car in New Orleans, Louisiana. While there, he visited and stayed a week with Zonian friends. He and a couple of friends got jobs at the shipbuilding yard in Pascagoula, Mississippi. Steve's girlfriend, Ann O'Donnell, a Zonian from Margarita whom he had known since the fifth grade, joined him within a month. They married and had two children, Samantha and Kyle. In the summer of 1979, due to shipyard lay-offs, they moved to Casper, Wyoming, based on a recommendation from another Zonian friend. Steve worked as a mechanic, and Ann worked in the postal service. They both retired and live in Casper, spending the winter months in Arizona.

Steve stated that his mother, Ina, said living in the Canal Zone was the happiest time of her and Jack's lives. Raising their children there was wonderful.

Irving Ike Spector
Tugboat Master • Panama Canal Company
US Navy, WWII Veteran

It was an exciting year in the Brooklyn borough of New York, where Irving "Irv" Ike Spector was born on June 11, 1916. For its baseball fans, there was a promising season. The Brooklyn Dodgers (nicknamed the Robins, who later became the Los Angeles Dodgers) won the National League championship and advanced to the World Series, losing to the Boston Red Sox and Babe Ruth.

Irv encountered some hardships in his early years. As a young teen, Irv sold newspapers for a penny along the boardwalk at Coney Island during The Great Depression. Years later, he got a job with the Civilian Conservation Corps, one of President Roosevelt's New Deal programs.

At age 20, Irv enlisted in the US Navy on May 13, 1936. After his military training, he was stationed in the Panama Canal Zone, on the Atlantic side of the isthmus, at US Naval Station Coco Solo, consisting of Coco Solo Submarine Base and Coco Solo Naval Air Station. He was a truck driver and crewmember of a landing craft mechanized (LCM).

On the opposite shore, across Manzanillo Bay from Coco Solo, is the seaport city of Colon. Military personnel from the various bases in the surrounding area would visit the city when off duty. While strolling the streets of Colon, Irv walked into a bakery to get a bite to eat and someone caught his eye. There, he met a young lady, Anjelica Alvarado, working at the bakery.

Anjelica was born in 1910 in the province of Veraguas in the interior of Panama. After losing her mother at age two, she and her two sisters were raised in a Catholic orphanage in Panama City. In young adulthood, she moved to Colon.

SNBM Irv Spector

Irv avidly visited the bakery several times, not for the delicious baked goods, but to see Anjelica ("Angelica" for English-speaking folks). They began a courtship and married on February 1, 1939. He became a stepfather for Angelica's two-and-a-half-year-old daughter, Digna Rosana Mathews, born in September 1936. They moved into Navy family quarters at Coco Solito, a couple of miles from Coco Solo and Colon. On May 22, 1940, Irv received his Navy discharge as a seaman first class from Naval Air Station Coco Solo. He reenlisted the following day. In June 1940, Irv and Angelica welcomed their first child, Herbert "Herb," born at Colon Hospital. A year later, their daughter, Sarah, was born in November 1941.

The Last Zonian

The following month, on December 7, the Imperial Japanese Naval Air Forces attacked Pearl Harbor, Hawaii, and on December 8, the United States declared war on Japan. The Panama Canal, a shortcut between the Atlantic and Pacific Oceans, became a vital waterway for US and Allied ships.

During World War II, Irv had sea service aboard ships and was sometimes away. In March 1943, he and Angelica welcomed their daughter, Helen, born at Gorgas Hospital in Ancon. Irv last served on the USS San Marcos (LSD-25). After completing two tours of duty, he left the Navy on September 8, 1945, as boatswain mate first class following the end of WWII.

Upon leaving the Navy, the family initially moved to the San Francisco neighborhood in Panama City, on the Pacific side, while Irv sought employment with the Panama Canal. He got a job as a small tugboat operator with the Dredging Division. He, Angelica, and the children moved to the small town of Gamboa, which was a bit isolated in the jungle along the Canal, about nine miles from the town of Paraiso and 17-and-a-half miles from the nearest hospital, traveling on a two-lane road. In January 1950, they celebrated the birth of their fourth child, Norman "Norm," at Gorgas Hospital at Ancon.

Gamboa, a little remote, had its uniqueness. Irv and Angelica enjoyed socializing and having parties with friends. Irv, at times, shared his musical talent by playing his accordion. Angelica loved cooking and playing bingo with the ladies. She took a break from her joy of cooking once a week when the family went to the Gamboa Golf and Country Club for dinner. Despite having two housekeepers to do the cleaning, laundry, and ironing, Angelica preferred to do her own cooking for the family. Irv's pastime was coin and stamp collecting, although he was an avid reader and spent much of his time immersed in a book.

The kids spent most of their time at the gymnasium and community swimming pool, fishing, and participating in school activities. The eldest son, Herb, liked the outdoors and hunting. On one occasion, while on a camping trip, after eating breakfast, he walked to a narrow creek in the jungle to wash his mess kit. He had an inner feeling as if something was watching him. When he looked up, a jaguar was staring directly at him from across the creek. Herb slowly reached to his side for his rifle, which he had left at the campsite. Realizing it was not with him, he threw his mess kit at the large cat, frightening it, and they both fled.

In September 1956, Irv was promoted to a towboat master in the Navigation Division. The family moved to 8455 Alcora Street in the town of Margarita on the Atlantic side.

The kids went right back to their active lives and sports activities. Herb participated in the grueling Sea Scout Explorer's Ocean-to-Ocean Cayuco Race. He was on a crew that won the race in the mid-1950s. Sarah was all about swimming, and Helen was in Girl Scouts. Norm built tree forts with his buddies in the jungle, chased royal blue butterflies, and was active in many sports, including Little League baseball, as he got older.

Angelica attended all the kids' sporting events. In high school, Herb was on many teams: football, wrestling, water polo, swimming, basketball, baseball, and soccer. Sarah played volleyball and water polo and was on the swim team. Helen was on the volleyball, basketball, softball, and swim teams. Norm, five years younger than his siblings, would also later exhibit his athleticism.

Angelica's support for her kids' endeavors was always visible. During the after-Christmas annual tree gathering event, which lasted a couple of weeks and culminated in early January with the town's bonfire, she sometimes protected Norm's stash of trees with a BB gun. That deterred other teams from messing with his team's stockpile.

Irv was a workaholic, spending much of his time working closely with Ben Brundige, Nelson Austin, and his best friend,

The Last Zonian

Charlie Jones. Sometimes, while working a day shift, he allowed Norm and a couple of his buddies to accompany him aboard the tugboat to experience the tug at work. Irv also worked part-time as a tugboat captain for Las Minas Bay, an oil refinery, towing barges on the Atlantic side.

When not at work, Irv hung out at the Cristobal Yacht Club and Elks Club. Every once in a while, he and Angelica enjoyed a weekend relaxing, barbecuing, and playing cards with friends at a house owned by other ship pilots near Pina Beach.

They often traveled stateside to visit relatives, sometimes using the Canal Zone Home Leave Program, which provided a travel allowance every other year. During their summer vacations from 1959 to 1964, Irv and Norm attended many New York Yankees baseball games. Two of those years, the Yankees won the World Series Championship in 1961 and 1962. In 1964, during the trip back to Brooklyn, the family attended the New York World's Fair, which was a memorable experience.

In the fall of 1970, Irv received the honor of traveling to Slidell, Louisiana, to pick up a new modern tugboat, Joseph C. Mehaffey, for its maiden voyage to the Canal Zone. He mastered other tugboats, including the Cardenas, Alahajuela, and Trinidad. The new vessel joined the Atlantic tug fleet for the Panama Canal.

After 36 years of living in Panama, Irv retired in 1972. He and Angelica moved to St. Petersburg, Florida, where other Zonian families and friends settled nearby.

Irv's enthusiasm for being on the water continued. For many years, he was the captain of the MV Tom Sawyer, a 400-passenger excursion vessel operating between St. Petersburg to Tampa.

One afternoon, while at work, Irv called his son Norm to ask him if he had ever heard of a guy by the name of Jimmy Buffet, who had chartered the entire boat and everyone was raving about. Norm informed his father that Jimmy Buffett, not Buffet, was a famous singer-songwriter. Irv met Jimmy when he came up to the bridge to thank him for his piloting of the vessel. Irv said he was a gentleman.

Spector family: (L-R) Sarah, Helen, Angelica, Norm, Irv, Digna, Herb

After 67 years of marriage, Angelica passed away on October 7, 2006, at age 96, in Seminole, Florida. Irv stayed occupied with his loving family. Ten years later, Irv passed away on June 1, 2016. He was 99 years old; ten days shy of his 100th birthday.

Digna left home in 1954 before graduating in the Canal Zone. She moved to Brooklyn, New York, to live with her step-grandmother. While in New York, she met and married Theodore Ashford. They had one child, Theodore. Digna passed away on December 12, 2020, in Norman, Oklahoma.

Herb graduated from Cristobal High School (CHS) in 1959 and then enlisted in the US Air Force with duty in Japan and Hawaii. He served from 1959 to 1962, then returned to the Canal Zone. He worked as a locomotive operator until 1963. Coincidently, at times, his father Irv's tugboat would hand off a ship to the locomotive team Herb was on to transit the vessel through the locks. In 1964, he attended Oklahoma State Tech in Okmulgee where he received his certification in both heating and air conditioning. He then moved to Richmond, Virginia, to be closer to his sisters, taking a job with Honeywell. He married Thelma "Pam" Brown. They had two daughters, Deborah and Carol. In 1972, Herb relocated to Seminole, Florida, following his parents' retirement. He started his own company, The Beacon Group, specializing in sales of commercial-grade heating, ventilation, air conditioning, and chillers. Herbert passed away on November 5, 2013, in Seminole, Florida.

After Sarah graduated from CHS in 1960, with the nickname "Little Hercules" (because of her athleticism), she remained in the Canal Zone. A year later, she married George West III, a soldier stationed at Fort Gulick. In 1961, they moved to Mechanicsville, Virginia. They had three daughters: Angela, Sherry, and Michele. After the marriage dissolved years later, she relocated to St. Petersburg, Florida, to be closer to family. Sarah retired from Barnett Bank and lives in Tampa. Her three daughters also live in the Bay Area.

After graduating from CHS in 1961, Helen went to Brooklyn, New York, to live with her grandmother. While there, she met and married Victor Musco. They had two children, Victor and Anthony. She and her family moved to the Richmond, Virginia, area, fairly close to her sister Sarah. After her parents retired to St. Petersburg, Florida, she and her family moved to the area to be near them. After her first marriage dissolved, Helen later married Ronald Gentry. After several years, they parted ways. Helen resides in Pinellas Park, Florida, near her sons.

Norm graduated from CHS in 1968, lettered in football, track, baseball, and basketball. He then attended Canal Zone College (CZC), receiving the CZC Outstanding Athletic Award and an associate degree in 1970. He earned his bachelor's in marketing from Florida Atlantic University in 1972, in Boca

Raton. While working at the Ocean Club of Florida in Ocean Ridge, he met Dawn Heck. They married in 1976 and have two girls, Kasilyn and Shaina. Retiring in 2021, Norm had 16 years in the restaurant business and 33 years in property management. Dawn worked 46 years as a registered nurse. They live in Vero Beach, Florida. Although retired, Norm kept his real estate associate's license active, using it part-time. He also utilizes his community association manager's license as he now consults for condominium and homeowner associations during their turnover phases.

Norm stated that his parents enjoyed chatting about their memories and the wonderful life they had in the Canal Zone. They said it was the time of their lives and that they were blessed to have had the opportunity to raise their family there.

Robert Graham & Alice Forsythe
Lead Lock Operator Machinist
Panama Canal Company
US Navy, WWII Post Era Veteran
And The Dressmaker

Nine years following the opening of the Panama Canal to ship transit between the Atlantic and Pacific Oceans, Robert "Bob" Graham Forsythe was born on September 6, 1923, at Colon Hospital in the seaport city of Colon at the Atlantic entrance of the Canal. In 1941, Bob, at age 18, started taking flying lessons and within a few months, he made his first solo flight. That same year, following the attack by the Imperial Japanese Navy Air Forces at Pearl Harbor, Hawaii, on December 7, 1941, the United States entered World War II. Bob graduated from Balboa High School in 1942. The following year, in July 1943, wanting to serve in the military, he attempted to enlist in the US Navy. He was denied due to a medical issue.

Bob worked at the Panama Air Depot (PAD) of the US Army Air Forces for his final six months of high school. Following graduation, he worked other jobs before being denied enlistment in the Navy. In 1945, while eating at the luncheonette and seeing friends at the PAD, he spotted and met Alice Taylor who worked at the eatery. Although Alice was already seeing another fellow, their encounter led to her dumping the other guy to date Bob.

Alice was born on January 14, 1920, near the town of Boquete, located in the highlands of the Chiriqui Province of Panama. Her loving grandparents raised her on their coffee plantation. As a young lady looking for her own opportunities in life, she left her scenic surroundings with its coffee plantations for the city of David and then moved to Panama City.

Bob was working as an apprentice in 1945 at the Balboa dry docks with the Mechanical Division of the Panama Canal. Previously denied military service, he was drafted into the US Navy in November 1945, despite the end of World War II with the surrender of Germany on May 8, 1945, followed by Japan on September 2, 1945. The Selective Training and Service Act of December 20, 1941, required Bob to register for military service. He served at Rodman Naval Station and Submarine Base on the Pacific side of the Canal Zone. During his time off, while at Rodman, he again took up flying for several months. Following his release from the Navy in July 1946, he returned to his job with the Mechanical Division.

Seaman Bob Forsythe

Bob and Alice celebrated getting married twice within a year. The first time was in September 1946 in Panama City. The following year, their daughter, Edna Mae,* was born in August 1947. They married a second time in September 1947 in the Canal Zone.

Bob worked at the Balboa dry docks in the Canal Zone, but the family lived in the Vista Hermosa neighborhood of Panama

City. He did not have the time-in-service or seniority to get government family quarters in the Canal Zone.

In late 1948, he became eligible for family housing, and they moved to Williamson Place in Balboa. Move-in day was busy with Bob making trips back and forth from their vehicle with boxes and items. Completely distracted, he was unaware of what was occurring in the house until opening the bathroom door. He was instantly startled, seeing a strange sailor in his bathroom, standing in front of a mirror, wearing a white Navy uniform looking at him. It did not take but a moment to realize the sailor was Alice. She laughed loudly at the surprised expression on his face. A humorous and loving moment in their life.

In 1950, with the closing of the dry docks, Bob received a job offer to work at the locks. He assumed the position would be at the Miraflores Locks, about five miles away, or at Pedro Miguel Locks, eight miles from Balboa. He was mistaken. The job was 50 miles away. The family moved to Gatun on the Atlantic side of the isthmus. The town was adjacent to the Gatun Locks. They initially received housing at 39 Lighthouse Road. They would move two more times years later, to house 111-B Bolivar Highway, which was just shy of a stone's throw from the locks, and finally to 414 Laurel Street on a hill overlooking the main road into town.

Bob, a lock operator machinist, sometimes worked in the tunnels located in the walls of the Gatun Locks. He maintained machinery and repaired mechanical breakdowns in the tunnels and other areas of the locks.

He and Alice became accustomed to living on the Atlantic side, it was less busy than the Pacific side and Panama City. A couple of years after they moved to Gatun, their son, Edward "Ed" John, was born in November 1952 at Colon Hospital, where Bob had been born 29 years earlier.

Having two young children did not deter Bob and Alice from traveling to Boquete to visit her relatives during the summer months and holidays. The road trip from Gatun to Boquete was long and slow, approximately 350 miles, and during the early to mid-1950s, it was not without hazards. The Pan-American Highway was gravel and dirt with sections of asphalt with potholes. Driving the highway segment from Panama City to Boquete, constructed through the jungle and mountainous terrain, worsened with flooding during the rainy season. They always enjoyed reaching the scenic view of their destination to visit family and relax in the beautiful surroundings.

The trips to Boquete, with their share of blow-outs and flat tires due to the poor road conditions and car mechanical failures, became less frequent as the kids got older. The family, like other Zonians, began taking advantage of the employee "Home Leave" entitlement, which paid for stateside transportation every other year. The road trips stateside to visit relatives from Florida to California had their share of adventures, but not due to the road conditions and flat tires. Instead, it was due to stopping and sightseeing while traveling across the country. Still, after their stateside vacations, they were always happy to get home.

Bob and Alice spent time with Edna and Ed, playing cards and board games and enjoying family time and laughs. Attending the annual Independence Day 4th of July celebration at the community barbecue pit with sack races and other activities was always fun. Going to the beaches on the Atlantic and Pacific sides of the isthmus was a norm, relaxing and seeing other families.

During the Fall months, in the tropical paradise, the holiday season's festivities were joyful times for the family. Taking the kids to the Halloween and Christmas parties in the gymnasium were fun community activities. However, Edna and Ed preferred going trick-or-treating throughout the town on their own. The town's annual after-Christmas tree bonfire event brought out the crowd for an evening of excitement with friends.

At home, when Bob's work shift changed to nights, and he needed to sleep during the day, the house was as quiet as a mouse. The kids spent much of their time with friends outdoors, which most Zonian kids did.

Alice enjoyed gardening and growing flowers, fruits, and vegetables. She also liked sewing, crocheting, and knitting. Her seamstress skills were renowned. What began as sewing clothing for her family led to assisting friends and others. She made casual wear, dresses, and cheerleader uniforms for Cristobal Jr. Sr. High School, ball gowns, wedding dresses, and gowns for the singing quartet of the Sweet Adelines International, Canal Zone Chapter. She was known as the "go-to" seamstress on the Atlantic side in the Canal Zone.

When Alice and Bob attended parties and socials, including the Shriners, Policemen and Firefighters, and New Year's Eve Balls, she would enter the gala wearing one of her beautiful gowns. Dancing was an activity they both enjoyed. So, with some socializing at the balls, Bob and Alice preferred to spend much of their time on the dance floor dancing the night away.

Alice & Bob Forsythe

In the early to mid-1970s, after 30 years, Bob got the flying bug again. He actively started flying at France Field with Bobby Parker. In August 1977, while visiting his daughter Edna in

Hayward, California, he flew numerous times, flying rental aircraft and taking Alice up into the skies.

After 37 years of government service, Bob retired from the Panama Canal Company. He and Alice left the Canal Zone in January 1979. They moved to Sacramento, California, where Edna was living.

Unbeknownst to them, the Swain family, Zonians they knew from Gatun, lived in Sacramento. Alice again put her seamstress skills to work after being asked if she would make a wedding dress for Nola Swain Boyer. Alice had watched Nola grow from a child to a young lady in the Canal Zone.

After retiring, Bob became a social butterfly, having more free time. He and Alice enjoyed the skies immensely, flying throughout California. In January 1985, Bob's dream of owning his aircraft became reality when he purchased a Cessna 182 Skylane (N1817X). Their grandest and longest adventure was flying cross-country three times from California to Florida to visit relatives.

Bob and Alice remained in California until September 2002 and then moved to Melbourne, Florida, to be near Edna and her daughter, who relocated to the area in 1995. Having sold his Cessna before relocating, Bob occasionally rented an aircraft at the Merritt Island Airport. A couple of memorable flights were taking his great-granddaughter, Abigail, to see her elementary school from the sky in 2006, and in 2014, he made a low pass of the NASA Space Shuttle runway. Alice continued with her joy in gardening of flowers and tending to an avocado tree at their new home in Melbourne. Being Zonians, they attended the annual Panama Canal Society Reunions in Orlando, which they did since the 1980s when it was in Tampa.

Bob and Alice enjoyed fellowship, including attending adult Sunday school before church, followed by the church service, Monday Bible study, and Wednesday fellowship meal and

Bible study. Additionally, every Sunday after church service the family got together. Celebrating birthdays and holidays and hosting visiting friends and relatives from out-of-state were also cherished times. Edna conveyed that the convenience of having family live within a radius of five miles was truly a blessing.

Sadly, after almost 70 years of marriage, Alice passed away on January 18, 2016, four days after her 96th birthday in Melbourne, Florida. In his 90s, Bob was still driving himself three days a week to the gym to exercise. Five years after Alice's passing, Bob joined her on June 14, 2021, at age 97, on the same month and day of his mother's passing.

Edna graduated from Cristobal High School (CHS) in 1965. She briefly attended Monmouth College in New Jersey. In early 1967, she returned to the Canal Zone. She worked at the Gatun Locks in the Time Office, then as secretary for the mechanical and electrical supervisors during the overhaul. In July 1968, she departed the Canal Zone for California. After completing Grace Ball Secretarial College in San Francisco in 1969, she worked with Pacific Gas & Electric Company. There, she met and married William Wilkinson in 1979. They had one daughter, Andrea. William passed away in February 1985. Edna later moved to Florida in 1995. She and her daughter's family live in the same neighborhood in Melbourne, Florida.

Ed graduated from CHS in 1970. After completing a four-year apprenticeship program in air-conditioning and refrigeration, he worked for the Panama Canal Company until 1979. That year, many Zonians retired or departed from the Canal Zone due to the implementation of the Panama Canal Treaty, which abolished the US unincorporated territory known as the Panama Canal Zone. Ed moved to Pennsylvania and married Cynthia Moore, a Zonian from France Field, in 1982. They had one child, Dylan. In the mid-1980s, they relocated to Florida; years later, the marriage dissolved. Ed later married Linda Shear in 1996 and took up residence in Palm Bay, Florida. Ed passed away on September 5, 2018, at age 65.

Edna stated that her family treasured the camaraderie of Gatun, the memories, and lifelong friendships. "After all," she said, "we were all born there, and our ancestry goes back to my grandparents, Dan and Grace Forsythe, who came to the Canal Zone in 1912, and my great-grandparents, Eduardo and Andrea Taylor, who pioneered Boquete in the El Interior of Panama. Our roots grew deep!"

* Edna is the last Zonian in the Forsythe family.

Robert John Blair
Lead Foreman Lock Operations
Panama Canal Company
US Navy, WWII Veteran

Robert "Bob" John Blair was born on May 3, 1914, in Philadelphia, Pennsylvania, in the year of two major world events: the commencement of World War I on July 28, 1914, and the opening of the Panama Canal to ship transit on August 15, 1914, connecting two oceans. Four years later, Bob survived the city's 1918 Spanish Influenza epidemic, which took thousands of lives.

During The Great Depression, the worst economic decline and stock market crash in United States history, which lasted from 1929 to 1939, Bob worked at the Biddle Estate of a prominent Philadelphia family. He often played cards with another estate worker, John Gallagher, an Irish American who lived on the estate with his wife, Pauline Marx, an Austrian immigrant, and their two children, older son John Jr. and daughter Eleanor Mary Gallagher.

Eleanor, an attractive young lady who was born in Philadelphia on March 12, 1922, caught Bob's eye. The attraction was mutual. By early 1940, Bob had left the estate and worked as a rigger at the Sun Shipbuilding and Dry Dock Company. Believing they would not get Eleanor's father's consent to marry, they eloped out of state. Bob, who was 26 and 17-year-old Eleanor, married on June 24, 1940, in Fredericksburg, Virginia. Concerned about her actual age, Eleanor annotated that she was 22 on the marriage certificate.

Bob and Eleanor returned to Philadelphia. Times were still tough, so he worked multiple jobs as a rigger, bartender, and an ice truck driver, delivering ice blocks to residents' homes. In those days, many households still had refrigerators that did not operate on electricity or have freon; they were literally iceboxes chilled with large blocks of ice.

Their first son, Robert John Jr., was born in February 1941. World War II was already raging in Europe. What started as an invasion of Poland by Nazi Germany in 1939 consequently included the United States entering the war following the surprise attack by Japan at Pearl Harbor, Hawaii, on December 7, 1941.

Times got tougher with food stamp rationing, which began in 1942. Bob had become an electrician, working as a lineman to support his family. A year later, when his toddler son, Bob Jr., was two years old, Bob enlisted in the US Navy in May 1943. After completing his naval training at Camp Perry, Virginia, he shipped out to the Pacific Islands to serve with the 104th Naval Construction Battalion, "Seabees," and quickly became a chief petty officer.

Eleanor also joined the war effort, driving a parcel post truck delivering packages after taking her son to school every day, maintaining the home, and praying that Bob would return home from the war so they could resume their normal life. Following the end of WWII on September 2, 1945, Bob was honorably discharged from the Navy in October 1945.

The family resumed their lives together and purchased their first home in Ridley Park. In March 1947, Bob reenlisted in the

Naval Reserves for three years while working as an electrician at the Philadelphia Navy Yard. In April 1947, they welcomed their second son, John "Jack" Robert. The family was finally settling down.

However, three years later, after Bob's Naval Reserve enlistment was complete, the Korean War began on June 25, 1950. Within two months, Bob was recalled to active duty in August and was discharged on November 9, 1950.

Living most of his life in the Philadelphia area, Bob wanted a change from working in the cold winters and an increase in his earnings. He informed Eleanor he was taking a job in the Panama Canal Zone. She loved her home, so she dug in her heels and told him that he should try living there first before she would uproot her family to move to a third-world country.

Bob arrived in the Canal Zone in late 1953 to work as a wireman lock operator electrician in the Locks Division at Gatun Locks on the Atlantic side of the isthmus. It took him two years to convince Eleanor that life in the Canal Zone was ideal for raising their boys. He conveyed it was a tropical paradise where she could enjoy beaches and swimming pools and shop for exotic wares from all over the world. Eleanor finally agreed to relocate in 1955. The family got housing in Cristobal and after a couple of years, they moved to the town of Coco Solo to 332 Lee Road.

Bob Jr., Jack, Eleanor, Bob

Eleanor enjoyed everything portrayed to her about the Canal Zone and Panama. She quickly came to love her adopted country. Besides visiting the favored sites, she stayed busy as a vigorous walker and attended the boys' Little League baseball games, Boy Scout activities, and the community swimming pool. She became a Red Cross 100+ mile swimmer with an envious lap log.

Bob was happy his family was with him and he was progressing in his job getting promoted to a lock operator electrician. The good news continued with the birth of their daughter, Marjorie, in July 1957 at Gorgas Hospital, Ancon.

Bob Jr., 16 years older than his sister, stayed busy at school with the glee and drama clubs, school newspaper, and yearbook. He also participated in the Reserve Officers' Training Corps (ROTC), hung out with friends, and was a lifeguard.

In 1961, Bob and co-worker Felix Karpinski were sent to Japan for several weeks to the Mitsubishi Company to study the performance and familiarize themselves with new towing locomotives for the Panama Canal. The locomotives, referred to as "mules," replaced the original mules in service since 1914.

In early 1962, the new locomotives arrived at the Gatun Locks with several Mitsubishi engineers. Bob and Eleanor became their hosts while they were in the Canal Zone. He also assisted as a tour guide, showing them the sites, and she returned the hospitality given to Bob in Japan by hosting many fabulous meals.

Bob, with four-year-old Marjorie, took the engineers on an adventure in his boat, disembarking at an island at Gatun Lake. When they finished exploring and wandering through the dense foliage, they could not find the boat. The engineers, thinking they were stranded, were a bit concerned. Bob resolved their anxiety by swimming around the island and returning with the boat.

A few years later, the family moved to Gatun, the town adjacent to the Gatun Locks and Gatun Lake. Initially, they lived at 132 Santa Rita Court and later moved to 131 Buena Vista Place. The Gatun Yacht Club became a favorite hangout for mingling with friends. Plus, Bob did a lot of work at the iconic club during various expansions and renovations. If the family was not at the yacht club, they were either at the beach, doing other outdoor activities, or socializing with Eleanor's brother, John Gallagher, and his wife, Dorothy. They followed Bob and Eleanor to the Canal Zone, where John became a locomotive operator at the Gatun Locks.

In 1964, Bob received a promotion from leader lock operator electrician to control house operator. And there was more good news that year. Jack was selected for the All-Zone Football Team.

Jack excelled in high school sports, playing football, basketball, and track. His younger sister and parents enjoyed going to the games to watch him play. In addition to being an athlete, Jack was a musician and organized a rock band called "The Roadrunners," which subsequently became "The Castaways." Eleanor became the "band mom" and loved driving them to venues.

Around the house, they always had pets, including dogs, cats, parakeets, cockatoos, and one that was unusual. Definitely odd. It all began with Bob's exploratory and inquisitive disposition. While driving on the gravel road to Pina Beach, he spotted a pathway that disappeared into the foliage. He parked the car on the side of the roadway and then followed the trail through dense vegetation until he came to a small village tucked away in the jungle. The villagers welcomed him. After seeing their meager existence, he occasionally visited to bring them groceries, mostly canned goods.

During one of these outings, going to Pina Beach with Eleanor and Marjorie, they stopped to take items to the villagers. Eleanor stayed in the car while Bob and seven-year-old Marjorie disappeared into the jungle. Marjorie was drawn to the chickens running around in the village. She picked up a juvenile to pet it. As they were getting ready to leave, the villagers gave her the young hen as a gift. When they returned to the vehicle, Eleanor, seeing Marjorie holding the chicken, told them it was not getting into the car. Marjorie pleaded that it was a pet. Eleanor finally gave in to please her daughter. They named the chicken "Sugar Babe."

The chicken became an indoor pet, learning to poop on a piece of newspaper and groom itself in front of a hallway mirror. When the hen went outside, she became a "guard chicken." Any stranger or pet that approached the house who Sugar Babe did not know quickly got chased away. Sugar Babe became a bit of a pet celebrity, appearing on a Southern Command Network television show, *The Most Unusual Pet*. Sugar Babe was a loved family pet for ten years.

By 1967, the boys had left the roost to pursue their own lives. Bob was promoted to lead foreman lock operations. He and Eleanor stayed busy with their regular routines and Marjorie's activities. They were actively involved with Marjorie at the Atlantic Stables, where Bob was the stable master. However, they were probably unaware of some of the places and distances that Marjorie rode, including walking her horse, La Mancha, across the steel-graded retractable bridges at the Gatun Locks and then riding to Fort Sherman and Devil's Beach, which was more than eleven miles from the stables.

When Eleanor worked part-time at the Gatun Theater ticket counter, Marjorie sometimes saw a free movie. Eleanor, being a remarkable swimmer, delighted in seeing Marjorie on the high school swim team and attended her competitions. She smiled when she went swimming at the community swimming pool and saw Marjorie sitting in the tall lifeguard chair.

Nearing retirement, Bob and Eleanor considered staying in Panama to become expatriates like other Zonians. Ultimately, in May 1976, after 27 years of government service, 22-and-a-half with the Panama Canal Company, they moved to Daytona Beach, Florida. They lived near their son, Jack "Dain," and

Blair Family: (L-R) Paulina (Marx) Gallagher, Bob, Bob Jr., Marjorie, Eleanor, Dain

Eleanor's brother, John, and his wife, Dorothy, in nearby Orange City. They later settled in neighboring Port Orange. Bob enjoyed his hobby as an avid photographer. Eleanor stayed fit by jogging on Daytona Beach and logging hundreds of miles, just as she did with swimming in the Canal Zone. She joined a health club and met many friends. Besides fitness, she loved going shopping.

After 61 years of marriage, Bob passed away on January 8, 2002, at age 87, in Port Orange. Eleanor lived alone, spending time with her three children and grandchildren. She was very independent and still drove her stick-shift sports car at age 93. Eleanor passed away on October 27, 2020, in Port Orange. She was 98.

Bob Jr. graduated from Cristobal High School (CHS) in 1959. He and his buddy, Gerarde Detore, joined the US Air Force together. He served two enlistments in the logistics field. After his military service, he attended the University of Maryland, earning a bachelor's in social science, and then married Patricia "Pat" Bittman. He went on to receive a master's in recreational therapy from the University of North Carolina at Chapel Hill. Bob Jr. was the first in the entire extended Blair family to attend college. After moving to Hagerstown, Maryland, he and Pat adopted two children, Keith and Jennifer. His career was as a civil servant, mostly working for the Veterans Administration. He relocated several times, including a tour working for the Panama Canal Commission from 1982 to 1985. Bob Jr. and Pat parted ways, and after returning stateside, Bob met and married Ernestina "Tina" Rivera through a chance encounter at church. They settled in Menifee, California. After three decades of a loving marriage, Bob passed away on June 12, 2021, at age 80.

After Dain graduated from CHS in 1966, he moved stateside to St. Petersburg, Florida, to be near his high school sweetheart, Beverly Dreyer, a Zonian from Margarita. While there, he attended St. Petersburg College. Dain and Beverly married, and they had one child, Dain Jr. They moved to Daytona, and Dain became a musician playing guitar and bass with touring bands. Dain and Beverly later parted ways. After touring, Dain was a radio personality, worked for Capital Records, and went on to start his own music production company, GrooveWorx, producing platinum-selling artists and composing music for national commercials, TV shows, and feature film trailers. He married Sharon Poole and had two children, Justin and Taylor. Dain and Sharon live in Brentwood, California.

Marjorie graduated from the CHS class of '75. She earned a degree in English and journalism from Stetson University in DeLand, Florida. There, Marjorie met Joseph "Joe" Bulone. She became a newspaper reporter and technical writer and eventually entered the corporate world in marketing and communications. She married Joe and had two children, Christopher and Lauren. Most of her 45-year career in the corporate world was in the biotechnology industry. Joe is a judge. Marjorie, Joe, her horse, Shakkan, and other pets live in Seminole, Florida.

Marjorie conveyed her mother's thoughts of living in the Canal Zone, "What she resisted emphatically for years became the happiest time of her life."

Charles Cunningham Loyd
Senior Powerhouse Operator – Gatun Dam
Panama Canal Company
US Navy, WWII Veteran

Charles Cunningham Loyd was born on February 19, 1922, in Pocatello, Idaho, where his father worked for the railroad. His family later relocated to Birmingham, Alabama. In high school, he excelled with numbers and was the math class vice president, although he aspired to be a radio announcer. Charles enlisted in the US Navy on October 26, 1942, ten months after Japan attacked Pearl Harbor, Hawaii. He served in the Pacific Theater during World War II.

Following his discharge from the Navy on November 28, 1945, Charles returned home and worked in maintenance for a power company. He later met Effie Elizabeth "Betty" Twining through mutual friends. Betty was born on December 2, 1926, in Birmingham. After attending Birmingham Southern College, she worked as a medical laboratory technician. Charles and Betty married on February 14, 1950. While they remained in Birmingham, Charles lived out of state for two years, traveling home whenever possible while attending a training program with the Tennessee Valley Authority.

Leopold J. Cimino

In June 1952, their son, Charles "Charlie" Cunningham Jr., was born in Birmingham. Shortly after that, the family moved to Memphis, Tennessee, where Charles worked at a power plant. In Memphis, Betty gave birth to daughter Anne Chesley in July 1956. As Charles's career progressed with another power plant position, the family moved to Nashville, "Music City." Along with the relocation, as with the earlier move, came a newborn, daughter Patricia "Pat" Colvin, * in April 1958.

While working for the US Army Corps of Engineers at a dam outside of Nashville, Charles received two job opportunities to relocate to another dam; one was in the Appalachian Mountains, and the other was overseas in the Panama Canal Zone. He chose the job with the Panama Canal Company. The family arrived in the Canal Zone on June 7, 1965. They got living quarters on the Atlantic side of the isthmus in Gatun's Old Town neighborhood at 105-A San Lorenzo Place, adjacent to the Gatun Locks.

They liked the small town. There were enjoyable amenities and community activities for the entire family, including the Gatun Yacht Club, community swimming pool, gymnasium, a small library, movie theater, cafeteria, ceramic club, and church-sponsored events, such as fish fries, spaghetti dinners, and church camp.

Charles's job as a senior powerhouse operator at the Gatun Dam was on the opposite side of the Gatun Locks from the town. It was a pleasant drive from his house with minimal traffic as he paralleled both sides of the locks to get to the dam less than three miles away.

When not working at the hydroelectric power plant, he spent some time working on his carpentry hobby, which led to him making improvements to the living quarters by building a room wall, a wall cabinet, and rolling cabinets. He also made smaller, heartfelt crafts and doll beds for his daughters.

The Last Zonian

Betty became a member of the Atlantic side Newcomers Club for women living less than two years in the Canal Zone. The club went on monthly excursions within the Canal Zone and other places of interest in Panama. After returning from a day trip to the San Blas Islands, she was glad to be home, conveying to the family that the aircraft she was on was held together with chewing gum and baling wire.

She was a Girl Scout troop leader for several years. During a camporee at the Canal Zone Girl Scout Council Camp Site in Gatun, they discovered an abandoned litter of three kittens with the mother nowhere to be found. Fearing the kittens' loss to the elements, they were all taken. Betty took two kittens. She and her daughters, Anne and Pat, named the kittens Samantha and Tammy. Later, realizing the kittens were actually males, Samantha became Sam, and Tammy kept his name.

Charles and Betty enjoyed chatting over coffee with friends Bud and Betty Balcer and neighbors Billy Joe and Elsie Brown. With an easygoing demeanor, Charles at times appreciated the quietness of relaxing at home. On the other hand, Betty got involved in the community as a representative of the Gatun Civic Council. She also stayed busy with her arts and crafts, going to the ceramic club, and doing some sewing.

Outings with the kids to surrounding areas on the Atlantic side were relaxing, and within ten miles of Gatun, they enjoyed the beaches at Fort Sherman Army base. Shimmy Beach was popular, having a snack bar, lifeguards, and a shark barrier. Devil's Beach and Hidden Beach were much smaller, secluded, and less crowded, but had no lifeguard. Additionally, down the road from the beaches, the family explored the ruins of Fort San Lorenzo, an old Spanish fortress seized by Henry Morgan's pirates in the late 1600s. Fort Randolph, another Army base near the town of Coco Solo, had a sandy shore area with sea urchins in its waters.

Trips to the Pacific side of the isthmus also raised the family's enthusiasm for the area. Attending church camp activities at Playa Santa Clara was fun for all and Betty enjoyed teaching arts and crafts. Plus, traveling to the mountainous region of Volcan in the Chiriqui Province of Panama close to the Costa Rican border brought some anticipation of scenic views.

As the kids got older, Charles taught them to drive a manual transmission car using a stick shift. On one occasion, he took his daughter, Pat, to an unused airstrip at France Field to practice in his Volkswagen (VW) Bug. As she shifted from second to third gear, he was looking out the window and talking aloud. Pat asked him, "Who are you talking to?"

He replied, "I'm talking to that bush pony over there." A small pasture with a few bush ponies was visible at the perimeter of the airfield.

"What did he say?" she asked.

"You'll never get it off the ground, lady," was his response, meaning she would never get the car to accelerate on the runway as she continued to fiddle with the gear shifter. Pat did master the skill and was one of a few teens in her group of friends who knew how to drive both automatic and manual transmission cars.

The teenage kids were doing their own thing, getting out with friends. Charlie, the eldest, did a lot of fishing with his buddy, Ted Bailey. He and Anne's friends spent time using the family billiard table. Charlie also hung out with friends who were in the Army. At times, he got around driving his father's VW Bug.

Pat, Charlie, Anne

Charles, wanting to spiff up his sky-blue VW Bug, hand-brush-painted the center trim on the hood fire-engine-red. Unbeknownst to him, he got help sprucing up the VW when his teenage daughter Anne and a friend painted the front and rear bumper bolts and radio antenna fire-engine-red. Seeing the additional highlights, he was not pleased. It was just a little too much for him, but he got over it. Although, that was not the only car to which Charles added flair to his liking. He also had an all-black '63 Mercury Comet that needed some style, so he hand-brush-painted the window trim and roof red.

All of the family members used the cars. Betty mostly drove the Mercury for all her errands and to work at the Christian bookstore in Cristobal. Anne drove one of the spiffy cars when available to hang out with her friends, go to the beach, and attend school activities. Or, she caught a ride with one of her friends. Pat spent time with her close friends, Cindy Ferguson and Nancy White, getting out and going to the Gatun Yacht Club.

The Tarpon Club near the Gatun Dam, with a casual restaurant, a bar, and a jukebox, was another hangout for residents, including teenagers. Its location provided an excellent view of the dam, the concrete spillway, and the Chagres River. The view for personnel working at the dam was just as good, overlooking the spillway, river, and potential safety infractions near the dam.

Charles, a senior powerhouse operator at the Gatun Dam, monitored and managed the hydroelectric generating plant water flow to ensure proper electrical power demands. At times, the dam employees, seeing trespassers and potentially hazardous situations on the spillway, would contact the Gatun Locks Security and Gatun Police to remove persons from the no-trespassing area. Teens would ignore the no-trespassing signs to fish or attempt to catch snook with large sticks, rocks, and a golf club on the dam's concrete spillway when the water level was shallow.

After their kids graduated from high school and moved on, Charles and Betty missed them. They were ready to return stateside, especially with Anne and Pat moving to Alabama, and knowing Charlie would be all right since he worked for a good company gave them solace.

After leaving the Canal Zone in 1977, Charles and Betty moved to Alabama. He transferred to Miller's Ferry Steam Plant, two hours south of Birmingham, with the Army Corps of Engineers for a few months before transferring to Norris Dam with the Tennessee Valley Authority north of Knoxville. Betty utilized her lab technician skills and worked at Oak Ridge Hospital. Both, being born in Tennessee, had family in the area. Charles retired in 1979 with 31 years of government service. They relocated to Birmingham and then moved south to the small town of Montevallo, about 45 miles away.

Charles & Betty Loyd

They attended the First Baptist Church and stayed involved with church activities. Around the house, they were busy working their half-acre vegetable garden and doing canning. They did some traveling, occasionally taking trips to the Smoky Mountains. What they enjoyed the most was spending time together, seeing their kids and grandchildren, and relaxing at home with their two cats.

Charles passed on January 14, 1990, in Birmingham, at age 67. Betty continued her church fellowship and spent time with family. Betty passed away on June 13, 2012, at age 85, in Birmingham.

Charles Jr. graduated from Cristobal High School (CHS) in 1970. He remained in the Canal Zone, trained in a four-year apprenticeship program, and then worked for the Panama Canal Company as an automotive machinist. He was briefly married to Sue Arbaugh and later to Patricia "Pat" Grimm Richards. She was a Balboa High School graduate of class '69. He and Pat had two daughters, Amanda and Valerey. He later relocated to Alabama. Charlie passed away in Birmingham on December 17, 1994, at age 42.

Anne graduated from CHS in 1974. She attended Canal Zone College for a year and then went stateside to receive an associate degree from the University of Alabama in Birmingham (UAB). She worked as a legal assistant in a law firm. After she met and married Dolf Seeds, they ministered to persons with addiction in Birmingham, Atlanta, New Jersey, and abroad in Ireland and Kazakhstan. Anne and Dolf had one child, Peter. Sadly, Anne passed away on July 20, 2010, in Montevallo, Alabama. She was 53.

After graduating from CHS in 1975, Pat attended the University of Alabama in Birmingham receiving a bachelor's in nursing and later, a master's degree. While working at UAB, she met Gary Boyd at a church Christmas party. He was studying to be a physician. She married Gary, and they raised four adopted children: Elizabeth, Andrew, Alex, and Katie. For a while, she worked in social work, and for 19 years, as needed, to assist Gary in his practice. Gary retired from his practice after 29 years, although he still works as a physician advisor. They enjoy traveling, exercising, and spending time with their grandchildren. Pat still sees and meets up with her close Zonian friends, Cindy and Nancy. She and Gary live in Birmingham, Alabama.

* Pat is the last Zonian in the Loyd family.

Robert Edwin McCullough
High School Teacher • Canal Zone Government
US Army, WWII Era Veteran

Robert "Bob" Edwin McCullough was born in the town of Lambert, Montana, on March 2, 1917. Established in 1914, Lambert was once just prairie grass. The immense farming of wheat and a railhead gave the town, which had a population of less than 1,000, some acknowledgment in its heyday. Bob's family moved from Montana to California twice between the early and mid-1920s before permanently settling in Sidney, Montana.

In Sidney, Bob's father, Edwin J. McCullough, worked as a clerk of the district court. His mother, Myrtle Allie Abelein McCullough, was a homemaker who raised five children: Neva, Robert, Richard, Alberta, and Julia.

In high school, Bob served on the records committee and as the class treasurer. In 1940, while attending his second year at St. Cloud State Teachers College in Minnesota, he was already working as a grade school teacher. That same year, he signed his military draft registration card in October.

Bob was deferred from military service after the United States entered World War II, following the attack from Japan at

Pearl Harbor, Hawaii, on December 7, 1941. This allowed him to complete his bachelor's degree before his enlistment on June 30, 1942. He served in the military until WWII ended on September 2, 1945, and was honorably discharged on January 8, 1946.

Bob's younger brother, Richard, also served during WWII. He was sent to the South Pacific and came home paralyzed from the waist down. He was very independent and drove his own car, always a Cadillac. He would drive his Cadillac to Texas in the winter and spend summers in Montana.

Following the war, Bob received a master's degree from Colorado State College of Education, now the University of Northern Colorado. He taught high school in the small city of St. Maries, Idaho, before taking a teaching position with the Canal Zone Government in the Panama Canal Zone.

Private Bob McCullough

Bob arrived in the Canal Zone on the SS Cristobal in July 1952. He received housing quarters in the town of Margarita on the Atlantic side of the isthmus. He initially taught and supervised shop classes at Rainbow City High School, a non-US citizen school for families of Panama Canal workers living in the Canal Zone.

A few years later, Bob transferred to Cristobal Jr. Sr. High School (CHS) in Coco Solo, a school for US citizens, where he taught early world history, social studies, and mechanical drawing 1. Well-liked by his students, he was known for being kind and passionate about his courses. Students' comments about him include that he was an excellent teacher, a good historian, enjoyed his class, and he was always nice. His kindness to all is evident in what he wrote under his photograph in a CHS yearbook, "Be kind to animals."

Although most of his students respected and liked him, there were a few who were insensitive and ignorant. For example, there was a rumor that Mr. McCullough was a prisoner of war (POW) during WWII and had a serial number tattooed on his forearm that he did not want anyone to see, so he always wore long-sleeved shirts to keep it hidden from prying eyes. Also, occasionally, a few callous kids purposely dropped a book on the hallway floor outside his classroom to watch his reaction to the loud sound. He always appeared to cringe momentarily.

Besides being a dedicated teacher, Bob stayed busy during his time off away from the high school. He was a firearms enthusiast and regularly visited the gun range at Rancho Ramos near Margarita. Liking the outdoors, he enjoyed hiking and attending other outside activities. Additional hobbies included coin and stamp collecting and reading.

Robert McCullough

Bob left the Canal Zone after his retirement in August 1977 with 29 years of government service. He returned stateside and settled in his hometown of Sidney, Montana. Bob never married. He helped out around the farm, became a caregiver to his 82-year-old mother, and took her to church. Occasionally, he went to the gun range with his various firearms and did his own ammunition reloading. He found relaxation in continuing his other hobbies of coin and stamp collecting and reading. Sadly, after only a little over six years following his retirement from the Canal Zone, he was diagnosed with cancer in December 1983. He immediately made his own funeral interment arrangements in order to not burden his family. Bob passed away eight months later, on July 27, 1984, at age 67. His mother, Myrtle, passed away five years later on December 9, 1989, at age 94.

Regarding the rumors of him being a POW and having a serial number tattooed on his forearm, here is the truth. Bob served in the US Army Air Forces (USAAF) as an aircraft mechanic for the B-29 Superfortress heavy bomber. Upon leaving the AAF on January 8, 1946, at Lowry Army Airfield in Colorado, he was a sergeant. Bob never served outside the continental United States and was not a prisoner of war. He was a patriot who honorably served his country. Bob's nephew, Harold A. Simard, debunked student rumors about a hidden tattoo by sharing that since Uncle Robert was fair-skinned, he always wore long-sleeved shirts to avoid sunburn. Also, as a gun enthusiast during his teaching years at CHS, when Bob heard a sudden bang, he instinctively lowered his head and flinched in response to the loud sound of a book dropped onto the hallway floor outside his classroom door.

Reflecting on his life in the Canal Zone, Bob wrote in a yearbook that he enjoyed living there because outdoor activities were possible nearly every day. His desire to be outdoors can be attributed to his upbringing in Montana.

Iris Esther Mary (Dedeaux) Hogan
Finance Branch Superintendent Postal Operations
Canal Zone Government

Iris Esther Mary Dedeaux was born on June 17, 1920, in Gulfport, Mississippi, where her father worked as a grocery merchant. In the mid-1930s, Iris arrived in the Panama Canal Zone with her parents, Leon Edward Dedeaux and Caroline Rosaline Lichtenstein Dedeaux. Her father worked as a carpenter with the Building Division in the Canal Zone, and the family lived in the town of Pedro Miguel.

At age sixteen, Iris graduated from Balboa High School in May 1937. She traveled back to Gulfport to visit family in March 1939 before proceeding to Chicago, Illinois, to stay with her Aunt Sophie while thinking about options for her future. Having previously lived in Chicago with relatives and attending a year of high school from 1933 to 1934, staying there was a consideration. She worked as a secretary for a short time while living with her aunt. Wanting to be closer to her family, Iris returned to the Canal Zone, and by early 1940, she found a job. She initially worked as a clerk-typist in the Quarantine and

Immigration Station at Fort Amador and then worked in offices within the Civil Affairs Bureau.

Iris met Paul Dexter Richmond on a double date after a friend asked Iris to accompany her on the date. Paul was born on December 21, 1914, in the town of Industry, Maine, with a population of less than 800. After graduating high school in 1933, he later entered the US Army and was stationed in the Canal Zone. He was a corporal in 1940, then got out and remained in Panama working as a civilian government employee for the Army. On February 14, 1942, Iris and Paul married in Balboa.

Their family grew when their first child, Leslie Jeanne, was born in November 1946 at Gorgas Hospital, Ancon. Iris became a stay-at-home mom, and in July 1947, they moved stateside to Portland, Maine, for a couple of years. Upon their return to the Canal Zone, Lois Ann was born in September 1949 at Ancon.

By 1950, Paul had progressed in his career to storekeeper. Later in the year, he took a position with the Canal Zone Government Civil Affairs Bureau Police Division, and the family moved to the Atlantic side of the isthmus, initially living in New Cristobal.

The family hired help that same year when Iris returned to the workforce, employed at the Postal Division in Coco Solo. Francesca assisted with house chores and taking care of the children. She spoke English and Spanish, which was great. However, years later, Iris had to cope with a sassy preschool-age Lois, who picked up some Spanish vocabulary and would only speak the acquired language to her. That phase faded after a while.

On another occasion, one morning, when Francesca went to check on the girls, she was shocked when she opened the bathroom door and stopped what was about to occur. Seven-year-old Leslie had lathered her three-year-old sister Lois with her father's shaving cream and was going to give her a shave.

She had watched her father shave himself a couple of times with his straight razor.

When the family moved to the town of Margarita, they had to hire new help. The girls liked Edna, so she quickly became part of the family.

A baby boy, Ralph Edward, born in November 1953 at Colon Hospital, brought the family joy in having a third child. Sadly, in September 1954, their fourth child, Paul Donald, passed away shortly after birth.

Staying busy working, Iris received a promotion with the Postal Division to a window and distribution clerk in 1956. Paul was a detective working with the Cristobal Police District. They welcomed their daughter Mary Elizabeth, born in July 1957, at Coco Solo Hospital.

The family grew again in January 1959 with the birth of Michael Anthony. However, after getting home with her baby, Iris hemorrhaged and was rushed to the hospital. Twelve-year-old Leslie, during her mother's recovery, and while her father was at the hospital or working, took care of her younger siblings and newborn brother in the evening after she got home from school. Mrs. Brooks, a neighbor, cared for two-year-old Mary and infant Michael during the day.

Maintaining a household with both Iris and Paul working full-time meant Edna, the longtime help, watched the kids grow up since she spent so much time with them. Years later, when Edna became a mother and left her employment with the family to raise her child, they were sad to see her go.

On days off, Iris and Paul sometimes just enjoyed relaxing at home or playing cards with friends. They valued their family outings, primarily on the Atlantic side. A favorite was day trips to Fort Sherman's Shimmy Beach, with a snack bar and protective shark barrier, and occasional picnics at Fort San Lorenzo, an old Spanish fortress on the Army base.

Leopold J. Cimino

Sometimes, they went to Pina Beach, which was more secluded and, for that reason, liked by many Atlantic siders who relaxed in the sun while the younger kids played in the sand and looked for shells. Venturing out from the Canal Zone brought the enjoyment of more scenic beaches on the Caribbean Coast, including Playa Maria Chiquita and Playa Blanca, with the intermittent sightseeing of Portobello, a natural harbor with remnants of another Spanish fortress.

The getaways to the picturesque mountainous terrain of El Valle in the Interior of Panama and the beaches on the Pacific side added some excitement. Paul, at Playa Gorgona, would swim out from the shore with an innertube and a burlap sack to do lobster hunting while Iris relaxed, and the kids strolled the beach and played in the tide pools.

Iris and the kids spent much of their time at the Gatun Swimming Pool, where her brother, Louis Dedeaux, was a swimming coach, there, and at Cristobal High School. Paul, on the other hand, was fully engaged in playing golf, and when his son, Ralph, was in grade school, he began teaching him how to play the game. They all liked going to the Margarita bowling alley. And, Iris also spent time playing tennis. They encouraged their kids to play sports during summer programs, which they continued at school. They also stayed active in neighborhood sports activities, riding their bicycles, skating on the streets, and roaming the town of Margarita. Leslie, the eldest, had a unique experience in high school, attending a few days of the US Army Jungle Warfare Training at Fort Sherman. It was a memorable venture.

In April 1964, Iris became the first female postal employee to become a Finance Branch Superintendent in charge of postal operations in the Canal Zone while working at the Coco Solo Post Office, one of 12 post offices. She worked at other post offices on the Atlantic side, including Gatun, Fort Davis, Fort Gulick, and Cristobal.

Iris and Paul parted ways in 1965. She continued working in her career and moved her family to 243 David Road, in Coco Solo. Iris raised her five kids as a sole parent. Inez, the help, assisted with the cooking, laundry, and caring for their poodle, Charlie. Iris continued doing family outings, although they lessened since the kids were older and had their own interests.

Leslie hung out with her friends, went to the beach, and spent time at a horse stable before going stateside to college. Lois spent time with her boyfriend, Charlie, and her other passion, artistic drawing. The three younger kids played in the neighborhood, climbing trees, playing football, fishing at the Pier 1 dock, and doing other activities.

Iris Esther Mary Dedeaux

Mary, the youngest of the girls, with her friends, would pull a red wagon to Pier 1 when a Navy vessel arrived at the dock to trade sodas for C-rations with sailors disembarking for shore leave. On one occasion, a sailor asked the grade schooler if she had an older sister. Mary said, "Yes," and walked him back to her house to meet Lois. Seeing her younger sister and a sailor walking toward the house, Lois hid in a closet from her sister while the unwanted suitor waited outside and finally departed alone.

Leopold J. Cimino

A year after Iris' promotion as branch superintendent at Coco Solo, she took charge of postal operations at Fort Davis for eight years before returning to the Coco Solo Post Office. She married Richard Hogan in January 1973, whom she met while working in the Postal Division. They moved to 8447 Espave Avenue in Margarita; the town was between Coco Solo and Fort Davis, about four miles in either direction. Iris remained at the Coco Solo Post Office for the following two years. She also served as a member of the Women's Advisory Council to the Governor.

Iris retired in June 1975 after 32 years of government service and 40 years living in the Canal Zone. Richard, a WWII veteran who pursued life in the Panama Canal Zone, retired in 1972 after 35 years of government service. They moved to Kerrville, Texas, around a community of other Zonian retirees.

Mike, Mary, Ralph, Iris, Lois, Leslie

After retiring, they enjoyed playing cards, bowling, golfing, and traveling, especially to see and spend time with family and friends. Iris stayed busy with the Hill Country Zonians Committee in Kerrville for many years, jointly organizing and planning events. Less than 11 years following their retirement, Richard passed away in February 1986, at age 68, in Kerrville.

Iris occupied her time with family, friends, attending the annual Panama Canal Society Reunions, working on her projects, and traveling abroad. She visited the former Canal Zone with family and friends. Interested in learning about her ancestry, she traveled a couple of times to France and Germany. She was also an excellent bowler and competed in a state bowling tournament. Iris passed away on March 25, 2014, at age 93, in Kerrville. She was a 25-year cancer survivor.

After graduating from Cristobal High School (CHS) in 1964, Leslie attended Mercy Hospital Street Memorial School of Nursing for two years in Vicksburg, Mississippi. She later moved to Portland, Maine, to live with her father. There, she met and married Raymond Winkelman in 1968. They later moved to Minnesota and had four children: Paula, Clint, Mosheh, and Amber. She worked various jobs while raising her kids, including as a school bus driver for 20 years. After she and Ray parted ways, she moved to Kerrville with her mother. While there, she married Bill Rogers. Leslie returned to healthcare, working in a nursing home and as a caregiver to Iris for several years before moving to Amarillo. After 20 years together, Bill passed away in November 2020. Leslie currently lives in Amarillo, Texas.

Lois graduated from CHS in 1968. The following year, in June 1969, she secretly married Charles "Charlie" Healan while he was home on military leave. Charlie was a classmate. He was drafted in 1968, entered the US Navy, served two tours in Vietnam, and left the Navy in 1972. Lois and Charlie had two sons, David and Charles. Charlie retired from the US Postal Service after 36 years of government service. Lois, from time to time, still does her artistic drawings. Charlie used to like tinkering with cars, doing bodywork and painting. Living a more tranquil life, they enjoy gardening while fending off squirrels and other critters who get most of the harvest. Lois and Charlie live in Deltona, Florida.

Ralph graduated from CHS in 1972 and attended Oklahoma State Tech. He married Cindy Mullens and they had two kids, Gregory and Christina. Later, after he and Cindy parted ways, he met Patty Eggleston Howard. Over the years, he worked in refrigeration and heating and escalator and equipment maintenance. Ralph and Patty live in Arlington, Texas. He is an avid golfer and enjoys going to the beach where he also likes to do metal detecting.

Mary, a CHS graduate of 1975, went to Texas State Tech Institute and received a degree in dental technology. Shortly thereafter, she met and married Eldon "Lee" Chiles and had two children, Jessica and Christopher. Following a couple of occupation changes, she retired after working 19 years in the public school system, helping children with disabilities and special needs. Lee retired after 31 years with the US Postal Service. Mary and Lee live in Fredericksburg, Texas. They stay busy, and she still enjoys riding her horse.

Mike graduated from Tivy High School in Kerrville, Texas. He works in maintenance. He enjoys collecting baseball cards and doing his drawing and paintings—a talent that runs in the family. While in high school, he won a scholarship for one of his drawings. Mike and Karen Marino, his longtime companion, live in Houston, Texas.

Paul Dexter Richmond retired from the Civil Affairs Bureau Police Division in June 1967, after 29 years and 11 months of service. He relocated to Portland, Maine, and later moved to Houston, Texas. Paul passed away on April 12, 1992, at age 77, in Houston.

Evelyn (Kuinlam) Barraza
Otolaryngologist • Canal Zone Government

Evelyn Josefina Kuinlam, born on November 20, 1925, grew up on a farm in the northern coastal town of Arecibo, 50 miles west of San Juan, Puerto Rico. Her childhood interest was in medicine. Studious in school, she skipped two grades and graduated early from high school. She received a bachelor's degree from the University of Puerto Rico before attending medical school at Tulane University School of Medicine in New Orleans, Louisiana, and receiving a scholarship from the Puerto Rican government.

In medical school, Evelyn met another pre-med student, Jaime Barraza, in 1945. Jaime was born on March 16, 1924, in the town of David, Chiriqui Province of Panama, a primarily agricultural region bordering Costa Rica. While living in Panama City, Jaime received his bachelor's degree and then attended medical school in the United States.

Evelyn and Jaime married in 1948, at the beginning of their final year in medical school. Upon completion, they received their Doctor of Medicine degrees in 1949. The young general practitioners initially moved to Puerto Rico for Evelyn to fulfill her government scholarship agreement for returning to work on the island. In Puerto Rico, they had their first child, a daughter who sadly passed away four days later due to a congenital heart defect. The tragic loss led to the physicians returning to New Orleans for specialty training. Evelyn initially wanted to go into obstetrics and gynecology (OBGYN) but changed her specialization to otolaryngology—ear, nose, and throat (ENT). Jaime, wanting to be a general surgeon, changed to ophthalmology. After they were done, Jaime received a commission as a captain in the US Army, so he incurred a two-year military commitment.

Evelyn and Jaime celebrated the birth of their second child, Jaime Jose, born in January 1954 in New Orleans. In the summer of 1954, they arrived in the Canal Zone to practice at Gorgas Hospital on the Pacific side of the isthmus. They got housing in the town of Diablo.

Living in the Canal Zone with their son and starting a full-time schedule, the new parents needed household assistance. So, Evelyn reached out to her mother-in-law to inquire and search for a housekeeper. Jaime's mother sent Rosa Castillo Fuentes, the help who had been working for the Barraza family for 30 years. At age 9, Rosa had watched over Jaime when he was an infant. Now, she volunteered to move to the Canal Zone to care for Jaime's son.

In September 1955, Dr. Evelyn Barraza and Dr. Jaime Barraza transferred to Coco Solo Hospital on the Atlantic side to open and take charge of an eye, ear, nose, and throat clinic. Evelyn was the sole otolaryngologist and ran the ENT side of the clinic. Jaime was the sole ophthalmologist. He ran the eye side of the clinic, performing elective and emergency eye surgical procedures, including many cataract surgeries.

The Last Zonian

Evelyn and Jaime got family housing in the small and quiet neighborhood of France Field, located close to Coco Solo, between the town and Coco Solo Hospital. Evelyn liked the neighborhood's proximity to the hospital, except during land crab mating season.

When the crabs were active in the mornings, Evelyn would look under her vehicle parked in the carport and find a bunch of crabs hanging out that she would swoosh away with a broom. Although it seemed a bit comical, that was not the end of the crab issue. During that time of year, Evelyn disliked driving the short stretch of the road, a quarter of a mile, from the entrance of her neighborhood to the main thoroughfare when crabs literally blanketed sections of the road. The surface appeared to shift and move from side to side. Driving slowly, Evelyn would straighten the steering wheel, then take her hands off it to place them over her eyes, peeking a little not to see the crabs, and stick her thumbs in her ears so she wouldn't hear the wheels crunching them. The smell was awful. And, seeing the crabs raising their claws on the edge of roadways as if they were waving or hitchhiking meant that crab mating season had certainly begun. Evelyn was not alone in her dislike of crab mating season; many Zonians shared her sentiment. There were also many flat tires.

Dr. Evelyn Kuinlam Barraza

The family grew with the addition of three more children while living at France Field. A year after moving in, Evelyn Maria was born in September 1956 at Gorgas Hospital, Rafael Lorenzo in March 1959, and Mayra Margarita seven years later in May 1966; the two youngest kids were born at Coco Solo Hospital. Rosa was still with the family to help.

It was not all work and no play; the Barrazas enjoyed life away from the clinic. Evelyn and Jaime were well-liked at the Coco Solo Hospital and within the community. They spent time with their close friends, the Moore family. They also enjoyed socializing with friends at their home in France Field, hosting elaborate cocktail parties with a bartender and large spreads of food, where the kids would sneak tidbits from a huge adored bowl of shrimp.

Like many Zonian families, going on beach trips to the Pacific side of the isthmus was fun for the kids and relaxing for Evelyn and Jaime. Additionally, Jaime enjoyed time on his boat docked at the Club Nautico Caribe Marina in the seaport city of Colon. He later became the president of the club.

Evelyn & children: (L-R) Evelyn Maria, Rafael, Mayra, Jaime Jose

The kids engaged in a variety of activities, including swimming, softball, archery, and other sports programs at the Coco Solo gymnasium. Living adjacent to the jungle allowed for exploration and building of hidden forts in the thick vegetation. Also, being close to the inactive France Field Army Air Station, they rode their mini-motor cycles on the airstrip and, at times, got chased by the military police as they sped away into trails. When not riding the minibikes, they shared riding their horse stabled at the Fort Randolph Riding Club. The kids had their own interests. Jaime Jose liked music and played a guitar in a local band in high school. Rafael liked water skiing along with baseball and soccer. Mayra loved to read and learn about plants. Evelyn Maria acquired a fascination with her mother's work in medicine.

Evelyn Maria remembers that her mother did many tonsillectomies often in her office. And, her mother would regularly be called into the emergency room to see patients with nose bleeds and foreign bodies in their ears, noses, or throats, such as beads and fish bones. Evelyn Maria often visited the clinic to visit and watched her mother with patients.

Dr. Evelyn loved traveling with her children, taking them to visit her family in Puerto Rico every summer and, at times, during holidays, traveling to the States so the kids could experience and see different sites across the country. Throughout the year, she took the kids to see theatrical plays on both sides of the isthmus. She liked shopping, so when she and the kids were on the Pacific side after staying the night at the Tivoli Hotel in the Canal Zone or the Hotel El Panama in Panama City, they ventured to the central shopping district in the city. The kids experienced quite a lot, including seven-hour-long road trips on the partially paved Pan-American Highway to visit Jaime's family in David, in the interior of Panama, close to Costa Rica.

After Evelyn and Jaime parted ways, she moved to the town of Balboa on the Pacific side with her daughter, Mayra, and housekeeper, Rosa. Jaime Jose, Evelyn Maria, and Rafael lived stateside, where some attended college. Evelyn transferred from the former Canal Zone Government Health Bureau to the US Army Medical Department Activity (MEDDAC), doing public health at Corozal until her retirement in 1982. When Evelyn left Panama, Rosa retired at age 67 and returned to David.

Evelyn moved to Stone Mountain, Georgia, where she worked at a medical clinic for several years, then fully retired to Rockledge, Florida, in 1989 to live near two close friends from the Canal Zone. Livia Strider lived in Rockledge. She and

Evelyn knew each other from living in Balboa. Wilma Moore lived less than ten miles away in Melbourne. They knew each other from the France Field neighborhood. Evelyn traveled extensively, visiting her children and throughout Europe. She later moved to Tampa to live with her daughter, Mayra. A few months of the year, she resided with her daughter, Evelyn Maria. Dr. Evelyn Barraza passed away on September 18, 2004, at age 78, in Tampa, Florida.

Jaime worked at Coco Solo Hospital until his retirement in the mid-1980s. He remarried and initially moved to Hayward, California. He later moved to Stockton, California, where he passed away on December 27, 2007. Dr. Jaime Barraza was 83.

Jaime Jose graduated from Cristobal High School (CHS) in 1972 and followed his parents' footsteps in the medical profession. He attended Tulane University School of Medicine, graduating in 1980, becoming an obstetrician-gynecologist (OBGYN) working for Kaiser Permanente in Oakland, California. He married Vivian Zee. They had two sons, Matthew and Andrew. Retired and a widower, Jaime Jose visits his sons, enjoys music, and still plays a guitar from time to time. He lives in Alameda, California. His son Matthew also attended Tulane University School of Medicine; he is the third generation in the Barraza family to become a physician trained at Tulane.

Evelyn Maria graduated from CHS in 1974. She attended Newcomb College and then received a National Health Service Corps scholarship to Tulane University School of Medicine, graduating in 1982. She worked for the Indian Health Service for four years to complete her scholarship commitment. In 1984, she married Thomas "Tom" Snider, a Zonian from Coco Solo. They flew to Panama for their wedding in the same Catholic church they attended as kids in Margarita. Evelyn and Tom had three kids: Kristin, Kyle, and Ryan. Evelyn later took a commission in the US Army. Her first duty station was to Panama from June

The Last Zonian

1988 to November 1991 in the former Canal Zone at Coco Solo Clinic, the former hospital where her parents practiced and two of her siblings were born. As the officer-in-charge of the clinic, Evelyn occasionally saw patients who retired from the Panama Canal Company and remembered her parents. Many would tell her that her father removed their cataracts, or her mother removed their tonsils years earlier.

While living in Army quarters at Fort Gulick Army Base, Rosa came out of retirement at age 73 to care for a fourth generation of Barraza family descendants. Rosa brought her niece Nuvia to assist Evelyn Maria, Tom, and the kids. Rosa enjoyed doing the cooking and caring for the children. Her niece did the laundry and other house chores. Rosa loved the Barraza family, and the Barraza descendants loved her. Rosa's niece met a soldier, and they married. Rosa retired again for the last time after Evelyn, Tom, and the kids left Panama. Evelyn retired as a Colonel in 2015 after 31 years on active duty. Evelyn and Tom live in Fox Island, Washington.

After graduating from CHS in 1977, Rafael attained a geology degree from Tulane University. He married Vicki Kenderdine. They live and work in the vicinity of Pensacola, Florida. They enjoy Civil War history, trips to Disney World, cheering for the University of Alabama football team, and living by the water in Pensacola Beach.

After leaving Panama, Mayra moved with her mother to Stone Mountain, Georgia. She graduated from Dunwoody High School and then received a bachelor's in horticulture from the University of Georgia. Following college, she joined her mother, who relocated from the Atlanta area to Rockledge, Florida. Mayra met and married her mother's friend Livia's son, Tom Strider. Tom had attended Balboa High School, while his father, an Army officer, was in Panama. After they married, they moved to Tampa, Florida. In 2006, they relocated to Panama and now live near the small city of Penonome in the El Interior, a little over two hours from Panama City.

Dr. Evelyn Barraza Snider stated, "One of the best things about living in the Canal Zone was the amazing sense of community. It was truly a great place to raise a family, enjoy so many outdoor activities, and make lifelong friendships."

Ronald Edward Moore
Obstetrician-Gynecologist • Canal Zone Government
US Army, Pre-Vietnam War Era Veteran •
Civilian Physician, Vietnam War

Ronald "Ron" Edward Moore, born on November 11, 1928, in Cincinnati, Ohio, could only wonder what awaited him as he began walking his path in life: love, family, and adventure. He was athletic during his youth, playing various sports. After earning a bachelor's degree from Hanover College in Indiana, he attended the University of Cincinnati College of Medicine.

While on a hospital rotation, Ron met Wilma "Willie" Lee Easton, who was studying at The Christ Hospital School of Nursing. Willie was born on November 17, 1932, across the Ohio River in Burlington, Kentucky. She grew up on a farm and was actively involved with various clubs during high school, including the rifle club. Ron, a city boy, and Willie, a country girl, were attracted to each other and hit it off.

During their courtship, Ron had an unusual way to ring the doorbell when visiting Willie at her apartment. He did it with his foot while in a handstand position. When Willie opened the door, he would walk in on his hands before hopping onto his feet. After a short period of dating, they married in June 1954.

After completing medical school, Ron's residency was at the District of Columbia General Hospital in Washington, DC. He and Willie both worked in the operating room; however, they could not be in the operating room together as a married couple.

Once he completed his residency, Ron took a commission as a captain in the US Army at Fort Knox, Kentucky in 1955. In December of that year, their daughter, Jane, was born in Cincinnati at The Christ Hospital where Willie attended college. Seventeen months later, in May 1957, they had another daughter, Maurie Dean, born at Ireland Army Hospital in Fort Knox. In late 1957, Ron received a notice for an overseas assignment. Initially excited about being stationed in Germany and having an opportunity to utilize some of his German vocabulary, he was disappointed when the Army reassigned him to Panama.

Ron, Willie, and the girls arrived in the Panama Canal Zone in October 1957. The family initially lived in New Cristobal, and Ron worked as an Army physician at Coco Solo Hospital on the Atlantic side of the isthmus. After living in the Canal Zone for a couple of years, he became fond of the place. In February 1960, the family grew with the birth of their daughter, Cynthia Lee, born at Coco Solo Hospital.

Seven months later, in September 1960, when Ron completed his Army service commitment, he informed Willie that he wanted to stay in the Canal Zone. He would take a civil service position with the Canal Zone Government Health Bureau and remain at Coco Solo Hospital. He was enjoying his calling of being a general practitioner to doing minor surgeries, including appendectomies, and performing childbirth deliveries. As a multi-skilled physician, his passion was being an obstetrician-gynecologist (OBGYN). Dr. Moore is thought to have delivered over 3,000 babies during his tenure in the Canal Zone. Many of the kids his children grew up with were infants he had delivered.

The Last Zonian

Dr. Moore believed in preventive medicine and did not hesitate to tell potential patients his thoughts. However, doing so was embarrassing to his daughter, Maurie. Occasionally, he conveyed his sentiment while she was riding with him in their Volkswagen. If he spotted a potentially hazardous situation, he would take action, especially on weekends when he was on call to work in the hospital emergency room. When he saw kids, at times, Maurie's friends, climbing around up in the trees, he would stop the vehicle and holler to them, "I'm on call at the emergency room. You need to get down off of that tree. I don't want to leave during my dinner to go fix your broken arm." It was embarrassing to Maurie, but realistically, his actions likely prevented some accidents.

In late 1966, less than a year following the official date of the first US Marine Corps combat troops entering Vietnam, Ron went to Vietnam with the Volunteer Physicians for Vietnam Program, administered by the American Medical Association. They assisted with providing medical treatment to the South Vietnamese people. He served two months, using his annual leave, working out of Nha Trang with other physicians before returning to the Canal Zone.

Willie, too, was on the go in 1966. With her friends, Cecilia Gove, Freda Stohrer, and Judy Thompson, they were a quartet known as "The Pan Canettes" and members of the Sweet Adelines International, Crossroads Chapter of the Panama Canal Zone. In April, The Pan Canettes competed and won their regional competition held in Clearwater, Florida. Later that year, they went on to compete in the Sweet Adelines International Convention held in Houston, Texas, placing eighth in the competition.

Over the years, the family moved a few times, but it was always less than five miles from Coco Solo Hospital. Initially, living in New Cristobal, then in the town of Coco Solo at house

239-D Bushnell Road, in Margarita at 8226 Cottage Place, in France Field at 0355 France Road, and back to Coco Solo at 254 King Road. Ron and Willie were active serving on the towns' civic councils.

When not at the hospital or attending a civic council meeting, Ron golfed on Saturdays or enjoyed fishing for peacock bass at Gatun Lake and tarpon on Chagres River. Willie stayed busy with the girls attending youth classes, such as tap and dance.

As the girls got older, taking an interest in more activities, and appreciating having their father around, Ron gave up golfing and dedicated his time to his daughters. He assisted them with their two horses at the Fort Randolph Riding Club and attended horse shows. He liked taking the girls water skiing, sailing, and fishing. On some weekends and weeklong vacations, Ron, Willie, the girls, and Gwendolyn (their help, who was more like family) traveled to the Pacific side of the isthmus to enjoy the calm waters and white sandy beach at Santa Clara, approximately a three-hour drive from their house on the Atlantic side.

Dr. Ron Moore

In 1968, Ron and Willie's adventurous spirit motivated them to take a big venture for their family vacation back to the United States. Rather than flying on Braniff International Airways or transiting aboard the ship SS Cristobal, they drove their 1965 Chrysler Newport from the Canal Zone to Ohio on the Pan-American Highway through Central America. The trip was an adventure, but the car was a lemon with some defects, including a hole in the exhaust that almost killed them. Fortunately, they only had three flat tires on the journey. On the return trip, the family opted to board and load their car on the SS Cristobal in New Orleans to relax for their voyage back to the Canal Zone.

The girls picked up their parents' competitive and athletic qualities, playing golf, tennis, softball, basketball, volleyball, and water activities. They also had some exhilarating antics at times evading the military police while riding their two minibikes on the France Field airstrip. On heavy rainy days, they participated in a thrill referred to as "ditching." The girls and friends would change into long pants, jump into a small flooded concrete drainage ditch in the back of the neighborhood, and ride the fast-flowing water, fearlessly, laughing, and screaming along the way.

In the Summer of 1974, Ron and Willie decided to leave the Canal Zone. Their daughter Jane had already left for college. They discussed their plan with Maurie since she was going to be a senior in high school and gave her the option to stay or move to the States. Supporting her parents, Maurie left the Canal Zone with the family in late summer. Ron accepted a management position with the Veterans Administration in North Carolina.

One afternoon, months later, when Maurie got home from school, her father asked, "Do you want to go back to Panama?"

A loud "Yes!" was Maurie's response.

Daughter Cindy agreed.

Dr. Moore called the hospital administrator in the Canal Zone to see if his position was still vacant. It was and he was welcome to return. The family was back in the Canal Zone in January 1975, only five months after their departure.

Upon their return, they were able to get their same help. Happy to see the family, Gwendolyn said, "Doctor Moore, you are the only family I know that takes their furniture with them on vacation."

In 1977, after the signing of the Panama Canal Treaty between the United States and the Republic of Panama, many Zonian families were uncertain about their future. Many began planning their departure for October 1, 1979, the day the Panama Canal Zone would be abolished and cease to exist as a United States unincorporated territory.

Ron and Willie left the Canal Zone when the treaty became effective. Jane, Maurie, and Cindy no longer lived in the Canal Zone. Willie departed on September 30, 1979, and Ron left

Willie & Ron Moore

on October 1, 1979. They relocated to Melbourne, Florida, but neither of them was ready to settle down into a retirement life. So, having an adventurous disposition, Ron worked for a government agency for several more years. He and Willie lived in Portugal, Saudi Arabia, and Sudan, enjoying their time together and traveling before finally retiring back to Florida.

Sadly, Ron passed away on December 6, 1993, at age 65, in Rockledge, Florida. He got it all: love, family, and adventure.

The Last Zonian

Willie stayed busy with her family and friends. A talented pianist, she enjoyed music and, for 18 years, took yearly rhythm and blues cruises. Being a Kentucky Colonel, she liked going to the Kentucky Derby at Churchill Downs in Louisville. Willie passed away on January 1, 2013, at age 81, in Melbourne, Florida.

After graduating from Cristobal High School (CHS) in 1974, Jane went to New York to attend college. Returning to the Canal Zone for the summer after graduating college, she met Leo Buss, who worked for the Smithsonian Institute. She and Leo married and had two children, Blake and Evan. Jane worked as an infectious disease physician. She and Leo presently live in Nicaragua.

Maurie graduated from CHS in 1975 and then moved to New Orleans, Louisiana, where she graduated from Tulane University. She had a medical career in diagnostic imaging. Now retired, she enjoys spending time with her family and friends, listening to blues music, going on blues cruises, and attending the annual Panama Canal Society Reunions. Maurie lives in Melbourne, Florida.

After graduating from CHS in 1978, Cindy attended Harcum College in Pennsylvania. She married Edward Forsythe, a Zonian from Gatun. They had one child, Dylan. Years later, they parted ways. She worked for the Harris Corporation and Raytheon. Cindy is married to Daniel Blom. She is enjoying her retired life—traveling, reading, and spending time with her two grandchildren. She lives in Malabar, Florida.

When Wilma left the Panama Canal Zone on September 30, 1979, the last day it existed as a US unincorporated territory, she wrote each of her daughters a letter. An excerpt from her letter to Maurie: "A happy experience for the Moores. Now the memories will scatter like dust to the whole world ... your childhood home was in the Canal Zone. It's gone tomorrow and change will wrought havoc with your beautiful homeland."

Lois Jeanne (Arnold) Nelson
Operating Room Nurse • Canal Zone Government
US Navy, Korean War Post Era Veteran

Lois "Jeanne" Arnold was born on March 23, 1931, in Springfield, Illinois, the state capital. Coal was the primary industry at the time. In 1950, women mostly worked in positions as secretaries, teachers, factory workers, and nurses. Jeanne went to college at St. John's Hospital and Training School for Nursing. She worked at the hospital until entering the US Navy in December 1953 as a lieutenant junior grade (LTJG) and registered nurse (RN).

With the Korean War ending five months earlier, on July 27, 1953, Jeanne remained stateside. While stationed at Naval Hospital Bremerton, Washington, Jeanne received

LTJG Lois Jeanne Arnold

the Navy Commendation Medal for her heroic actions on August 30, 1955, in saving two other nurses from a mentally deranged male patient wielding a 10-inch carving knife.

In the fall of 1955, Jeanne and some other nurses went to the Naval Station Officers' Club. While there, she met Joshua "Josh" Jacob Nelson, a Navy lieutenant and gunnery officer.

Josh was born in Galveston, Texas, on February 23, 1929. After completing high school in Houston, he worked as a bank teller. He enlisted in the Navy Reserves in March 1951 while attending the University of Houston. He was called to active duty but received a four-month deferment to complete his bachelor's degree. He then attended Naval Officer Candidate School and received a commission in May 1953 with an assignment on the USS Wright.

Jeanne left the Navy in the autumn of 1955 but remained in the inactive Naval Reserves. She moved to Springfield, Illinois, to continue working as a nurse. In April 1956, she returned to active duty at Naval Hospital Oakland, California. Jeanne and Josh married in May 1956 in Alameda, California, and four months later, she hung up her uniform. The following year, they celebrated the birth of their son, Mark Morris, in January 1957 in Oakland. They had two more sons, David Robert, in March 1959, and Joshua Jr., in June 1960, both born in the city of Fremont, California.

The family lived in California, Japan, Virginia, and Hawaii. Mark remembers the family going to dinner in Waikiki with film

Jeanne & sons: Mark, Joshua Jr., David

director Otto Preminger, director of the film *In Harm's Way*. Mark's father had met Preminger several years earlier in Hawaii while filming aboard his ship, the USS St. Paul. Actor Kirk Douglas stayed in Josh's cabin aboard the ship. Kirk and Josh became lifelong pen pals. While at the dinner table, nine-year-old Mark recognized Preminger from his role as Mr. Freeze in the Batman television series. So, he asked him if he was Mr. Freeze. Josh, a strict disciplinarian often at sea, was not privy to American TV and instantly got irritated with Mark, thinking he was being a smartass. Preminger immediately stopped Josh, telling him that his son was correct.

In the summer of 1970, the family arrived in the Panama Canal Zone aboard the SS Cristobal. They got living quarters on Fort Amador at 15ND on the Pacific side of the isthmus. Josh, a Navy Commander, was in charge of the Military Sealift Command. In his role, he frequently accompanied military vessels transiting through the Canal and got to know many Panama Canal Company pilots. Jeanne maintained the household and watched over the boys.

The boys traveled off base to their schools by bus. Josh Jr. attended Diablo Elementary School, approximately six miles away. It was the same routine, getting picked up and passing through a military guard gate as the bus exited Fort Amador. The kids endearingly called their bus driver "Cap." One afternoon, Cap accidentally became aware that if he turned the bus key from on to off while driving, the exhaust would backfire loudly. This discovery led to a prank. While passing the security gate after a military guard waved the bus through, Cap initiated the exhaust backfire, startling the guard. Josh Jr. and the other kids erupted in laughter, begging Cap to do it again the next day. He obliged the kids' enthusiasm from time to time.

Jeanne and Josh immediately began embracing their life in Panama, learning to speak Spanish with the kids, taking road trips into the interior provinces and the scenic highlands, enjoying the many beaches, and discovering places within Panama City. Their favorite for milkshakes and expressos was the Golden Frog in the city's La Cresta neighborhood near the Cathedral Iglesia Nuestra del Carmen on Via Espana.

Like many families living in the Canal Zone, they enjoyed scouting, swimming, surfing, ocean diving, and fishing. They also enjoyed not having to clean their catch after a day of fishing for a seafood meal when they went to the Rodman Naval Station Officers' Club for surf and turf dinners.

Jeanne and Josh parted ways in 1972. She put her surgical nursing skills back to work and took an RN position with the Canal Zone Government Health Bureau. She worked as an operating room nurse at the main health facility in the Canal Zone, Gorgas Hospital, in Ancon. She later became president of the union for employees at Gorgas Hospital.

Jeanne and the boys moved to 790-A Tabernilla Street in the town of Balboa. As a single mother working and raising three boys, she ensured the boys still enjoyed activities, including Boy Scouts, scuba diving and freediving, and surfing on the Atlantic and Pacific coasts. Living in the Canal Zone and Panama, Jeanne and the boys thrived, making close, enduring Zonian and Panamanian friendships. As the boys got older, they were doing their own thing.

Mark, the eldest, reached a pivotal age when he turned 18, the legal drinking age for young adults living in the Canal Zone. He and some of his friends celebrated what he later referred to as a naively perceived milestone in his youth. They drank their share of Cerveza Panama at his house on the ground-floor patio and in the carport. At midnight, they piled into Duke Petersen's parents' Plymouth Belvedere station wagon and drove to the west bank of the Panama Canal near the Miraflores Locks to the Third Locks Excavation site. The site was part of a plan to build three new

The Last Zonian

locks with longer and wider chambers across the isthmus that commenced in 1940 before the United States entered World War II and abandoned it in 1941. Mark, standing atop a 30-foot cliff, leaped in the darkness into the water below. Having jumped off the cliff in the daylight, this was a different experience. Hitting the water and surfacing he was fine, fortunately.

While life changed for Jeanne when the boys graduated high school and moved on to live their lives, she was always happy to hear from them. They chatted about their news and laughed at times at their stories, like Josh Jr.'s fishing escapade.

In the mid-1980s, Josh Jr. worked for a construction company supervising the repairs to pier columns at the Rodman Naval Station. Fishing at the pier was bountiful for several reasons, one being it was prohibited to the public. His boss, the company's owner and avid speargun fisherman, asked if Josh would take him under the pier after hours to avoid notice. So, one late afternoon, Josh, his girlfriend, and his boss set off in a small aluminum boat. Reaching the pier, his boss entered the water with his speargun and within minutes surfaced, throwing a 30-plus pound snook into the boat. Josh immediately hit the large fish with a club to knock it out. As his boss rolled back in, the still-alive fish began pounding its tail against the bottom of the boat. Seeing the big fish flopping around, Josh's girlfriend attempted to flee the vessel. Josh immediately calmed her down and, again, hit the fish.

In 1988, Jeanne moved from Balboa to a condominium in Panama City. Most of the residents of the former Canal Zone had moved stateside and more of her close friends were living in Panama City. She preferred the cosmopolitan and culturally stimulating environment of the city rather than the uneventful and dwindling community remaining in the former Canal Zone.

During "Operation Just Cause," the US Invasion of Panama from mid-December 1989 to January 1990, Americans living outside the former Canal Zone were not safe. In the first days of the invasion, Jeanne, a nurse, was called into work at Gorgas Army Hospital but was unable to get there due to Noriega's armed Dignity Battalions roaming the streets and searching door-to-door for Americans living in Panama City. Her friends and neighbors at the condo, when questioned, denied any "Gringos" were living in the building, thereby shielding Jeanne in her condo from harm. Jeanne told the hospital staff that unless they were going to send an armored vehicle to pick her up, she was remaining in place. She eventually was able to get to Gorgas Hospital after a couple of days, where she assisted with the wounded, most of whom were reportedly Panamanian.

In the spring of 1990, after 20 years of living in Panama, Jeanne took an early retirement from Gorgas Army Hospital and left the country. She moved to Safety Harbor, Florida, and worked at a surgical clinic. A few years later, she moved to Seattle, Washington, to help Josh Jr. and his wife, Mary, care for her second grandchild and worked part-time as a mobile phlebotomist. Several years later, she moved to Peoria, Illinois, to live near her sister Sharon. They traveled some, including a genealogy fact-finding mission to England. She later moved to Chicago to be closer to her sons, Mark and David, and her grandchildren. Jeanne, who shared her passion for the arts with her sons at a young age, continued to paint well into her elderly years. Jeanne passed away on June 3, 2021, at age 90, in Chicago, Illinois.

Josh Sr. married Ingrid Sandra Aleman. They left the Canal Zone in 1975 with their one-year daughter, Eva. He retired from the Navy in December 1978 in New Orleans, Louisiana. He and Ingrid had three more children: Ari, Moshe, and Chaim. He worked for an offshore drilling and exploration company as a relief captain, barge mover, and accident investigator for a few years before moving to Florida. Years later, the marriage dissolved.

Josh's daughter, Eva, became a US Naval officer and RN. After being moved from his condo in Florida to Maryland, Josh passed away on May 30, 2019, at age 90, in Silver Springs, Maryland.

Mark graduated from Balboa High School (BHS) in 1975. He attended Canal Zone College, the University of Panama, and then the National School of Arts in Panama to pursue his passion. He worked several jobs with the Panama Canal Company, US Army, and US Air Force, including locations at Miraflores Locks, Corozal, Howard Air Force Base, and Gorgas Hospital while attending fine arts school. He completed his bachelor's from the School of the Art Institute of Chicago and a master's at the University of Illinois at Chicago. He married Giselle Mercier, and they had a daughter, Gabrielle. After he and Giselle parted ways, Mark later married Anna Kong. He is an accomplished artist and painter in Chicago. In 2007, the US State Department purchased a painted mural from him for the embassy consulate in the former Canal Zone. After 30 years, he retired from teaching grades K-8, high school, and as a college adjunct. Mark and Anna reside in Pilsen, where he has an art studio in the historic neighborhood of Chicago.

David graduated from BHS in 1978. He earned a bachelor's from Florida State University in 1984. He returned to Panama during summer and winter breaks, working one summer for the fire department. A few years later, in 1987, David received his master's degree from Washington University in St. Louis, Missouri. He married Amy Yurko, and they had a son, Samuel. They later parted ways. David retired during the COVID-19 pandemic after 25 years with the School of the Art Institute of Chicago. Nowadays, he primarily works on his sculptures in his Chicago studio. He lives 10 minutes from his brother, Mark.

Josh Jr. graduated from BHS in 1979. He went to a tech school in Waco, Texas, and then relocated to Seattle, Washington, to work for Boeing. While in Seattle, he earned his bachelor's and master's and became a tool engineer for Boeing. He married Mary Louise Jablonski in Florida, and they had a son, Evan. He later transferred to the Boeing facility in Charleston, South Carolina. Josh Jr. and Mary live in Mt. Pleasant, across the harbor from Charleston.

Mark stated that his parents liked the ambiance of the Canal Zone and Panama. He said, "I have great lifelong memories of the place and friends. There was so much I was able to do while growing up and working in the Canal Zone, and becoming proficient in speaking a new language. All these experiences created a diverse and rich foundation that helped me on my journey."

THE LOST TOWNS

The Atlantic Side

The town of Gatun, adjacent to the Gatun Locks, was the best place to live in the Canal Zone. The truth be told, every Zonian will tell you that the town they lived in was the best in the Canal Zone. They were all special and unique. Gatun was certainly a fabulous place to reside.

Most families arriving to the Canal Zone came during the summer, either by commercial aircraft or passenger ship. Those arriving by ship certainly had a feeling of excitement seeing the seaport inside the breakwater, a sea barrier that protects Limon Bay and the entrance for ships transiting the Panama Canal from the Atlantic side of the Isthmus of Panama.

Imagine you are a passenger aboard the SS Cristobal, a Panama Canal Company cargo and passenger ship. As the vessel slowly passes through the breakwater, traveling in a north-to-south direction as it enters the harbor, to your far right is Fort Sherman Army Base, and to the left is Fort Randolph and the town of Coco Solo.

Leopold J. Cimino

While looking from the ship's bow, a small boat is spotted heading toward one of the anchored cargo vessels inside the breakwater. It probably carries a Canal Zone Admeasurer official like, Leland Snider, who will inspect the ship and do physical measurements, figure out the tonnage of the vessel, and then calculate the rate it is charged to transit the Canal.

After the inspection, the appropriate documentation usually takes approximately three days to complete. Once a vessel is cleared to travel the Canal, a Panama Canal Company ship pilot, like Gerald Oster, with unique training and expertise, takes control of the vessel while it transits through the Panama Canal. Additionally, tugboat pilots such as Ted Bailey and Irv Spector assist in the movement of large ships using towlines to help guide, push, pull, and tow a ship, especially with the alignment and approach to the locks.

On the SS Cristobal, as you proceed forward in the harbor, the seaport city of Colon, Panama's largest municipality on the Atlantic side of the isthmus, and the Port of Cristobal are more visible. As the ship nears the docks, on the port side, a short distance away, people can be seen walking along Front Street with its colorful shops and bazaars stocked with elegant linens and merchandise from around the world. It is a place to shop for something unique or find a one-of-a-kind item.

At the pier, after disembarking from the SS Cristobal, all the passengers proceed to get processed through Canal Zone Customs. Waiting to greet you is a family member (or a friend of the family) who arrived in the Canal Zone sometime earlier to get established with their job and await family housing quarters. Upon completing customs and carrying your luggage outside of the warehouse, the hustle and bustle of the port, observing a crane unloading a car from your ship, and hearing the chatter and elation of passengers seeing and hugging family as you make your way to a vehicle, adds to the excitement and delight of being in a new place. Friends you met aboard the ship wave at you and your family, saying, "I hope we see each other again."

Knowing that your new residence is in Gatun, you must travel approximately seven and a half miles from the port. After leaving the pier, your family member who is driving exits the port on Terminal Street. While he begins narrating the ride to Gatun, you gaze at your surroundings, seeing people going about their everyday lives, some hastily walking and others driving vehicles. On your right, a short distance from the port gates, people go in and out of a three-story building that houses the Cristobal Post Office, police station, courthouse, library, and other offices. It is where Paul Richmond works for the Police Division. A little further along Terminal Street, the name changes to 13th Street at the railroad tracks. On the left, people are waiting for the train's arrival at the Cristobal Train Station.

Continuing on 13th Street, just two blocks past Front Street and Balboa Avenue, you stop at the intersection with Bolivar Avenue. It is the main thoroughfare for the small city of Colon.

Here, a glimpse of the city reveals the commotion and busyness of locals walking and talking on the sidewalks and crossing the bustling streets as vehicles honk their horns. Others ride colorful multi-painted "Chivas," (small buses) zipping through the city. Colon is adjacent to the town of Cristobal and the Port of Cristobal, which are in the Canal Zone. The only thing defining the Canal Zone territorial boundary separating the Cristobal area from Colon is simply a street and, in other places, a chain-link fence.

After turning right onto Bolivar Avenue to leave the city, the road connects into Bolivar Highway. Coming to a fork in the road less than half a mile from the port, Rainbow City is on the left, a town for non-US-citizen Panama Canal workers in the Canal Zone. Randolph Road, the left fork, leads to Fort Randolph, Coco Solo, France Field, Coco Solo Hospital, and the

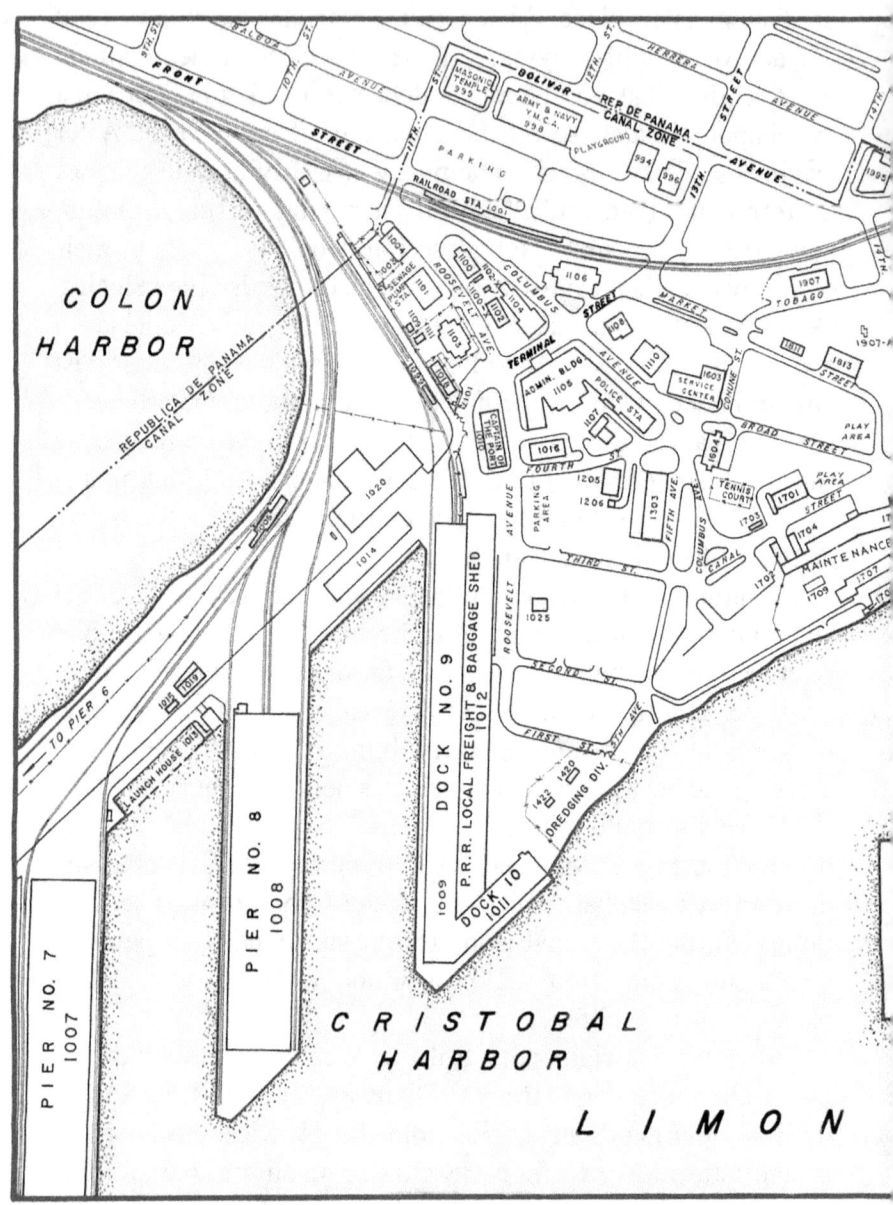

Canal Zone: Cristobal Harbor Piers

The Last Zonian

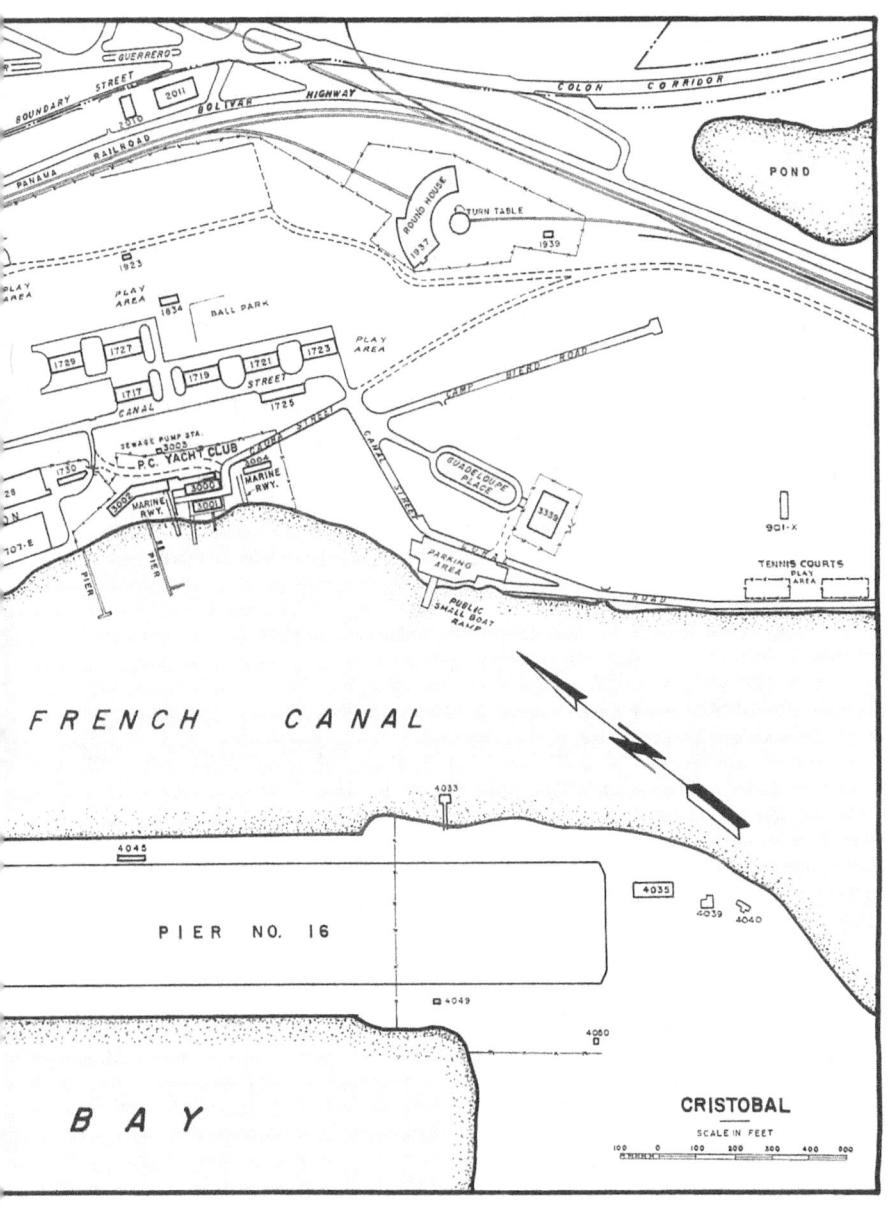

Canal Zone: Cristobal

Roosevelt Transisthmian Highway, connecting the Atlantic side to the Pacific side.

Proceeding to the right on Bolivar Highway after passing the Rainbow City baseball park, just a bit further, an appetizing aroma fills the car. "Yum," is heard as the driver explains the smell is coming from the bakery. Cash Paulson, the general manager, oversees the distribution facilities in the Mount Hope warehouse complex, the location of the Canal Zone Atlantic side bakery. On the opposite side of the road, in a canal next to Limon Bay, are the Marine Industrial Division docks and workshops where John O'Donnell works as a leader marine machinist.

Next to the bakery complex, headstones are noticeable on a hill. The Mount Hope Cemetery, established in the 1850s, is the primary burial location on the Atlantic side. The cemetery is divided into sectors by nationality, with a little over four percent of the 37,000 graves being US citizens, including veterans.

Across the road from the cemetery, seeing water spraying into the air at a fenced-in facility piques your curiosity. "What is it?" you ask your family member at the wheel.

"Mount Hope Filtration Plant, built in 1914 and subsequently upgraded, provides purified water to the Canal Zone on the Atlantic side and the city of Colon," he replies.

A short distance later, there is more suspense upon approaching an intersection with three roads. Which direction to travel? Straight ahead is Margarita Avenue, which enters the town of Margarita, visible directly across the intersection. Margarita is the largest town in the Canal Zone on the Atlantic side, only two and a half miles from the port. A left turn at the stop sign on Diversion Road leads to the Roosevelt Transisthmian Highway, Coco Solo Hospital, France Field, Coco Solo, and Fort Randolph, approximately four miles from Margarita. Taking a right curve at the intersection, you continue on Bolivar Highway leading to Gatun, about five miles away. After leaving Margarita, just a hop up the road on the left is the turnoff to Gulick Road that leads to the Brazos Brook Golf and Country Club, Rancho Ramos, Brazos Heights neighborhood, and Fort Gulick Army Base. Bolivar Highway then changes into New Bolivar Road.

Suddenly, after traveling less than a mile along the two-lane road, an unpleasant scent interrupts your family's chatting and the fascination of the trip. A stinking smell is apparent in everyone's facial expressions. The driver smiles since he knows where it is from, and he points to the left. The Mindi Dairy is a Canal Zone facility with a herd numbering more than 1,000, including cows, calves, and bulls on approximately 2,000 acres of pastureland. On the opposite side of the road is the narrow East Diversion waterway, which runs parallel for about a mile and a half before disappearing into the jungle and exiting into the Panama Canal. Caiman, similar to crocodiles, are sometimes visible, basking in the sun.

While taking in the surroundings, the driver of a vehicle traveling in the opposite direction raises his hand out his window as he passes. It is a hello gesture of greeting from a neighbor of the family member who picked you up at the port.

Further down the roadway on the left is Andrews Road. A short distance along that road is a military police checkpoint monitoring vehicles entering and exiting Fort Davis Army Base. After rounding a right curve onto Keys Road, built on a strip of land crossing over the Third Locks Excavation, horses graze in the pastures of the Atlantic Horse Stables and stroll along the traces of the excavated waterway.

Before the United States entered World War II, a plan commenced in 1940 for third locks across the isthmus to build new locks with longer and wider lock chambers at Gatun, Pedro Miguel, and Miraflores; they abandoned the plan in 1941. The excavation of the third locks at Gatun is visible on both sides of Keys Road. On the right, the waterway stops approximately 45 meters before reaching the road and on the left, about 10 meters from the road. The Third Locks Excavation is more evident when looking left and seeing the remnants in the distance of the abandoned canal and its steep dirt side walls dugout through elevated terrain adjacent to the town of Gatun, ending at a tall, sloping hill before reaching Gatun Lake.

Passing the horses in the pastures and looking straight ahead, a ship can be seen transiting the Panama Canal, towering behind a warehouse next to the waterway, moving slowly toward the Gatun Locks. Opposite the warehouse, along the inside corner of a left curve in the road, several cars are parked in a small gravel parking area at a roadside Chinese fruit and vegetable market. People are picking up fresh produce, looking at it, and making purchases at the front opening of a small structure. Ironically, despite the market's fruit trees and vegetable gardens around the hut, some of the produce is sometimes gathered by Gatun kids from the jungle and then sold to the owners of the market who then sell it to the kids' parents and other Zonians.

After traveling around the curve from the market onto Jadwin Road and being informed by the driver that Gatun is just ahead, you are eager to see it. A short distance further up on the left, more horses are grazing in a pasture at the Gatun Horse Stables. Across from the pasture is Schoolhouse Road which heads in the direction of the Gatun Locks and weaves its way back into the town of Gatun. At the corner of Schoolhouse and Jadwin roads, the American Legion Post has the best Chinese food and wontons. It is a hangout for Zonians and military personnel. Continuing on Jadwin and proceeding up a hill, as the vehicle crests the top and crosses over railroad tracks, you see the sign: white, red, and blue with the word Gatun.

The town of Gatun was originally built in 1904 as a tent city to support workers constructing the Canal. Over the years, new construction for family and bachelor housing was built for US employees who worked at the locks. However, not all the employees who live adjacent to the Gatun Locks or other housing areas in the Canal Zone work at the locks.

Gatun has two primary neighborhoods derived from the town's expansion years ago. Old Town is closest to the Gatun Locks, Gatun Train Station, and a small public boat ramp, and has some housing quarters on hill ridges with the best views of the locks and Gatun Lake. New Town is near the abandoned Third Locks Excavation and closest to the community swimming pool, gymnasium, and the road that leads to the Gatun Yacht Club. There are other housing areas on Pomarosa Street and Schoolhouse Road next to and behind the Gatun Elementary School; Laurel Street and Halcon Place have houses on a hill across from the elementary school that is on Jadwin Road, and High Street, located on the left at the entrance to Gatun has a few housing quarters.

After passing the Gatun sign, a group of kids are screaming and laughing as they slide down a steep hill from the top of Laurel Street on their buttocks and using cardboard boxes. Seeing them having fun, there's an inner temptation to join in and try it yourself, no matter your age. Across the road at the Gatun Elementary School, the bicycle racks are empty, but kids fill the racks with their bikes during the school year. It is their main mode of transportation to get around and explore. No more than 30 meters from the school, the Masonic Lodge near the intersection of Jadwin Road and Laurel Street is a gathering place in the morning for kids before riding or walking to school. Policeman Gayle Fortner controls traffic to ensure kids cross Jadwin Road safely. He was well-liked by the kids because of his interaction with them.

A tad up the road, in a field near the entrance to Laurel Street, kids are playing sandlot football behind some family housing quarters and a church. The kids are wet and muddy

Leopold J. Cimino

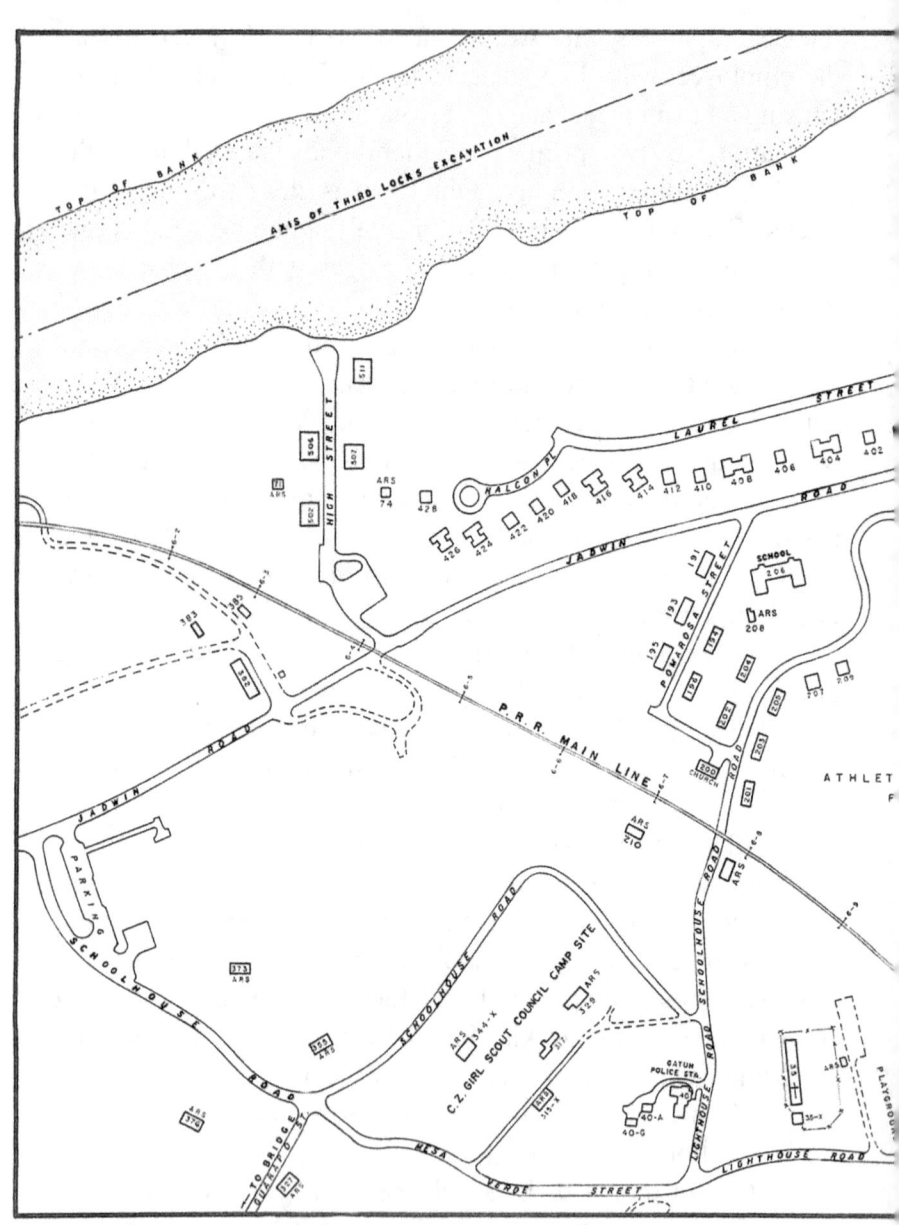

Gatun: Jadwin Road Entrance

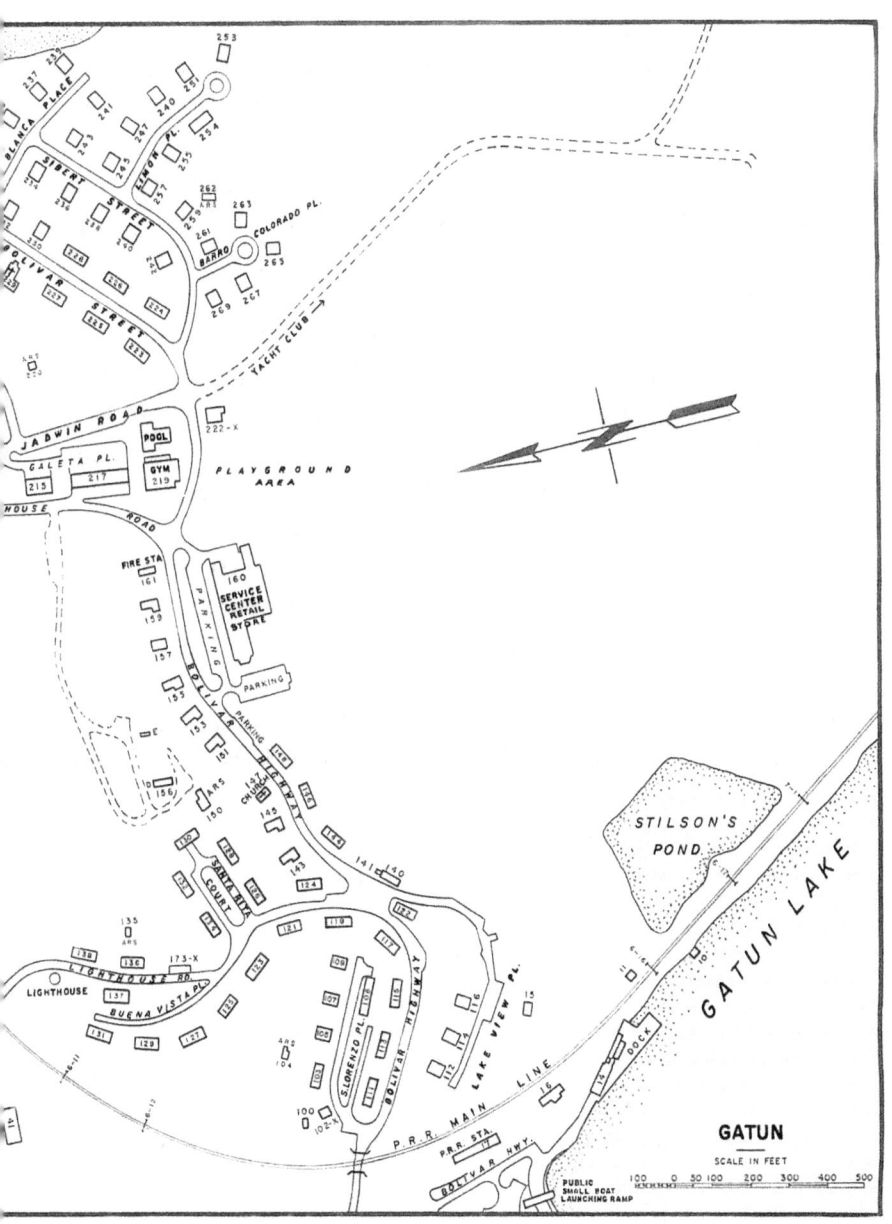

Gatun: New Town (top), Old Town (bottom)

from an earlier rain shower but don't care. Upon reaching an intersection, Jadwin Road ends. On the left, three kids throw something up into a tree next to a small bus stop on the corner. They are throwing rocks at mangoes hanging from branches high up in the tree. Many kids get pretty good at mastering knocking mangoes out of the trees. Behind the bus stop is a housing area. The driver divulges that your family quarters are located in the New Town neighborhood.

After the stop sign, an unnamed road continues straight from Jadwin Road and disappears into the jungle. You later learn it leads to a popular hangout on Gatun Lake.

Lively shouting, bellowing, and whistle-blowing draw attention to the right through a tall chain-link fence where kids are swimming and jumping off a diving board at the Gatun Swimming Pool. The pool is across the street from the bus stop and on the opposite corner of the intersection from the mango tree. On Wednesday nights, the swimming pool has extended hours until 8:45 PM. It is a gathering place for kids of all ages to sit, chat, listen to music, play four square, water tag, water polo, and do cannonballs off the diving board. Many kids receive swim lessons at the pool from Louise Russon and go on to become advanced swimmers and lifeguards, compete on township and high school swim teams, and participate in the Canal Zone Boy Scout Olympics.

After deciding to tour Gatun further, the driver obliges by turning left at the intersection from Jadwin Road onto Sibert Street to enter New Town. As the street veers to the right, kids appear ahead: two boys riding their bicycles in the street and twin girls skating on the sidewalk.

Slowly passing by the kids and two cul-de-sacs, Barro Colorado Place and Limon Place, you notice that royal palm trees line the streets. The houses appear inviting, with the outside stairways and concrete support columns painted white and the houses' wooden siding painted off-white. The neighborhood's brightness is in the trim of the houses, with the garage doors, porch stairway handrails, entrance doors, windows, and the fascia trim around the roof line painted in pastels: light blue, light green, yellow, and tan. To top it off, the weathering of the copper roofing to a blue-green patina color helps to give the streets a charming tropical ambiance.

Additionally, the housing quarters have a carport on the ground floor and stairways at the front and side of the duplex buildings, which lead to the main floor and living areas. Continuing on Sibert Street, it ends by connecting into Loma Blanca Place. There are a few houses to the right on the street, which is a dead end. Directly behind the houses on Loma Blanca Place is the jungle and the abandoned steep dugout canal of the Third Locks Excavation. There are a couple more housing quarters to the left on Loma Blanca Place before the street stops at Bolivar Street near the Protestant Church. The church hosts enjoyable community functions, including fish fries and spaghetti dinners. Bolivar Street heads in one direction, to the left, connecting with Sibert Street to complete a circular pattern in the neighborhood.

At last, after seeing your living quarters, you leave the neighborhood, turning left at the Jadwin Road intersection onto the unnamed roadway. Slowly moving along, the vehicle disappears into a sea of tall sawgrass until it goes up a hill surrounded by thick jungle foliage. At the top, the road then descends down a long steep hill. Most kids riding their bikes down the hill use their brakes a lot, although there are a few daredevils. Gatun Lake is visible near the bottom of the hill, where the road curves to the left. Around the corner, cars are in a parking lot along railroad tracks. Beyond a walkway crossing the tracks in a tall chain-link fenced area is the Gatun Yacht

Club. The view from outside the facility grounds includes many people enjoying themselves in and out of the water.

The yacht club is a great hangout for families. It is a place to relax, get some sun, enjoy some music, socialize with friends, go swimming, do some boating, and have a cookout at a pavilion. The indoor clubhouse is known for having great burgers. Some kids and teens who are not members climb over the fence at the furthest point so no one sees them. Parents who know they are not members ignore it and let them enjoy being with their friends as guests. Many swim to a floating wooden platform just offshore from the yacht club, tethered to the bottom of the lake to restrict its movement, for a place to sit and chat. A thrill is swimming beyond the floating platform to a buoy that is a channel marker for ships transiting the Canal. Once reaching the buoy and climbing to its top, the excitement is in trying to rock it back and forth.

After getting a glimpse of the yacht club, it's time to turn around in the parking lot, and head back up the hill. Three teens are seen walking alongside their bikes. It is just too steep and long for them to ride up, although it can be done. At the Jadwin Road intersection, the driver turns left onto Bolivar Highway. The thoroughfare truly is not a highway; it is a two-lane road that runs along the ridge of a hill leading to the Gatun Locks.

While passing by the swimming pool, a lifeguard sitting in a tall chair starts blowing her whistle at some kids in the pool, making you chuckle at the memory of it also happening to you. Next to the swimming pool, there are a few bicycles parked outside the entrance of the community gymnasium. It is a terrific place for youngsters and teens to participate in or learn an indoor and outdoor sports activity, including ping pong, badminton, tumbling, kickball, battleball, and survival, which is a free-for-all with one ball, basketball, volleyball, tennis, and archery. The activities, like those at the swimming pool, help the kids build confidence, camaraderie, and teamwork. Some go on to compete on higher-level sports teams.

Across the street from the gym's entrance in a small field is the community outdoor picnic area with a fireplace and grill, a view of Gatun Lake, and a large commercial swing set. In the picnic area, a teen is straddling his bicycle, watching two other young teens, a girl and a boy, swing as high as they can go, as if attempting to reach the sky. The small field next to the community picnic area is where the annual after-Christmas tree bonfire event is held under the supervision of the fire department. Teams throughout Gatun gather the discarded trees for the bonfire. It is awesome to see the teams emerge from various directions, hauling their trees to the central location with bicycles and automobiles, leaving a trail of tinsel on the streets. Upon arrival, the trees are counted. The winning team receives movie tickets along with popcorn and bragging rights.

Just beyond the gymnasium on the right is Schoolhouse Road, which branched off from Jadwin Road next to the American Legion Post near the entrance of Gatun. The road weaves its way past the Canal Zone Girl Scout Council Camp Site, the Gatun Police Station, a housing area behind the elementary school, and ends at Bolivar Highway at the top of the ridge between the gym and the Gatun Fire Station. The ingenuity of kids is sometimes seen on Schoolhouse Road when they race their homemade, unmotorized go-karts down the long descent of the hill toward the elementary school.

The fire station at the corner of Bolivar Highway and Schoolhouse Road is between the New Town and Old Town neighborhoods. It is where Lanky Flores worked as a firefighter. Several housing quarters aligned next to the fire station have a great view from the back of the house, looking down a hill at the tennis courts, archery field, and elementary school.

Across the street from the fire station and the adjacent houses is the community service center building. The Gatun Post Office, where Pat Finneman works, with the town's centralized mailboxes, is in the same building with a barber shop, small library, snack bar, movie theater, ceramic craft shop, and an open area with tables, chairs, and vending machines, used on occasion for activities. The building once also had a commissary.

Hungry, everyone decides to stop to stretch their legs, check the mailbox, and get a quick bite to eat. After checking the mail and entering the seating area, seeing people eating and chatting at tables increases your appetite. You notice a couple of kids each shaking a small brown bag as they exit the snack bar. They smile and say hello as they walk by, shaking their bags. It is a favorite for kids in town: the best crispy hot French fries, drenched with ketchup and shaken together.

While eating and chatting at a table, a colorful movie poster marquee next to the indoor ticket booth catches your eye. "Hmm. I wonder what's playing at the theater?" First-timers attending the theater receive tips from friends and neighbors or learn from experience on what to do and expect while at the movies. The theater has no air conditioning, so the exit doors are opened during the evening show to allow a breeze to enter the cinema. The breeze is not the only thing that comes through the open doors. This is when the tips are useful. Keep your feet off the floor so mice won't walk over them. And, if you begin seeing black spots moving in the air as you view the screen, keep your head down to avoid the bats that also enter the open doors. At times, there are further interruptions to the show when Mrs. Baldwin, the theater manager, swings a broom at a bat in an attempt to get it out while the movie is still playing. And, if that is not hilarious, it is funnier when she temporarily stops the movie and turns on the theater lights to get the bat out. That is when you see how many people have their feet off the ground and propped up against the seat in front of them, looking down at the floor around their seats. Those are just the theater tips for a newcomer to Gatun; there are more for this uniquely special place.

Back in the vehicle and sightseeing along Bolivar Highway, just beyond the community service center on the right, is a small Catholic Church. There are more housing quarters on both sides of the street as it begins a slight descent from the ridge to a parking lot of a two-story building at a three-way junction. The building has a dental clinic and medical dispensary later utilized by the Boy Scouts of America, Gatun Troop 12.

The junction's left fork, Lake View Place, disappears behind the building and dead ends on a hill. The houses on this street have the best view of Gatun Lake and ships passing through the south end of the Gatun Locks. It is also a shortcut for kids carrying their fishing tackle to the docks at the bottom of the hill.

The right fork, Lighthouse Road, continues down a hill by the housing quarters in Santa Rita Court on the right. Thirty meters farther is Buena Vista Place, which veers off to the left up a hill and dead-ends at the top. The last house, 131, at the end of the street, has the best view of the Gatun Locks control house and the north end. As Lighthouse Road continues downward, a lighthouse is on the left below house 131 before the road crosses the railroad tracks. A bit further, Lighthouse Road stops and connects to Mesa Verde Street near the Gatun Police Station.

The Canal Zone Girl Scout Council Camp Site is a tad down the road. During Girl Scout camporees, Gatun boys quietly move through the jungle around the camp site to meet the girls. Truly, kids have explored everywhere in and around Gatun on foot or bicycle, leaving no unturned stone.

Continuing the tour, driving slowly along Bolivar Highway on the center fork in the road with the windows down, allows a slight breeze to flow through the car while at the same time listen to your surroundings. Ahead of the vehicle, three teens are racing bicycles down the roadway, speeding by houses on the right side of the street and a hill on the left. As the vehicle descends the hill, the south end of the Gatun Locks comes into view.

Near the bottom of the roadway, a street branches off to the right. San Lorenzo Place has some living quarters tucked away behind the houses on Bolivar Highway. Just past San Lorenzo Place, the teens on the bicycles stop at the left side of a small bridge overlooking the railroad tracks and the Gatun Train Station. After making a sharp left curve from the bridge, it's time for a pit stop to refill the vehicle at a small two-pump gas station on the right. Behind the gas station is the massive structure of the Gatun Locks, with the sounds of its daily operations. The boys on their bikes zoom by the filling station while just ahead, across the road, passengers are boarding the Panama Canal Railway train heading to the Pacific side of the isthmus.

Gatun Lake is straight ahead. After the vehicle is topped off, the driver slowly heads toward the lake. Arriving at a small public boat launching ramp, the boys sitting on their bikes wave at you as the vehicle pulls up next to them in the parking area overlooking the boat ramp. A few kids throw their seining nets into the water to catch minnows as bait for bigger fish. A girl shouts, "I've got some!" as she rummages through a net already pulled in. It is not often that kids go home empty-handed without a bigger catch.

On the right, a short distance from the small boat ramp, a large ship loaded with cargo containers is entering the Gatun Locks from Gatun Lake after transiting the Panama Canal from the Pacific side of the isthmus, passing through the Miraflores Locks and Pedro Miguel Locks. A tugboat is moored at a docking area in the opposite direction of the ship and close to the kids seining.

On some mornings, the dock is bustling with people, several small launches, and some trucks. Panamanian locals from villages along the shores of Gatun Lake travel by boat to bring and unload their produce, cattle, and other goods that get transported by trucks and sold at the markets in the city of Colon. On one occasion, two steers got loose before being loaded on trucks. The steers roamed the streets of Gatun before being captured. Kids were happy they were already on the school bus that day rather than standing at the bus stop.

The Aids to Navigation building across from the docking area is known for having the best steamed hotdogs in the area. The building, with a bar and over-the-counter snacks, is also utilized as an employee hangout for the Atlantic Locks Employees Association. An adjacent structure houses the docks for boat launches to transport Panama Canal workers to and from ships transiting the locks. It is also a good place to fish for peacock bass, yellow jack, and perch, only from the outer pier.

After leaving the boat ramp parking area and heading back toward the bridge overlooking the railroad tracks, you turn left just before reaching the gas station onto Locks Road, which runs parallel to a tall chain-linked fence next to the Gatun Locks. Family members are in awe of the one-mile locks with its three pairs of chambers up close, peering out the vehicle's window while leisurely traveling from the south end of the lake toward the north end of the locks in the direction of the Port of Cristobal, where they arrived in the morning.

Halfway down the road is another stop upon reaching a parking lot at the Gatun Locks security entrance for employees and visitors. Depending on the day and time, you may encounter David Reed or Ted Finneman, who work lock security. After clearing security, the family heads to the visitor's observation tower.

The tower is across from the locks control house, which is situated between two water lanes. From the tower, you can better perceive the magnitude of a ship moving through the three chambers in each lane. A control house operator, like John Klasovsky, operates the gates of the locks and regulates the water flow in the chambers, which raises and lowers ships passing through the locks.

In view from the observation tower, the large ship loaded with containers that entered the locks from Gatun Lake is being lowered into one of three chambers. The ship is tethered to locomotives called "mules" on each side to control spacing and braking as the ship moves forward. Locomotive operators such as Jack Barger become experts in assisting with the movement of vessels through the locks.

Unbeknownst to visitors, numerous unseen employees assist in the daily operations of the locks. Professional occupations include mechanics, machinists, electricians, and others. For example, the maintenance of electrical and mechanical equipment in tunnels within the thick concrete walls of the locks requires people like Bob Blair, a lock master electrician, and Bob Forsythe, a leader operator machinist, to maintain machinery and repair mechanical breakdowns in the tunnels and other areas of the locks.

After leaving the Gatun Locks and continuing on Locks Road, the same boys on their bicycles are seen some distance ahead of the vehicle as they hastily race down the slight downward slope of the road from the elevation of the man-made Gatun Lake toward sea level at the north end of the locks. Reaching the end of the thoroughfare, the boys turn left at a road, entering into the locks. A raised checkpoint barrier indicates the passage is open. The boys and a locks security officer wave at each other as the teens proceed to dismount from their bikes and walk on the pedestrian walkway to cross over the two retractable bridges within the water lanes of the Gatun Locks. Who knows where the boys are heading off to explore? The locks security officer likely knows the teens' parents. Gatun is a small town, so many residents know each other's kids. It is not uncommon for a parent to tell a friend or neighbor that they saw their kid somewhere.

On the other side of the Gatun Locks is a jungle playground for many Gatun kids. And there is more to do. Taking a left on a two-lane paved road leads to some recreational sites and the Gatun Dam, known as "the spillway." Before reaching the dam, a huge open field with some sporadic clusters of trees is sometimes used for camping and motocross racing. The Gatun Dam provides hydroelectric power to the Gatun Locks and controls the water level in Gatun Lake by raising or lowering gates, which is performed by a professional like Charles Loyd, a senior powerhouse operator.

The Tarpon Club adjacent to the spillway has a casual dining area, a bar, and a pool table, and is another hangout for many Zonians. It was once an exclusive membership club for fishing anglers on the Chagres River, known for having silver tarpon and snook. The river stops at the Gatun Dam. It is approximately six-and-a-half miles long from the apron of the dam's concrete spillway to its mouth, which exits into the Caribbean Sea near Pina Beach and Fort San Lorenzo.

The two-lane paved road narrows next to the Tarpon Club to cross a one-lane bridge over the Gatun Dam spillway. On occasion, people driving across the bridge can see teens below on the spillway striking the shallow water with a stick and even dropping rocks in an attempt to hit fish. Using a large stick to stun and catch snook often works, but rarely with a rock.

On the other side of the bridge, a dirt road branches off to the right, which leads to a small dock and boat ramp on the river and a trail that leads to the spillway apron on the opposite side of the Tarpon Club. It is a great fishing spot. The two-lane paved road continues up a slope next to the dam, then curves away from it, following the shoreline of Gatun Lake on its left. On the opposite side of the road is another massive open field, which is actually a part of the enormous earth dam. The paved road stops about a mile from the bridge at the fringe of the dense jungle, then changes to a dirt and gravel road as it vanishes into the thick rainforest. A picnic pavilion and gravel beach area, referred to as the "Ski Docks," are located a short distance from the disappearing road. Beyond what may look like impenetrable vegetation is a road that weaves under the jungle canopy only to emerge into the light at Pina Beach on the Caribbean Sea. It is one of many beaches frequented by Zonians.

Going to the right from the Gatun Locks bridge, the two-lane paved road leads to more recreational areas, a military parachute drop zone and training sites, Fort Sherman Army Base, the Atlantic breakwater, and an old Spanish fortress. The road, surrounded by jungle on both sides, parallels the Canal for about a mile and a half as it heads north in the direction of Limon Bay and the breakwater. Along the way, some excellent fishing spots on the west bank of the Canal, are hidden by the jungle vegetation from the road. Less than half a mile farther on the left, invisible from the road, is a military drop zone and mock village used for training. Both areas are well-known explored sites by Gatun kids, who have also driven a bulldozer at the location. Past the drop zone, the road skirts the west shoreline of Limon Bay until it reaches Fort Sherman, which is approximately ten miles from the Gatun Locks.

Fort Sherman is on a peninsula with the Caribbean Sea coastline on one side and Limon Bay on the other. It is home to the US Army Jungle Operations Training Center for military personnel receiving jungle warfare training. Shimmy Beach, located on the base, is another favorite place for military and Zonian families. Beyond the beach's shark barrier are views of Limon Bay, ships anchored within the breakwater, and in the distance across the bay, the city of Colon, the town of Coco Solo, and Fort Randolph. The west breakwater that juts out from Fort

Sherman and the east breakwater, which projects out from Fort Randolph, create the Atlantic entrance to the Panama Canal and help make Limon Bay a safe harbor. A small zoo on the base containing animals and reptiles is open to the public. It is part of the Army jungle training center, which allows troops to see wildlife they may encounter. Devil's Beach and Hidden Beach, which are on the Caribbean Sea coastline of the base, are more secluded hangouts for individuals and families, but they do not have a lifeguard or shark barrier. The beaches are less crowded than Shimmy Beach due to its limited access on a quarter-mile narrow dirt road and beach parking away from the main thoroughfare that leads to the historic Spanish fortress of Fort San Lorenzo. The old fortress, located at the mouth of the Chagres River, sits on high rock embankments overlooking the coastline and Pina Beach across the river.

After a long day and hearing about what is on the other side, rather than following the boys across the locks' bridge, everyone decides to continue the sightseeing of Gatun. Turning right onto Guarapo Street leads to the intersection of Schoolhouse Road and Mesa Verde Street across from the Canal Zone Girl Scout Council Camp Site. Turning left on Schoolhouse Road, you stop at the American Legion Post to order takeout of Chinese food before turning right onto Jadwin Road, which leads back into Gatun. Passing the Gatun sign again, you realize your tour was a circle of the town. Arriving and unloading at your residence in New Town, you hear, "This is home."

After a satisfactory night of sleep, during breakfast, a family member comments, "I can't wait to get our own furniture." As everyone begins to load into the vehicle, hearing and seeing a flock of 20 to 30 green parakeets chatting loudly in a small tree next to the house is a pleasurable sight to start the outing. Parakeets, coatimundis, and iguanas are commonly seen in Gatun, along with the occasional sight of a sloth hanging on a tree branch.

Driving through the neighborhood to continue sightseeing and purchase more groceries at the Coco Solo Commissary, kids are already outside skating, sitting, reading, and riding their bicycles. A couple of boys are washing a car, which is a way for kids to earn a little money.

On the way to take a quick tour of the town of Margarita, five miles from Gatun, a family member has their hand out the window playing the airplane floating game with the wind flowing against their palm as if it were flying. Passing the Mindi Dairy pastures, that unpleasant whiff hits everyone again. Rolling up the windows is useless and does not help.

Upon reaching a familiar intersection, Bolivar Highway heads left to the Port of Cristobal and the city of Colon. Straight ahead, a few cars are spotted on the left side of the road parked at another Chinese fruit and vegetable market on Diversion Road, which leads toward the town of Coco Solo. Upon making a right turn onto Margarita Avenue, the fire station, community health clinic, and Union Church are located at the entrance of the town. A right turn on First Street, at the opposite end away from the fire station, is a gas station across from the Knights of Columbus.

Margarita has similar facilities as other towns with a few additional amenities. Just up the street from the health clinic is the service center known as the "Club House," which has a post office, movie theater, cafeteria, convenience store, barber shop, small library, and the only bowling alley on the Atlantic side.

Sharing the same parking lot is the old commissary building, referred to as the "Red Barn," after being converted into a community center for hosting events, and is a teen hangout. The gymnasium is around the corner from the Red Barn, with a basketball court on the second floor and a skating rink on the first floor—many youngsters and young teens on the Atlantic side frequent this facility. The baseball field, situated behind the gymnasium, Red Barn, and Club House, gets a lot of use by the community, especially during Little League season.

Margarita was established in the late 1940s. Its first resident was C. E. Borgis, a locomotive crane operator with the Municipal Engineering Division. He and his family moved into an apartment on Christmas Eve 1940. The town is bigger, newer, and built with many one-story houses. With a larger population, it has more neighborhoods, identified primarily by street names, such as Cocobolo Street, Campana Place, Brazos Boulevard, Espave Avenue, Alcora Street, Hevea Place, and Sixth Street. One housing area not known by the street name is called Snob Hill. While touring the town, the family notes that Margarita has more churches than Gatun.

A noticeable similarity between the two towns is kids riding bicycles. On Brazos Boulevard, South Margarita Elementary School is bigger since it is for students in kindergarten through sixth grade. Gatun Elementary School is kindergarten to fourth grade, so kids are bused to Margarita for fifth and sixth grade.

Beyond the elementary school, Brazos Boulevard ends at Gulick Road. A few additional facilities in that vicinity include the Brazos Brooks Golf and Country Club, Cristobal Gun Club and skeet range, Rancho Ramos police range and picnic area, Benevolent and Protective Order of Elks (BPOE) Elks Club, and Veterans of Foreign Wars (VFW).

Making a U-turn at the school to head toward Snob Hill to see the north side of town, kids are spotted in front of their house on Cedro Place playing jump rope and hopscotch. At the intersection, the driver turns right onto Espave Avenue, another thoroughfare into the town starting by the gas station near First Street, passing the Catholic Church and more housing, and ending at Alcora Street. On Alcora Street, there is a dead end to the right. Going left through the neighborhood, the only thing visible is the jungle behind the houses, a playground for Margarita kids

Leopold J. Cimino

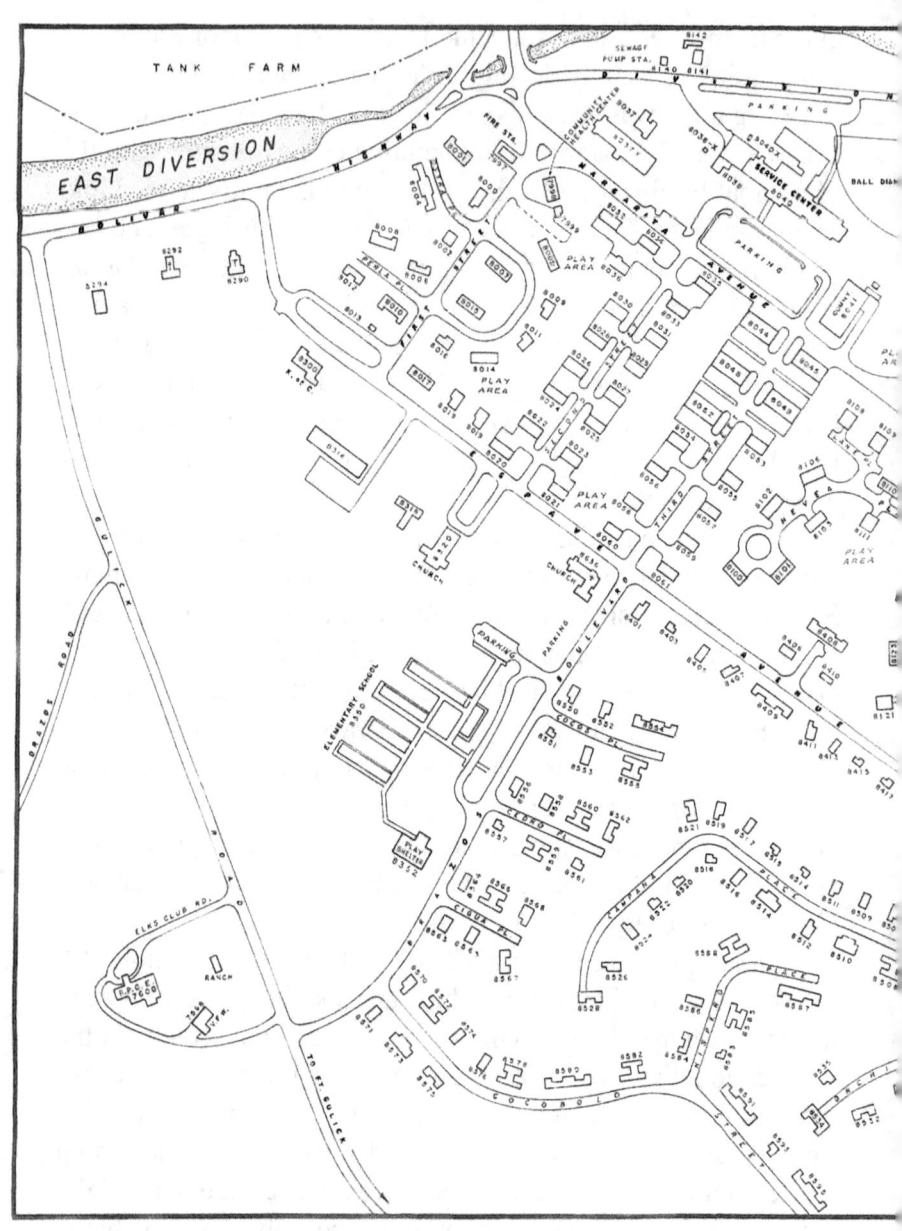

Margarita: Map 1

The Last Zonian

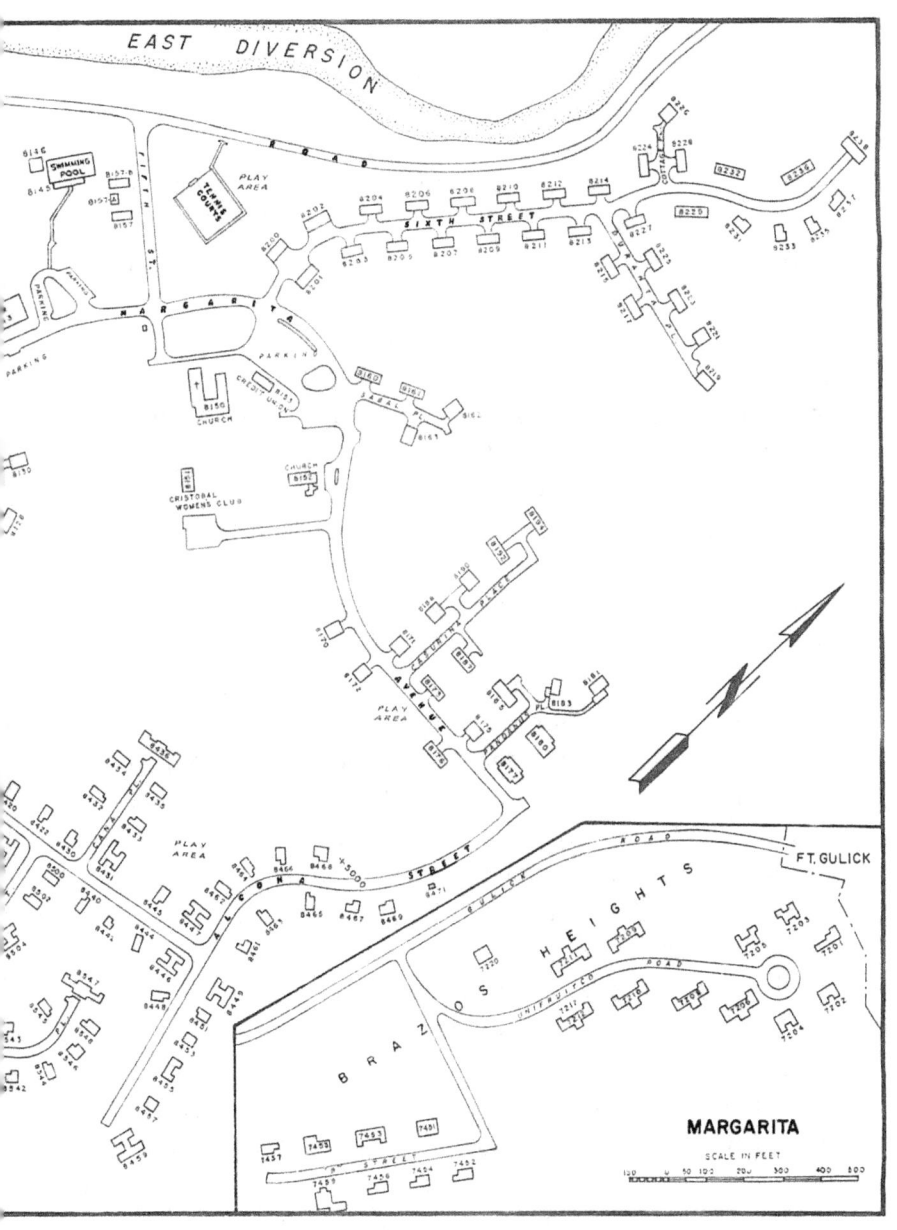

Margarita: Map 2 / Brazos Heights Map (bottom right)

to explore and build forts. Alcora Street ends connecting with Margarita Avenue, the main thoroughfare into town that starts next to the fire station on First Street. After making a left turn and heading back from the farthest end of Margarita Avenue, the Snob Hill neighborhood, which is actually Pandanus Place and Casuarina Place, comes into sight. Truly, there is nothing in particular that stands out. The houses are similar in structure to others and are also bordered by the jungle. A little further down the street are the Cristobal Women's Club, two churches, a credit union, and the Sixth Street neighborhood. Rounding a left curve on Margarita Avenue before reaching the gym and skating rink, you turn right on Fifth Street.

Done touring the town of Margarita and exiting from Fifth Street, the sound of a whistle is heard coming from the community swimming pool on the left. Here, too, kids are having fun. On the opposite side of the street, two adult couples are playing a tennis match at the courts. Having seen both Gatun and Margarita, it is obvious that residents from each town patronize the other to enjoy the different facilities and amenities.

After turning right at the end of the street onto Diversion Road (known locally by Zonians as "Snake Road" because of its curves), you travel about half a mile to where Diversion merges into Randolph Road. A short distance further, Randolph Road intersects with the Roosevelt Transisthmian Highway. Going left leads to Mt. Hope, Rainbow City, the Port of Cristobal, and the city of Colon. Taking a right on the Roosevelt Transisthmian Highway less than two miles on the left is the Coco Solo Hospital, where doctors Evelyn and Jaime Barraza and Ron Moore work. The primary health facility in the Canal Zone is Gorgas Hospital in Ancon where Jeanne Nelson works as a surgical nurse. To get there by automobile, one must continue on the two-lane Roosevelt Transisthmian Highway, weaving the steep hills and curves for approximately 50 miles to get to the Pacific side of the isthmus. Proceeding straight at the intersection leads to France Field, Army France Field, the town of Coco Solo, Navy Coco Solo, and Fort Randolph.

The Randolph Road and Roosevelt Transisthmian Highway intersection can get busy, especially with cars, buses, and trucks coming from and going to the surrounding towns and the Pacific side. Drivers and bus passengers have witnessed some quirky occurrences with teenage drivers at the four-way stop, called the "four corners." The young drivers play silly games with their friends, including the driver and passengers exiting the vehicle, running around it, jumping back into the car, and then proceeding from the blinking red light. Another example is when two vehicles full of teenagers stop at the intersection and, while holding up traffic, entertain onlookers by cramming as many passengers as possible into one of the vehicles. Rumor is that nine teens got into a Volkswagen Beetle.

About a mile from the intersection, the France Field neighborhood is on the right. Randolph Road is known for its unpleasant occurrence during crab mating season. Portions of the road get covered with crustaceans, and the stench of crabs crushed by vehicles is awful. Even rolling up vehicle windows does not provide an escape from the terrible smell.

On the opposite side of the neighborhood, aircraft hangers are visible that were part of the former France Field Army Air Station constructed in 1918. Before and during World War II, France Field had various air squadrons used for reconnaissance and protection of the Panama Canal. In 1949, the US Air Force inactivated the base. It became Colon Airport, and the US Army also used it.

A little further up the road is the town of Coco Solo, which has two areas: Coco Solo North and Coco Solo South. In 1914, following the official opening of the Panama Canal, the military completed the construction of bases in the area by about 1920.

Leopold J. Cimino

Naval Station Coco Solo consisted of Submarine Base Coco Solo and Naval Air Station (NAS) Coco Solo, a seaplane base with a small runway. It also had a squadron of fighter aircraft at one time. During WWII, these Naval assets served, along with anti-torpedo nets and Army air and ground forces, to protect the Panama Canal's Atlantic entrance. The Pacific side had military air, sea, and ground assets to guard the Pacific entrance to the Canal.

In 1957, due to a reduction of Naval forces in the Canal Zone, the Canal Zone Government (CZG) acquired the majority of the former Naval Station Coco Solo land, housing quarters, and other buildings. This acquisition led to the CZG having the town of Coco Solo, with approximately 300 Zonian families moving to their new residences, primarily in Coco Solo North, starting in January 1958. The Navy kept parts of Coco Solo South, including some housing quarters.

Randolph Road is the only thoroughfare to Coco Solo, Fort Randolph, and Galeta Island. Driving the long straight road bordered by dense jungle on the right side heading north, a notable realization during the sightseeing is that everything is fenced by the jungle. Coco Solo is on the eastern shore of Manzanillo Bay across from Colon. Fort Randolph is approximately a mile and a half farther north at the eastern breakwater and the Caribbean Sea.

Nearing the town, Cristobal Jr. Sr. High School comes into view. Seventh to twelfth graders from the other Zonian and military communities are bused to this school. The high school opened in 1917, with its first classes in a building on Colon Beach. A new building was constructed in 1933 at New Cristobal, a Canal Zone residential section in Colon. The high school later relocated to Coco Solo in 1959 to a building once a Navy barracks.

The Last Zonian

Touring the town from Coco Solo South and turning left onto Taxiway, the former Naval Air Station (NAS) Coco Solo is noticeable, with some housing quarters, warehouses, and other buildings still used by the Navy: Coco Solo Annex, Rodman Naval Station. A massive concrete area is visible next to Manzanillo Bay with aircraft hangers, a control tower, and ramps for seaplanes used during WWII.

Making a right turn on Maile Street, opposite the Navy Annex, is the high school campus. The old three-story Navy barracks converted into a junior-senior high school has a great view of Manzanillo Bay behind it. The school mascot name, "TIGER," is painted above the front entrance of the gymnasium. The bike racks outside the gym have several bicycles parked in them. Peering in through the open double doors, you see kids playing basketball. A softball field is on the opposite side of the street. The gym's summer program, like that at Gatun and Margarita, offers various sports activities and crafts. Adjacent to the gym is the main junior-senior high school building where Bob McCullough teaches social studies. Behind the building are tennis courts. Across the street from the school is the swimming pool, football stadium, and two athletic practice fields. The junior-senior high school utilizes the services of Alice Forsythe, a renowned "go-to" seamstress on the Atlantic side, to make cheerleader uniforms.

From the swimming pool come the familiar sounds of kids having fun, shouting, jumping into the water, playing the game of foursquare, and, of course, a lifeguard blowing a whistle at someone running on the pool deck. The swimming pool, with three diving boards, lounge chairs, bleachers, and a snack bar, is a town hangout open every day and in the evening on Wednesdays. Some kids spend their days at the pool, getting money from their parents for lunch and returning home late in the afternoon. Having a snack bar on site is convenient for

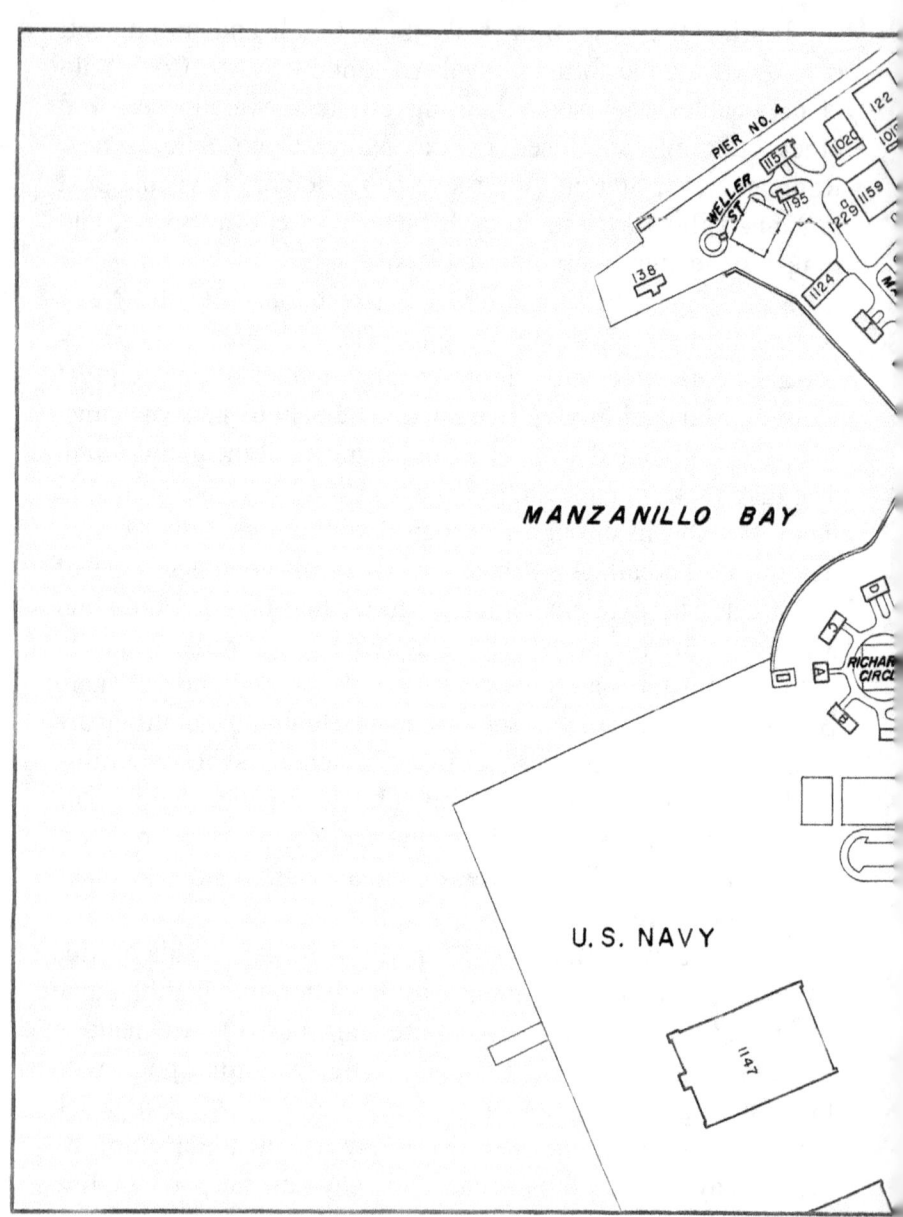

Coco Solo South: Map 1

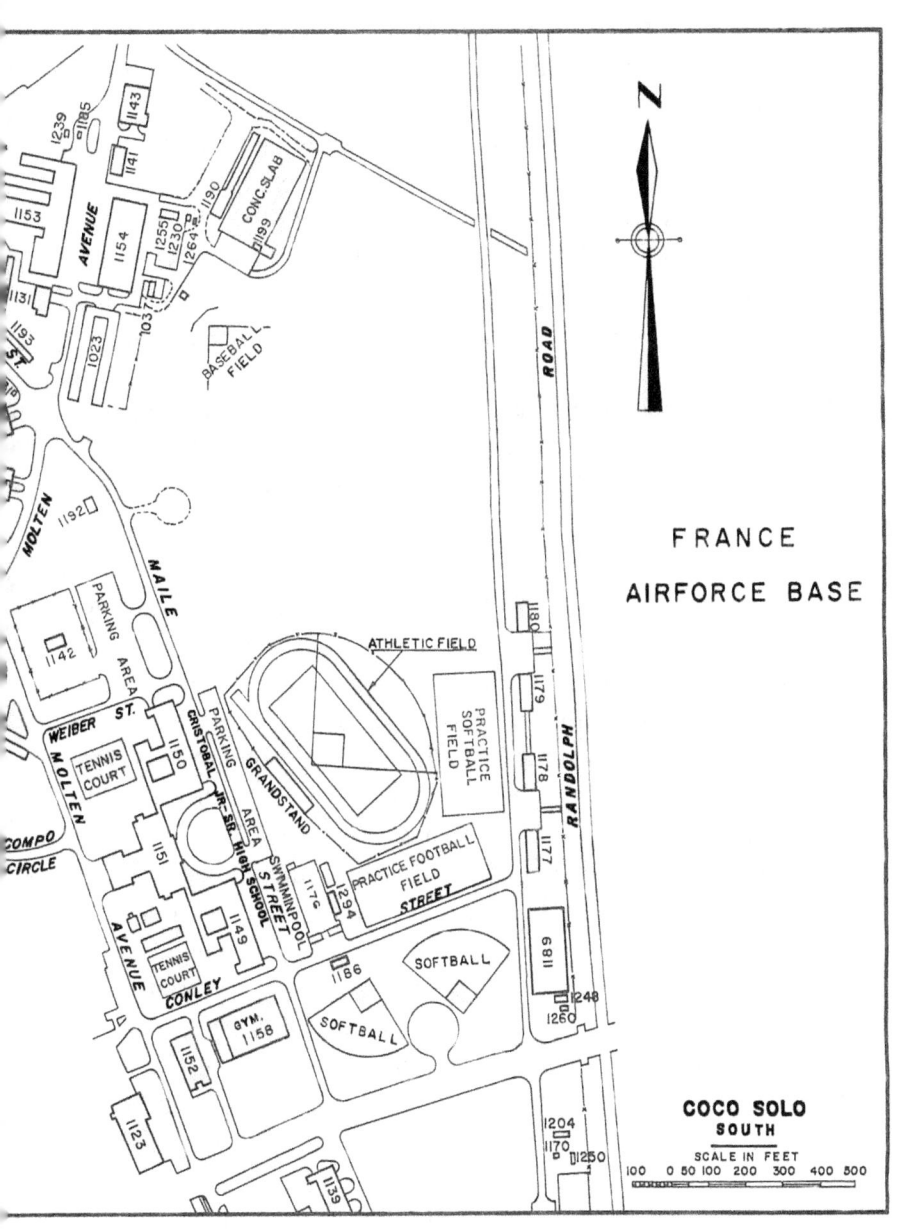

Coco Solo South: Map 2 (Cristobal Jr. Sr. High School)

getting a burger, fries, and soda and then attempting to quickly go back into the pool, only to be told by a lifeguard, "You have to wait 30 minutes before going back into the pool."

Just beyond the high school and a parking lot, on the left, of the street lined with royal palm trees, the houses that border a small cove have a nice view of Manzanillo Bay. On the opposite side of the road is a huge open field where kids are flying their kites. It is a great day for it, with a refreshing breeze flowing through the lowered car windows. Veering to the right, a little further up the route, a small warehouse at the corner of Maile Street and Johnston Avenue is pointed out as a busy place during the holiday season. It is the primary location on the Atlantic side for families to shop for a real Christmas tree shipped in from stateside.

The residents in Coco Solo North live in neighborhoods identified as the two-bedrooms and four-bedrooms. Going left onto Johnston Avenue next to the bay, the four piers used by the former Navy submarine base are visible. Pier 1 extends the furthest with a warehouse and smaller buildings and is a dock for Naval vessels. The vacated buildings are hobby shops for the residents. Near the end of Pier 1, boys are fishing. One is sitting on a small wooden box, and the other standing. They are likely trying to catch a red snapper, jack, or barracuda for the challenge.

Continuing north past Pier 1 is the Coco Solo Elementary School next to a cove facing the bay. With no air conditioning, the breeze through open louvered windows ventilates the classrooms. Kids walk or ride their bikes to school except for children bused in from nearby neighborhoods outside of Coco Solo North. Adjacent to the school is the Breakers Club, which was once a Navy Officers Club. It is an excellent place to dine, with great views: Manzanillo Bay adjoining Limon Bay, the Atlantic breakwater and entrance to the harbor, Colon, and, way across the bay, Fort Sherman. The Lions Club, just up the street

The Last Zonian

from the Breakers Club at the northwestern tip of the town, has the best, obstruction-free view.

Families living in the four-bedroom neighborhood opposite the elementary school and clubs also benefit from the blowing winds from the bay and Caribbean Sea. Several housing quarters at the town's northern shore have a great view across the bay of the eastern breakwater. Residents sometimes look to see how choppy the waves are hitting the breakwater and check the clouds to determine the weather for the day.

Zigzagging through the neighborhood from Lake Road to David Road, Cushing Road, and then Sperry Road, it is noticeable that, like the other towns, the streets are lined with royal palm trees. The concrete houses are uniformly painted off-white, with pastel-colored trim, and clay terra cotta shingle roofing. Passing 228 Sperry Road, twin boys can be seen riding their bikes. Nearby, a few kids are sitting on a curb. A girl and a boy appear to be negotiating an exchange of comic books.

Turning right onto Holland Road, across from Holland Court, a group of kids is spotted playing football on a small field near a playground while others are crouched and sitting on a dirt patch. "What are they looking at?" someone utters in the car.

"I know what they're doing. They're playing marbles or jacks," another responds.

Resuming the zigzagging from Holland Road to Bushnell Road and then to King Road, which parallels the town's northern shoreline, there is an excellent view of the eastern section of the breakwater. While continuing the drive through the two-bedroom neighborhood on Lee Road, Calhoun Road, and Severn Road, you see a lady strolling along, holding her baby, while her toddler pedals his tricycle at her side.

Turning onto Fulton Road, the main thoroughfare entering Coco Solo from Randolph Road, and then veering into a parking lot located behind the houses on Severn Road and Calhoun Road,

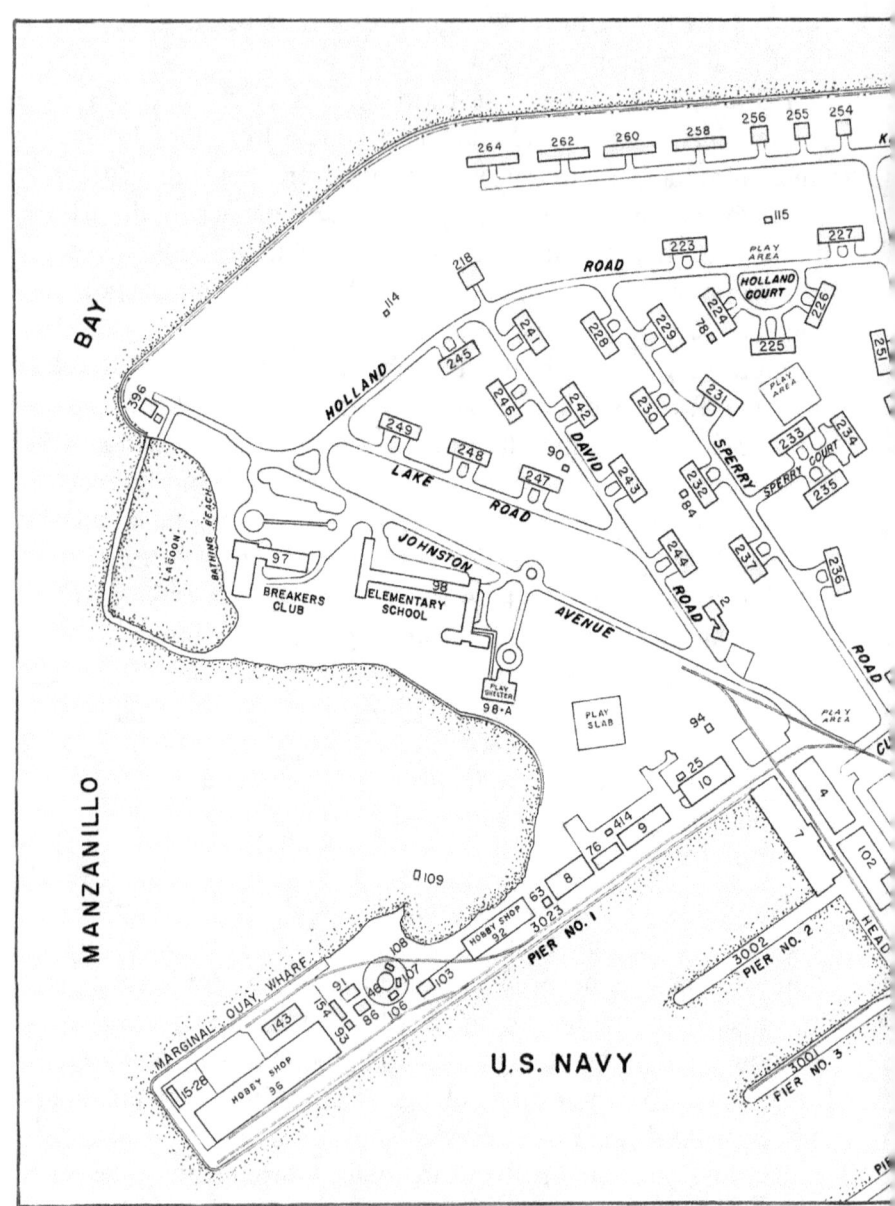

Coco Solo North: Map 1

The Last Zonian

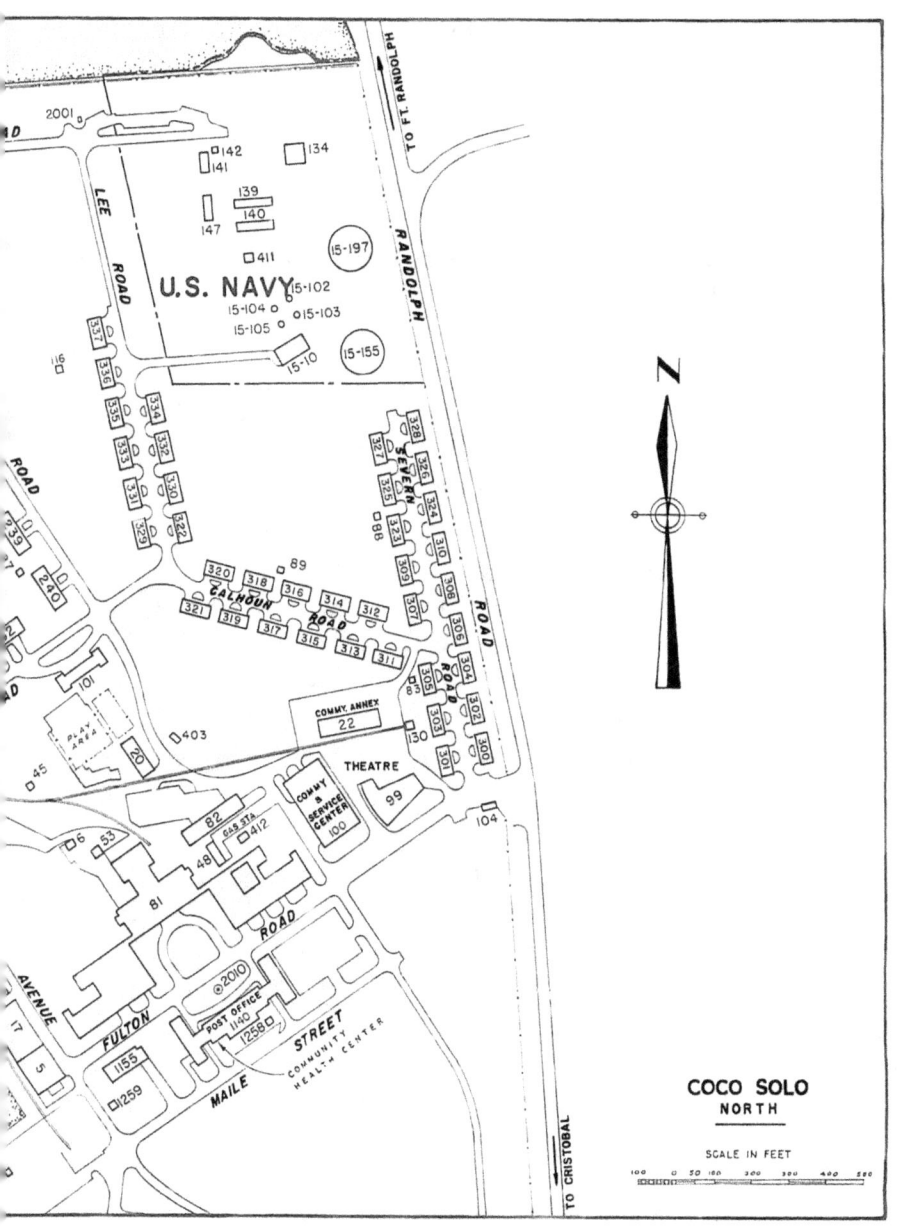

Coco Solo North: Map 2

it is a busy place with numerous cars. The parking lot is shared by three buildings: the Canal Zone Government retail stores, the commissary, and a theater. Everyone in the car is hungry, so it is a perfect time to stop and eat at the cafeteria before walking through the retail stores and then getting some groceries before heading home.

The cafeteria and commissary are located in a two-story building along with a clothing and shoe store, a record store with the latest long-playing (LP) vinyl records, a barber shop, a beauty salon, and a quick-stop convenience store. A small building next to the commissary has toys and sporting goods. Across the parking lot is the air-conditioned cinema, with stadium seating only at the rear. With air conditioning, they don't need to open the doors, so the movie is free from intermission and bats flying around the theater, disrupting the show.

After strolling through the retail stores, meeting and chatting with other Zonians, and walking the aisles in the commissary, everyone is ready to load the groceries in the car and head home. It's been another long day.

Coco Solo has facilities similar to those of other towns, including a church, a teen center, a gas station, a post office, and a community center for town council meetings and dances. The post office is where Iris Hogan works as the supervisor. A benefit for families living in Coco Solo is that their kids can attend kindergarten through twelfth grade without being bused out of town. Additionally, the Fort Randolph Riding Club is just up the road for equestrian enthusiasts. Fort Randolph is great for snorkeling and spearfishing from the shore at a reef in the Caribbean Sea. On the downside, though, the town has no police or fire station due to its proximity to Cristobal. So, the fire department is on-site during the annual after-Christmas tree bonfire, where the event organizers give kids a nickel per tree.

And, even though there is low crime, police patrols are done frequently in the town.

After leaving Coco Solo, a teenager is hitchhiking on Randolph Road heading out of town, most likely going to Margarita or Gatun. Unfortunately, the car has no room to give him a ride. From time to time, a hitchhiker is seen on the road or waiting at a bus stop. Occasionally, when a hitchhiker gets a ride, the driver knows them, or when asked their name, the driver knows a family member, and vice versa, the rider may know a member of the driver's family or has heard their last name.

The Atlantic side Canal Zone community is relatively small. Most towns and military bases are within a ten-mile radius of each other except for Fort Sherman, ten miles from the Gatun Locks and farther from other towns. The Atlantic side is referred to as the "Other Side" to people living on the Pacific side. They consider it isolated compared to the more populous Pacific side. In reality, it is a paradise.

Returning home from another day of sightseeing, all agree that each town has its own appeal. And as the years pass, you have heard it all about living in Gatun. Some outsiders think it is boring and in the boonies, although it's true that Fort Sherman is farther away and more secluded. After residing in Gatun and making lifelong friends, you know it is a hidden paradise that you have come to love. And, how true the words you heard upon the first day of arriving in the town came to be, "This is home."

Gatun: Then and Now

My family lived in 235-A Loma Blanca Place, in Gatun's New Town neighborhood, when my father retired from the Panama Canal Company. Behind the house was the Third Locks Excavation, abandoned in 1941.

New Town and everything left of the Gatun sign at the town entrance on Jadwin Road, including the houses on High Street, Halcon Place, and Laurel Street, parallel to the Third Locks Excavation, no longer exists. They are gone, erased from the earth. The demolished housing areas and removal of the dugout terrain from which they once stood were consumed by the expansion of the newer Agua Clara Locks.

What remains of Gatun is now, in reality, an island surrounded by water from Gatun Lake, the Gatun Locks on one side, the Agua Clara Locks on the other, and the Canal that leads to Limon Bay. If you ever have the opportunity to travel through the Agua Clara Locks aboard a ship or go to its visitor observation tower, look across the locks. You can still see what used to be the Gatun Elementary School and Gatun Swimming Pool, remnants of an amazing place to have lived that many of us Zonians called home.

At the top of the photograph is Gatun's New Town beside the abandoned Third Lock Excavation. The Gatun Swimming Pool is at the top right on Jadwin Road, next to New Town. The houses on Laurel Street, Halcon Place, and High Street are at the bottom.

The Agua Clara Locks was constructed at the location of the abandoned Third Locks Excavation and the destruction of Gatun's New Town, Laurel Street, Halcon Place, and High Street. It opened for ship traffic on June 26, 2016. The Gatun Elementary School, three other buildings, and the Gatun Swimming Pool aligned with the one-time Jadwin Road are visible on the right side of the locks, starting at the bottom of the lateral water-savings basin next to the second chamber. Some houses behind the elementary school and in Gatun's Old Town are still standing.

Coco Solo: Then and Now

When my father worked for the Navy at the Coco Solo Submarine Base, we lived in Coco Solito. After he began working for the Panama Canal Company, we moved to Canal Zone housing in Coco Solo to 308-B Severn Road. We later moved to Gatun, where I began kindergarten.

The town of Coco Solo, which Zonians called home, is gone and demolished. The landscape has drastically changed and is unrecognizable. What used to be a vibrant town is now a container port. Passengers aboard a ship transiting the Panama Canal entering Limon Bay from the Atlantic breakwater, looking from the port side, see cranes and a myriad of stacks of cargo containers. It is the site of a lost town.

Although the town no longer exists, Brian Allen, a Zonian who lived in Coco Solo, writes of his adventures in the Canal Zone in his book *My Paradise Lost*. While chatting about Coco Solo in one of our conversations, he asked me, "Do you remember that song by Joni Mitchell, Big Yellow Taxi, They Paved Paradise? It's real for Coco Solo."

Coco Solo North, with Pier 1 at the top left, close to the four-bedroom housing quarters, and a portion of the eastern breakwater is at the top of the photograph. The two-bedroom quarters, shopping center, and Randolph Road are visible in the bottom half of the photograph.

The Colon Container Terminal began operations in October 1997. Remnants of the town of Coco Solo are visible at the bottom left of the photograph, showing dilapidated two-bedroom housing quarters on Calhoun Road and Severn Road, which parallel Randolph Road. At the top, Pier 1 is still used after construction improvements. The city of Colon is on the other side of Manzanillo Bay.

What happened to Margarita? The town still exists, remaining mostly the same, but it is not maintained as it was with the Panama Canal Company.

Here's Where the Story Ends

As of the time of publishing this book, the last-born Zonian in the Canal Zone is 44 years old. He or she was born on or just before September 30, 1979. That infant was the last-born Zonian since, on October 1, 1979, the US unincorporated territory known as the Panama Canal Zone was abolished and ceased to exist per the execution of the Panama Canal Treaty.

Unfortunately, attaining the person's name, gender, date, and time of birth is nearly impossible. The US Department of State (DOS) maintains the birth certificates from the Canal Zone, issued between 1904 and 1979. A request for a birth certificate can only be done by the individual on the document, a legal guardian of the individual, a person with notarized written approval from the individual, or from an authorized government agency. Additionally, the National Archives and Records Administration (NARA) holds the medical records for the Canal Zone, however, their response to the information request was that it would involve pulling thousands of boxes from shelves and scouring through thousands of records. Hence, the search is too time-intensive for the records center. Rather than pulling thousands of patient records, an easier search would be to pull only the Maternity and Pediatric Department records for newborn deliveries in the month of September 1979. Both DOS and NARA have the information.

If the last-born Zonian is still living today, he or she is not "The Last Zonian," as inferred in the title of this book. The truth is, no one will ever know who "The Last Zonian" will be to walk on this earth. The Panama Canal Society (PCS) organization, founded in 1932 and located in Florida, has a large membership. Still, many other Zonians are not associated with the PCS or other Canal Zone groups. Some Zonians live across the United States and abroad. The numbers are unknown. We will never know who "The Last Zonian" is.

Every Canal Zone town, from the Atlantic side to the Pacific, has entire Zonian families that are deceased today. The number of Zonians dwindles each year. When the last Zonian perishes, the United States will have lost a populace that is a part of history, which began with building one of the world's engineering marvels, the Panama Canal.

For those of us who lived there, the old Canal Zone we knew is gone. Living in that era was as good as living in a slice of paradise, which it was, except that place no longer exists. We are members of a distinct family of Americans now living from coast to coast across the US and abroad. At our gatherings and reunions, our numbers are obviously diminishing. Our faces reveal our journey. We were once the kids written about in these stories but are now senior citizens soon to follow the generations before us. We are vanishing. Although each of us has our unique story, we share a special commonality. We are Zonians.

Epilogue

As the years pass and I look back, I attribute the joy in my life to my parents, being born and raised in the Canal Zone, an upbringing in faith, my marriage to my beautiful wife Rhonda of 41 years, being gifted with loving children and grandchildren, and having wonderful friends. I am thankful and grateful every day for the blessings I receive in my life.

Living with faith, love, and joy matters. Kindness to others is a reflection of the heart. Surrounding myself with like-minded friends strengthens my spirit. All of this, woven into my own story, has made me a better person.

Life certainly has its peaks and valleys, but it is the happy times that get ingrained into the memories we hold close as our family members and friends pass on one by one. Life is so precious and short. Rhonda used to say, "No one is promised tomorrow." A verse that says it all is, "What is your life? You are a mist that appears for a little while and then vanishes." James 4:14 (NIV).

Generations will pass, and pictures may not last; it is the memories and stories that endure as time passes. So, how do you want to be remembered?

Leopold J. Cimino, July 2024

References

Hay–Bunau-Varilla Treaty United States-Panama (1903) – pg vii Preface
https://www.britannica.com/event/Hay-Bunau-Varilla-Treaty

An American Legacy In Panama, A Brief History of the Department of Defense Installations And Properties, The Former Panama Canal Zone, Republic of Panama – pg vii Preface
https://www.govinfo.gov/content/pkg/GOVPUB-D-9c7ec1da44988da2a99cf78b969dc6ab/pdf/GOVPUB-D-9c7ec1da44988da2a99cf78b969dc6ab.pdf

Panama Canal – pg vii Preface
https://www.history.com/topics/landmarks/panama-canal

Panama Canal Locks – pg vii Preface
https://en.wikipedia.org/wiki/Panama_Canal_locks

Panama Canal Zone – pg vii Preface
https://en.wikipedia.org/wiki/Panama_Canal_Zone

Canal Zone Region, Panama – pg vii Preface
https://www.britannica.com/place/Canal-Zone

1914 Panama Canal Open to Traffic – pg vii Preface
https://www.history.com/this-day-in-history/panama-canal-open-to-traffic

SS Ancon – pg vii Preface
https://en.wikipedia.org/wiki/SS_Ancon

Building the Panama Canal, 1903-1914 – pg vii - viii Preface
https://history.state.gov/milestones/1899-1913/panama-canal

References

How the Panama Canal Took a Huge Toll On the Contract Workers Who Built It – pg viii Preface
https://www.smithsonianmag.com/history/how-panama-canal-took-huge-toll-on-contract-workers-who-built-it-180968822/

William Crawford Gorgas – United States Army Surgeon – pg viii Preface
https://www.britannica.com/biography/William-Crawford-Gorgas

8 FAM 302.7 Acquisition By Birth In The Panama Canal Zone – pg ix Preface
https://fam.state.gov/FAM/08FAM/08FAM030207.html

Birth of US Citizens and Non-Citizen Nationals Abroad – pg ix Preface
https://travel.state.gov/content/travel/en/international-travel/while-abroad/birth-abroad.html

Chapter XII Forging the Defenses of the Canal – pg xxii Memories
https://history.army.mil/books/wwii/Guard-US/ch12.htm

Fortifications of the Panama Canal – pg xxii Memories
https://storymaps.arcgis.com/stories/44e0b1e30a71455987b4f179d709b5d4

Anthrax Strike: The 1976 Outbreak of Labor Militancy in the Panama Canal Zone by Michael Murphy, October 2005 – pg 3 A Slice of Paradise
https://www.czbrats.com/Builders/anthraxstrike.htm

The Panama Canal Review, February 5, 1954, How Do Zonians Work And Play? This Is What They Have To Say – pg 4 A Slice of Paradise
https://www.govinfo.gov/content/pkg/GOVPUB-W79-8f76b43a0c27d7ff8c302b1f4ace11fa/pdf/GOVPUB-W79-8f76b43a0c27d7ff8c302b1f4ace11fa.pdf

Panama Yellow-Head Amazon Parakeet – pg 4 A Slice of Paradise
https://en.wikipedia.org/wiki/Panama_amazon

Coatis, Raccoons, and Ringtails – pg 4 A Slice of Paradise
https://www.nps.gov/sagu/learn/nature/coatis-raccoons-and-ringtails.htm

Coati, Nasua spp. And Nasuella spp. – pg 4 A Slice of Paradise
https://animals.sandiegozoo.org/animals/coati

References

Gatun Lake – pg 5 A Slice of Paradise
https://en.wikipedia.org/wiki/Gatun_Lake

List of former United States military installations in Panama
– pg 5-8 A Slice of Paradise
https://en.wikipedia.org/wiki/List_of_former_United_States_military_installations_in_Panama

Peacock Bass – pg 9 A Slice of Paradise
https://en.wikipedia.org/wiki/Peacock_bass

Cayuco – pg 10 A Slice of Paradise
https://en.wikipedia.org/wiki/Cayuco

From the Stacks: Cayuco Race – pg 10 A Slice of Paradise
https://pcmc.domains.uflib.ufl.edu/uncategorized/from-the-stacks-cayuco-race/

Volcan, Panama – pg 12 A Slice of Paradise
https://en.wikipedia.org/wiki/Volcán,_Panama

The Panama Canal Review, August 3, 1951 Panama Canal Company and Canal Zone Government Organization Directory
– pg 13-14 Occupations and Operations
https://www.govinfo.gov/content/pkg/GOVPUB-W79-1db1cb67c1916f032a933e0c3db29501/pdf/GOVPUB-W79-1db1cb67c1916f032a933e0c3db29501.pdf

Organization of the Panama Canal Zone 1964
– pg 13-14 Occupations and Operations
https://www.czbrats.com/Builders/canalorg.htm

Logan, Kansas – pg 17 Snider
https://en.wikipedia.org/wiki/Logan,_Kansas

Battle of Inchon, Korea – pg 17 Snider
https://en.wikipedia.org/wiki/Battle_of_Inchon

Patrick Peyton "The Rosary Priest" – pg 21 Snider
https://en.wikipedia.org/wiki/Patrick_Peyton

References

The Bronx – pg 27 Oster
https://en.wikipedia.org/wiki/The_Bronx

Occupation of Japan – pg 27 Oster
https://en.wikipedia.org/wiki/Occupation_of_Japan

The Korean War and Japanese Ports: Support for the UN Forces and Its Influences by Ishimaru Yasuzo – pg 27 Oster
http://www.nids.mod.go.jp/english/publication/kiyo/pdf/2007/bulletin_e2007_5.pdf

Air Raids on Japan – pg 28 Oster
https://en.wikipedia.org/wiki/Air_raids_on_Japan

Able Seaman (AB) Merchant Ship Rank – pg 28 Oster
https://en.wikipedia.org/wiki/Able_seaman

Seafarer's Professions and Ranks – pg 28 Oster
https://en.wikipedia.org/wiki/Seafarer%27s_professions_and_ranks

USNS Private Leonard C. Brostrom – pg 28 Oster
https://en.wikipedia.org/wiki/USNS_Private_Leonard_C._Brostrom

New Orleans Weather 1923 – pg 35 Bailey
https://www.extremeweatherwatch.com/cities/new-orleans/year-1923

United States Merchant Marine – pg 37 Bailey
https://en.wikipedia.org/wiki/United_States_Merchant_Marine

Palo Seco: A Leper Colony in Panama, by Enrique Chaves-Carballo – pg 41 Bailey
https://hekint.org/2022/12/16/palo-seco-a-leper-colony-in-panama/

Panama's Leprosy Patients Fear Loss of Home, November 5, 1977 – pg 41 Bailey
https://www.washingtonpost.com/archive/politics/1977/11/05/panamas-leprosy-patients-fear-loss-of-home/2961f0d2-500a-4146-bd93-916bfcbb4a18/

A Boom in Boomerangs – pg 42 Bailey
https://spinoff.nasa.gov/node/8975

References

Eighteenth Amendment to the United States Constitution – pg 45 O'Donnell
https://en.wikipedia.org/wiki/Eighteenth_Amendment_to_the_United_States_Constitution

Navy Ship USS PC 1221 – pg 46 O'Donnell
https://www.hullnumber.com/PCRF

City of Corry, Pennsylvania – pg 53 Paulson
https://www.corrypa.org/corry-history

Naval Historical and Heritage Command (PBY Catalina Aircraft) – pg 53 Paulson
https://www.history.navy.mil/content/history/nhhc/search.html?q=PBY

Mildred Elley (Secretarial Program for Women) – pg 54 Paulson
https://en.wikipedia.org/wiki/Mildred_Elley

Civil Functions, Department of the Army Appropriations, 1954, Hearing HR 5376, Bakery Production, Panama Canal Company, Commissary Division, Mount Hope and Clubhouse Division La Boca (page 147) – pg 56 Paulson

Abbreviations Used for Navy Enlisted Ratings – pg 64 Fortner
by Charles A. Malin, Bureau of Naval Personnel, 1970
https://www.history.navy.mil/research/library/online-reading-room/title-list-alphabetically/a/abbreviations-used-for-navy-enlisted-ratings.html

Panamanian Professional Baseball League – pg 64 Fortner
https://en.wikipedia.org/wiki/Panamanian_Professional_Baseball_League

Panama Coup, Memorandum From the President's Assistant for National Security Affairs (Kissinger) to President Nixon (Washington, December 18, 1969) – pg 66 Fortner
https://history.state.gov/historicaldocuments/frus1969-76ve10/d525

The New York Times, Panama Protests U.S. Aid to Fugitives – pg 66 Fortner
https://www.nytimes.com/1970/06/29/archives/panama-protests-us-aid-to-fugitives.html

References

Balboa High School (Panama Canal Zone) – pg 67 Fortner
https://en.wikipedia.org/wiki/Balboa_High_School_(Panama)

Connecting Continents – The Panama Canal Expansion Program – pg 68 Fortner
https://ch2mhillalumni.org/the-panama-canal-expansion-program/

San Carlos (Canton), Costa Rica – pg 69 Flores
https://en.wikipedia.org/wiki/San_Carlos_(canton)

Encyclopedia of Arkansas, Brinkley (Monroe County) – pg 77 Reed
https://encyclopediaofarkansas.net/entries/brinkley-monroe-county-941/

The Panama Riots of 1964: The Beginning of the End for the Canal – pg 79-80 Reed
https://adst.org/2016/07/panama-riots-1964-beginning-end-canal/

Martyrs' Day (Panama) – pg 79-80 Reed
https://en.wikipedia.org/wiki/Martyrs%27_Day_(Panama)

The Panama Canal Riots, Treaties, Elections, and a little Military Madness, 1959-1973 – pg 79-80 Reed
https://www.archives.gov/research/foreign-policy/panama-canal

Joe Cicero (MLB Baseball Player) – pg 85 Finneman
https://sabr.org/bioproj/person/joe-cicero/

Gatun Dam – pg 87 Finneman
https://en.wikipedia.org/wiki/Gatun_Dam

Youngstown, Ohio – pg 93 Klasovsky
https://en.wikipedia.org/wiki/Youngstown,_Ohio

Climate and Monthly Forecast Gatun, Panama – pg 94 Klasovsky
https://www.weather-atlas.com/en/panama/gatun-climate

Harrisburg, Illinois – pg 101 Barger
https://en.wikipedia.org/wiki/Harrisburg,_Illinois

US Army Technician Fifth Grade (T/5 or Tec 5) – pg 103 Barger
https://en.wikipedia.org/wiki/Technician_fifth_grade

References

1916 Brooklyn Robins Season – pg 111 Spector
https://en.wikipedia.org/wiki/1916_Brooklyn_Robins_season

Naval History and Heritage Command – pg 111 Spector
NH 82338 Naval Air Station (NAS) Coco Solo, Canal Zone
https://www.history.navy.mil/content/history/nhhc/our-collections/photography/numerical-list-of-images/nhhc-series/nh-series/NH-82000/NH-82338.html

Coco Solo Naval Base, Submarine Base and Naval Air Station – pg 111 Spector
https://members.tripod.com/william_h_ormsbee/cocosolo_naval_base_hist_p01.htm

USS San Marcos (LSD-25) – pg 113 Spector
https://en.wikipedia.org/wiki/USS_San_Marcos_(LSD-25)

Selective Service System (History and Records) – pg 120 Forsythe
https://www.sss.gov/history-and-records/

Selective Service Training and Service Act of 1940 – pg 120 Forsythe
https://en.wikipedia.org/wiki/Selective_Training_and_Service_Act_of_1940

Inter-American Highway (Pan-American Highway) – pg 122 Forsythe
https://en.wikipedia.org/wiki/Inter-American_Highway

Philadelphia 1918: The Flu Pandemic Hits Home – pg 127 Blair
https://www.jefferson.edu/alumni/connect/alumni-bulletin/summer-2020/the-flu-pandemic-hits-home.html#:~:text=19%2C%201918.,threatening%20the%20city%27s%20social%20fabric.

Penn and the 1918 Influenza Epidemic – pg 127 Blair
https://archives.upenn.edu/exhibits/penn-history/flu/

The History of Ice and The IPIA – pg 128 Blair
https://www.packagedice.com/history-of-ice.html

The Great Depression and The Rise of the Refrigerator – pg 128 Blair
https://psmag.com/environment/the-rise-of-the-refrigerator-47924

References

Naval History & Heritage Command, 104th Naval Construction Battalion (Seabees) – pg 128 Blair
https://www.history.navy.mil/content/dam/museums/Seabee/UnitListPages/NCB/104%20NCB.pdf

GrooveWorx – pg 134 Blair
https://en.wikipedia.org/wiki/GrooveWorx

The Panama Canal Review, January 1, 1960 (Page 2, Gatun Dam) – pg 138 Loyd
https://www.govinfo.gov/content/pkg/GOVPUB-W79-2855ff909b10f3bb99663f61d9e91ed7/pdf/GOVPUB-W79-2855ff909b10f3bb99663f61d9e91ed7.pdf

The Attack on Panama City by Henry Morgan (Walter E. Piatt, MAJ, USA) – pg 139 Loyd
https://apps.dtic.mil/sti/pdfs/ADA350055.pdf

Pirates of the Original Panama Canal (Samir S. Patel) – pg 139 Loyd
https://www.archaeology.org/issues/79-1303/features/543-pirates-henry-morgan-panama-city-raid

The Gatun Tarpon Club (article appeared in the August 6, 1954 issue of *The Panama Canal Review)* – pg 141 Loyd
https://www.angelfire.com/tx/CZAngelsSpace/MyHomeTown6.html

US Bureau of Labor Statistics, Occupational Outlook Handbook – pg 141 Loyd
Power Plant Operators, Distributors, and Dispatchers
https://www.bls.gov/ooh/production/power-plant-operators-distributors-and-dispatchers.htm#tab-2

Lambert History (Montana) – pg 145 McCullough
https://www.roundupweb.com/story/2014/07/02/special-editions/lambert-history/4901.html

St. Cloud State University (Minnesota) – pg 145 McCullough
https://en.wikipedia.org/wiki/St._Cloud_State_University

Richland County, Montana (Genealogy and History) – pg 145 McCullough
http://genealogytrails.com/mon/richland/index.html

References

Boeing B-29 Superfortress – pg 148 McCullough
https://en.wikipedia.org/wiki/Boeing_B-29_Superfortress

National Archives, Records of the Army Air Forces (AAF),
Record Group 18, 1903-64 (bulk 1917-47) – pg 148 McCullough
https://www.archives.gov/research/guide-fed-records/groups/018.html#18.1

National Archives – pg 148 McCullough
World War II Prisoners of War Data File, 12/7/1941-11/19/1946
https://aad.archives.gov/aad/

Industry, Maine (from *Maine: An Encyclopedia*) – pg 150 Hogan
https://maineanencyclopedia.com/industry/

Arecibo, Puerto Rico – pg 157 Barraza
https://en.wikipedia.org/wiki/Arecibo,_Puerto_Rico

David, Chiriquí – pg 157 Barraza
https://en.wikipedia.org/wiki/David,_Chiriqu%C3%AD

Chiriqui Province – pg 157 Barraza
https://en.wikipedia.org/wiki/Chiriqu%C3%AD_Province

Vietnam War Timeline (History Channel) – pg 167 Moore
https://www.history.com/topics/vietnam-war/vietnam-war-timeline

Volunteer Service From American Physicians During the Vietnam War
– pg 167 Moore
https://journalofethics.ama-assn.org/article/volunteer-service-american-physicians-during-vietnam-war/2019-09

National Archives, Women at Work in the 1950s – pg 173 Nelson
https://text-message.blogs.archives.gov/2018/03/27/women-at-work-in-the-1950s/

SS Cristobal, *The Panama Canal Review,* October 1, 1981 (pg 56)
– pg 183 The Lost Towns
https://www.govinfo.gov/content/pkg/GOVPUB-Y3_P19_2-ab21c6b7f9401aa6ec28d4dc5cb1cdeb/pdf/GOVPUB-Y3_P19_2-ab21c6b7f9401aa6ec28d4dc5cb1cdeb.pdf

References

Colon, Panama – pg 184 The Lost Towns
https://en.wikipedia.org/wiki/Colón,_Panama

Disposition of Cemeteries in the Panama Canal Zone Where American Veterans are Buried, March 1, 1978 (including Mount Hope)
– pg 188 The Lost Towns
https://www.govinfo.gov/content/pkg/GOVPUB-Y4_J89_2-f86f66f378c67ef565253b647a8ee0b0/pdf/GOVPUB-Y4_J89_2-f86f66f378c67ef565253b647a8ee0b0.pdf

The Panama Canal Review, August 4, 1950, Mindi Dairy
– pg 189 The Lost Towns
https://ufdc.ufl.edu/UF00097366/00223/pdf

The Panama Canal, The Third Locks Project, June 1941
– pg 189 The Lost Towns
https://www.govinfo.gov/content/pkg/GOVPUB-W79-37ac6b0aaa65c0df3ec488d34fa66b8c/pdf/GOVPUB-W79-37ac6b0aaa65c0df3ec488d34fa66b8c.pdf

Gatun – pg 190 The Lost Towns
https://en.wikipedia.org/wiki/Gatún

The Panama Canal Railway Company – pg 200 The Lost Towns
https://en.wikipedia.org/wiki/Panama_Canal_Railway

Map of Margarita – (reviewed only, not utilized)
https://www.gifex.com/images/0X0/2009-09-17-6348/Map_of_Margarita_Panama.gif

Army Air Forces Historical Studies: Prepared by AAF Historical Office January 1946 Air Defense of the Panama Canal January 1, 1939, to December 7, 1941, including France Field – pg 211 The Lost Towns
https://www.afhistory.af.mil

Building the Navy's Bases in World War II Volume II (Part III) Chapter XVIII Bases in South America and the Caribbean Area, including Bermuda
– pg 212 The Lost Towns
https://www.history.navy.mil/research/library/online-reading-room/title-list-alphabetically/b/building-the-navys-bases/building-the-navys-bases-vol-2.html

References

Building the Navy's Bases in World War II: Chapter XVIII Bases in South America and the Caribbean Area, Including Bermuda
– pg 212 The Lost Towns
https://www.ibiblio.org/hyperwar/USN/Building_Bases/bases-18.html

Naval Base Panama Canal Zone – pg 212 The Lost Towns
https://en.wikipedia.org/wiki/Naval_Base_Panama_Canal_Zone

Coco Solo, from *The Panama Canal Review,* January 3, 1958
– pg 212 The Lost Towns
https://ufdc.ufl.edu/UF00097366/00164/images/3

Galeta Island, US Navy – pg 212 The Lost Towns
https://en.wikipedia.org/wiki/Galeta_Island_(Panama)

1967 Caribbean Vol 50, Cristobal High School, Fifty Years of Progress (pg 20) – pg 212-213 The Lost Towns
https://ufdc.ufl.edu/UF00093680/00050/images/20

Cristobal High School History – pg 212-213 The Lost Towns
https://aoshs.org/collections/school-histories/na/yy/732/

Panama Canal Commission Maps from Telephone Directory 1967
Canal Zone Town Maps – pgs 192, 193, 208, 209, 214, 215, 218, 219
The Lost Towns

The Other Side (pg 12), *The Panama Canal Review*, October 1, 1980
– pg 221 The Lost Towns
https://www.govinfo.gov/content/pkg/GOVPUB-Y3_P19_2-bceabefd6bb4e5e0417f736cd275e444/pdf/GOVPUB-Y3_P19_2-bceabefd6bb4e5e0417f736cd275e444.pdf

Gatun (image ownership and photographer unknown), found on various social media sites, including So You Lived In Gatun, Facebook Group
– pg 224 Gatun: Then and Now

Agua Clara Locks (image ownership and photographer unknown), found on social media site– pg 225 Gatun: Then and Now

References

Coco Solo North (image taken by the Panama Canal Company)
– pg 228 Coco Solo: Then and Now. Also, found on the following website
http://www.czimages.com/CZMemories/Photos/photoof151.htm

Colon Container Port (image ownership and photographer unknown)
– pg 229 Coco Solo: Then and Now
panamaadvisoryinternationalgroup.com

Miscellaneous References:
Margarita, Excerpts from *The Panama Canal Review*, December 3, 1954
https://www.czbrats.com/Towns/Margarita.htm

Library of Congress, US History Primary Source Timeline, World War II
https://www.loc.gov/classroom-materials/united-states-history-primary-source-timeline/great-depression-and-world-war-ii-1929-1945/world-war-ii/

The Panama Canal: An Army's Enterprise
https://history.army.mil/html/books/panama/panamacanal/CMH-70-115-1-PanamaCanal.pdf

Panama Canal Company, Canal Zone Government (Annual Report 1962)
Fiscal Year Ended June 30, 1962 (Introduction page 108)

Coto War (Panama and Costa Rica)
https://en.wikipedia.org/wiki/Coto_War

US Merchant Marine, Liberty Ships Built During World War II
http://www.usmm.org/libyards.html

Panama Canal Museum Collection, George A. Smathers Libraries
(University of Florida)
https://pcmc.uflib.ufl.edu

www.ingramcontent.com/pod-product-compliance
Lightning Source LLC
Chambersburg PA
CBHW072149070526
44585CB00015B/1065